Premiership

The Development, Nature and Power of the British Prime Minister

Andrew Blick and George Jones

SOCIETAS
essays in political
& cultural criticism

imprint-academc.com

Published by
Imprint Academic, PO Box 200, Exeter EX5 5YX, UK

Published in the USA by Societas
Imprint Academic, Philosophy Documentation Center
PO Box 7147, Charlottesville, VA 22906-7147, USA

ISBN: 9781845401689

A CIP catalogue record for this book is available from the British Library and US Library of Congress

Contents

Authors' Acknowledgements

The authors wish to thank Professor Peter Hennessy, Professor Paul Langford, Professor Kevin Theakston and Dr. Mark Bennister for their comments and advice on our work. All conclusions and errors of fact and omission are our own. We would also like to thank Anthony Freeman and Keith Sutherland at Imprint Academic; and Nicola and George Blick, and Diana Jones.

About the authors

Dr. Andrew Blick is Senior Research Fellow, Democratic Audit. During 1999 he worked in the Prime Minister's Office, No.10 Downing Sreet. His other works include two books: *People Who Live in the Dark: the history of the special adviser in British politics* (London: Politico's, 2004); and *How to go to War: a handbook for democratic leaders* (London: Politico's, 2005). His current research interests include Parliament, the Civil Service and possible federal structures for the UK.

Professor George Jones has from 2003 been Emeritus Professor of Government at LSE where he was Professor of Government between 1976 and 2003. Since 2003 he has also been Honorary Professor at the University of Birmingham and Visiting Professor at Queen Mary, London. Harold Wilson once remarked of him that he 'really has got the feel of what No.10 is about' and that he had a 'perceptive understanding of the prime minister's dual political and administrative role'. He has authored, co-authored and edited a number of books, chapters and articles on British central and local government, including the acclaimed biography of Herbert Morrison: B. Donoughue and G.W. Jones, *Herbert Morrison: Portrait of* *a Politician* (London Weidenfeld and Nicolson, 1973) and (London: Phoenix Press, 2001). He has written about advising the Prime Minister and Cabinet in recent times in J.M. Lee, G.W. Jones and J. Burnham, *At the Centre of Whitehall* (Basingstoke: Macmillan, 1998); and a study of prime ministers in G.W. Jones (ed.), *West European Prime Ministers* (London: Frank Cass, 1991), as well as numerous chapters and articles about prime ministers and the Cabinet. He wrote the first study of the private secretaries of prime ministers in G.W. Jones, 'The Prime Ministers' Secretaries: Politicians or Administrators?' in J.G. Griffith (ed.), *From Politics to Administration* (London: Allen and Unwin, 1975).

Introduction

Uncovering the 'Mysteries or Secrets' of the Premiership

'There are certain Mysteries or Secrets in all Trades from the highest to the lowest, from that of *Prime Ministring* to this of *Authoring*, which are seldom discovered, unless to Members of the same Calling'.[1] These words, written by Henry Fielding, first appeared in print in February 1742. The previous month had seen the forced, final exit from government of Robert Walpole, the politician traditionally regarded as the first British premier, of whose ascendancy Fielding had been a prominent critic. Since the eighteenth century the office Walpole helped establish has undergone substantial changes and transformations – but the observation made about it by Fielding still resonates.

The reference to '*Prime Ministring*' as the 'highest' of 'Trades' was laced with irony. Walpole was often portrayed by contemporary satirists as a corrupt scoundrel hiding behind a façade of respectability. The term 'Prime Minister' was at the time more one of abuse directed at a person than a description of an office, since such a body, which was not yet institutionally entrenched, was regarded as constitutionally illegitimate.[2] Nonetheless Fielding was at the same time rightly acknowledging that the role performed by Walpole was important, as head of an embryonic institution lying at the apex of the political system. It has retained this prominence until now – and is universally accepted as doing

[1] The quote comes from the novel *Joseph Andrews*. Henry Fielding, *Joseph Andrews/Shamela* (Oxford: Oxford University Press, 1999), p.76.

[2] See eg: Brian W. Hill, *Sir Robert Walpole: 'Sole and Prime Minister'* (London: Hamish Hamilton, 1989), p.2.

so, whatever the particular interpretations placed upon it. An understanding of the premiership is vital to those who are or seek to be within government, or wish to observe its operation from the outside.

But the subject of the office of the British Prime Minister presents difficulties to those seeking to analyse it, not least because the formal basis for its existence, though greater than it was in the time of Fielding and Walpole, remains slender. Discourse about this institution suffers from both the overlooking of crucial evidence and the application of inadequate analysis. As a consequence, the premiership remains an institution surrounded by 'Mysteries or Secrets'. The purpose of the present work is to dispel them.

The application of history

This book draws upon methods from two academic fields. The first is that of history. Interpretations of the premiership often involve consideration of the extent to which it has changed over time. Some have argued that the 1997–2007 tenure of Tony Blair saw a transformation in the way the office operated. In their biography of Alastair Campbell, the media aide to Blair, Peter Oborne and Simon Walters referred to Blair's 'attempt to govern Britain in an entirely different and new way';[3] and Christopher Foster described 'Blair's replacement of Cabinet by prime ministerial government'.[4] In 2002 Blair himself used an historical reference to make the opposite case. When asked about his establishment of units in the Cabinet Office answering directly to him, he noted: 'I would say it is in the tradition of what Governments and Prime Ministers have done over a long period of time ... These things will come up from time to time ... I do not think we should see that as some great constitutional innovation'.[5]

If such views are to be tested then a discipline concerned with the systematic study of how events have played out

[3] Peter Oborne and Simon Walters, *Alastair Campbell* (London: Aurum, 2004), p.358.

[4] Christopher Foster, *British Government in Crisis, or the Third English Revolution* (Oxford: Hart, 2005), p.174.

[5] House of Commons Liaison Committee, Minutes of Evidence, 16 July 2002, Question 14.

over time is invaluable. Accordingly, notable additions have recently been made to the debate over changes to the office of Prime Minister by two historians, Paul Langford[6] and Peter Hennessy.[7] While Professor Langford looks forward from the eighteenth century, Professor Hennessy faces back from the twentieth and twenty first. In this work both perspectives are taken into account.

The historical discipline enables a comparison between events and trends in different periods and the discernment of underlying tendencies and patterns. As well as a thorough assessment of the development of the premiership, it makes possible consideration of how it has been interpreted at different times. When portrayals of the premiership from various eras are considered alongside each-other, significant similarities and contradictions can be revealed.

Potentially of use both to the critical assessment of existing theses about the office of Prime Minister and the development of new interpretations is the emphasis placed in historical method on the exhaustive and scrupulous analysis of sources. It can be applied to the gathering and processing of data from any period, from the distant to the contemporary. The need for a careful scouring of the evidence arises partly because of the long tradition for UK constitutional arrangements to be defined by deeds and the often loose conventions surrounding them, and not to be strictly codified: tendencies exceptionally strong for the premiership. Given the importance of actions to its composition it is apt that the Fielding passage quoted above uses a verb – *'Prime Ministring'*, rather than a noun. No comprehensive official delineation of the office of prime minister has ever been publicly issued; and it is doubtful one exists internally within Whitehall. Relevant information exists in diffuse form. In 1841, when – on behalf of Prince Albert – Queen Victoria requested details about the premiership from the former premier Viscount Melbourne, he, displaying an impressive instinctive grasp of the task of the British constitutional historian, explained:

---

[6] Paul Langford, 'Prime Ministers and Parliaments: The Long View, Walpole to Blair', The Annual History of Parliament Lecture, 2005, *Parliamentary History*, Vol. 25, pt.3 (2006), pp.382–94.

[7] See eg: Peter Hennessy, 'Rulers and Servants of the State: The Blair Style of Government 1997–2004', *Parliamentary Affairs*, Vol. 58 No. 1, 2005.

> the work of conducting the executive government, has rested so much on practice, on usage, on understanding, that there is no publication to which reference can be made for the explanation and description of it. It is to be sought in debates, protests, in letters, in memoirs, and wherever it can be picked up.[8]

One means developed for this work for uncovering the discrete development of British governance is through the technique called here 'constitutional etymology'. It involves tracing the usage of particular words and phrases. Like any other technique it has limitations, including being subject to potential technological fallibility and the possibility that different words may have been used to convey the same or a similar meaning. But it is useful in uncovering indicators of changing practices and perceptions. The availability of electronic databases – including the *Times Digital Archive*, covering the period 1785–1985 (thereafter it is stored elsewhere); the British Library and National Archives on-line catalogues; and an historic Hansard search engine extending back to 1803 – makes such an approach increasingly fruitful. In the chapters that follow, constitutional etymology is applied to words and phrases related to the premiership, No.10 staff, and Cabinet government.

There is also an attempt to identify and gather quantitative data that have a bearing on the nature of the office of Prime Minister. Use is made of statistics on the occurrence of Cabinet meetings – obtained partly through a request under the *Freedom of Information Act 2000* – and numbers of staff attached to the premiership. Using the online 'UK Statute Law Database' we have been able to measure the volume of legislation referring to the Prime Minister and other posts.

In this book particular emphasis is placed on accounts provided by those whom Fielding described as 'Members of the same Calling'. Included within this definition are not only prime ministers but the aides who have, throughout the history of the office, supported them. While the perspective of premiers and their assistants should not be accepted uncritically, it tends at present to be undervalued.

---

[8] Arthur Christopher Benson and Viscount Esher (eds), *The Letters of Queen Victoria*, 3 vols, Vol. 1, *1837–1843* (London: John Murray, 1908), Viscount Melbourne to Queen Victoria, 1 November 1841, p.358.

As well as primary sources – that is first-hand versions of events – we draw on secondary interpretations. Historians have worked in some detail on the origins of the premiership.[9] In the 1950s and 1960s respectively Byrum E. Carter[10] and F.W.G Benemy[11] wrote books on the institution that included some consideration of its development from the eighteenth century onwards. More recently Hennessy has produced a work that – though focused primarily on the office and its individual holders since 1945 – contains introductory material providing a long-term perspective.[12] But there is no single full-length account of the office from its origins to the present. There is a body of literature which seeks to place the contemporary premiership in international perspective[13], but the same efforts have not been made to compare different stages of its development.

Fortunately no such deficiency exists in a genre that deploys techniques associated with the historical discipline – biography. Accounts of individuals are of heightened importance in a consideration of the premiership, since the relatively informal nature of the role means the way in which it is exercised and develops can, to a large extent, be determined by the particular actions of those involved, including premiers, their staff and their associates. Yet at present, as the political scientist Kevin Theakston has noted, while 'There are innumerable political biographies and historical studies of British prime ministers ... these are neglected as a basis for comparison, generalization and theory testing or evaluation'.[14]

---

[9] See eg: Sir Lewis Namier, *Crossroads of Power: Essays on Eighteenth-Century England* (London: Hamish Hamilton, 1962).

[10] Byrum E. Carter, *The Office of Prime Minister* (London: Faber & Faber, 1956).

[11] F.W.G. Benemy, *The Elected Monarch* (London: George G. Harrap & Co., 1965).

[12] Peter Hennessy, *The Prime Minister: the office and its holders since 1945* (London: Allen Lane, 2000).

[13] See eg: G.W. Jones (ed.), *West European Prime Ministers* (London: Frank Cass, 1991); Michael Foley, *The Rise of the British Presidency* (Manchester: Manchester University Press, 1993); Sue Price, *Presidentializing the Premiership* (Basingstoke: Macmillan, 1997); Ludger Helms, *Presidents, Prime Ministers and Chancellors* (Basingstoke: Palgrave Macmillan, 2004); and Thomas Poguntke and Paul Webb (eds), *The Presidentialization of Politics* (Oxford: Oxford University Press, 2005).

[14] Kevin Theakston, 'Political Skills and Context in Prime Ministerial

The approach of employing academic techniques for the study of the past as a means of better understanding the present is known as 'applied history'[15]. It utilises two forms of reasoning: by analogy and by sequence. The former entails comparing and contrasting events occurring in different periods; while the latter involves examining the chain of developments leading up to a particular set of circumstances. One particular goal of applied history is the broadening of existing discussions. Debates, including about whether the premiership has grown in strength at the expense of institutions such as the Cabinet and Parliament, need to be considered from new perspectives. Another objective of applied history is to move backwards, in time the conventional starting points for analysis. Existing theories of the office, while often implicitly acknowledging the worth of history through referring to developments over time, tend to place a premium on more recent periods. Less interest is attracted by the first half of the twentieth century than the second; the nineteenth century receives only scant attention; and the eighteenth is ignored virtually altogether.[16] It is unsatisfactory that potentially revealing evidence is not drawn upon.

Applied history – and particularly the use of analogical reasoning – is controversial within the discipline with which it is associated. The present authors' rationale for deploying it, is that those engaged in any form of study whose work yields knowledge relevant to an important contemporary subject have a duty to share it. John Tosh and Seán Lang make a strong case for this approach. 'Historians may argue that since their expertise concerns the past not the present, it is not their job to draw out the practical import of their work'. But if they do not, 'then others who are less well informed and more prejudiced will produce ill-founded interpretations'.[17] Within

---

Leadership in Britain', *Politics and Policy*, Vol. 30, No. 2, June 2002, p.283.

[15] See: John Tosh, 'In defence of applied history: the History and Policy website', February 2006, http://www.historyandpolicy.org/papers/policy-paper-37.html

[16] See: Chapter One.

[17] John Tosh with Seán Lang, *The Pursuit of History: Aims, methods and new direction in the study of modern history*, Fourth edition, (Harlow: Pearson, 2006), pp.49–50. See as well: Margaret Macmillan, *The uses and abuses of history* (London: Profile, 2009).

debates about the premiership references to its supposed development over time are already rife. Often they are poorly-informed and frequently seem driven by agendas other than an impartial inquisitorial spirit.

It might be argued that, if the past can be so easily mishandled or manipulated, it is better not to introduce it into contemporary discussions. But the best corrective to pseudo-history is the genuine article. A common example of such malpractice is the construction of a premiss that events repeat themselves precisely within arbitrary parameters constructed by particular observers. Ironically one of the best means of dispelling notions of this nature is through reference to errors that have arisen in history through such outlooks. Anthony Eden's ill-fated 1956 policy towards Egyptian nationalisation of the Suez Canal came about partly because he interpreted circumstances as a replication of those of the 1930s that had culminated in the outbreak of the Second World War.

History has many possible values if applied to debates about the premiership. It can challenge the selective use of precedent to emphasise or downplay the significance of any particular action: a practice which needs to be supplanted by a fuller historical consideration, enabling the identification and assessment of the genuinely new or rare. Another tendency which can be counteracted is that of secular millennialism. The claim that the end is nigh, or upon us, can be correct at most, at only one moment. Yet for more than a century the demise of Cabinet, with its effective replacement by an hegemonic No.10, has frequently been identified as imminent, underway – or even as having already occurred. A related deficiency present in some theories, resting on a view of the past, is that of the simplistic, unilinear interpretation of developments. In accounts of the premiership it can involve claims that the person occupying the post has, in some sense, become a greater focus for media and public attention; or that those working within No.10 are subject to a continuously-increasing workload. Subsequent chapters show that there is a need to reconsider these and other commonly-advanced views. Our dual objective is to correct errors and open up rather than close off debate. Imperfect theories may have some truth within them, which needs to be qualified and understood in a broader setting.

Political science and history

Despite its wide potential as a tool of analysis of the premiership, the historical discipline has limitations. It provides a firm empirical basis but not a theoretical framework, creating the danger that accounts of the institution become a formless succession of events. Additional techniques are required.

Political science can add particular value to the consideration of the issue rightly treated as central by many analysts of the office of Prime Minister. The premiership matters most as an institution, involved in the exercise of power, a concept defined here as the ability to achieve desired outcomes.[18] Individuals who become prime ministers or senior No.10 aides tend to do so wishing to affect the course of events in some way; and the impact of the office upon outcomes is often highly rated by observers. But how should the differences it makes be assessed? Political scientists have devoted significant attention to the issue of power. Sophisticated models have been developed. The implications for and applicability to the premiership of one of them, the 'core-executive' framework, have been the subject of consideration.[19] There is scope for more work on this topic, undertaken here.

In particular, the present exploration and analysis of the office of Prime Minister, investigate the idea promoted by some theorists, that the attainment of goals should be considered in a multi-faceted sense. They suggest that power should be regarded as having different faces or dimensions.[20] This book approaches the premiership in this spirit, showing that existing theories of the institution fail to consider it in a sufficiently nuanced or broad manner.

---

18 See eg: Peter Morriss, *Power: A philosophical analysis* (Manchester: Manchester University Press, 2002); David Beetham, *The Legitimation of Power* (Basingstoke: Macmillan, 1991), p.43.

19 For an application of the 'core-executive' approach to the premiership see: Martin J. Smith, *The Core Executive in Britain* (Basingstoke: Macmillan, 1999), pp.71-105. For a critical assessment of this outlook, see: Richard Heffernan, 'Exploring (and Explaining) the British Prime Minister', *British Journal of Politics and International Relations*, 2005 Vol. 7, pp.605–620.

20 See eg: Steven Lukes, *Power: a radical view* (Basingstoke: Palgrave Macmillan, 2005); John Gaventa, 'Finding the Space for Change: A Power Analysis', *IDS Bulletin*, Vol. 37, No. 6, November 2006, pp.23–33.

One way in which outlooks present in political science can be utilised and built upon is through introducing into its theoretical setting the historical method. Every interaction through which participants seek to achieve particular goals takes place over time. The framework within which it plays out may change while it occurs, with implications for the outcome. A given process both operates in an environment affected by such earlier activities, and has implications for the setting within which subsequent activities take place. For all these reasons history – concerned as it is with events in a temporal trajectory – can enhance political-science understanding of power. The emphasis placed by some within the discipline on biographical analysis has uses as well. If power is the ability to achieve desired objectives, then its assessment requires an understanding of these aims. They can exist only in the consciousness of individuals, either seeking their own personal goals or pursuing shared agendas in a group. Institutions – though they may be configured in such a way as to encourage certain predilections on the part of those attached to them – do not possess ends in their own right. Consequently the study of power-processes necessitates the examination of particular people and their objectives.

More broadly, if political scientists are in the business of establishing universal laws about concepts such as power, then it is important to test the applicability of their theories across different time periods. History can help identify a spread of case studies from various eras that enable the verification, modification or refutation of particular models. If there is a point in the past before which a particular idea cannot be seen to apply, this phenomenon needs to be explained.

It is possible that political science can enhance history. If historical change in the premiership is to be understood, it is necessary to establish, amongst other things, whether the office has had an underlying role which has remained throughout, with alterations only to the ways and means through which this basic function is performed. The idea that this basic function may be that of public leadership, as discussed extensively in political-science literature[21], is explored here.

---

[21] See eg: Paul 't Hart and John Uhr, *Public leadership: perspectives and practices* (Canberra: Australian National University E Press, 2008); Jean

Though not proposing to resolve the many ongoing areas of debate associated with this subject, we consider the concept of public leadership in relation to the premiership as it has developed.

Using methods from history and political science, both individually and in conjunction, we seek to elucidate the office of the British Prime Minister. Chapter One describes recent interpretations of the institution that have been advanced. Chapter Two compares them with accounts that have been provided of the premiership since its early development, and considers the various themes that have been raised over time in the light of the available evidence. Chapter Three sets out an explanation of the development of the premiership over time, including its underlying public leadership role and the part played by the processes of 'zigzag' and 'administrative fusion and fission'. Chapter Four considers the viability of the resource dependency model upon which core-executive interpretations of the premiership rest and proposes a new 'matrix' for the analysis of exercises of power by No.10. Chapter Five, the conclusion, summarises the arguments presented in the book and considers their applications for both practitioners and observers of central government.

Throughout this work the focus is upon the *institution* of the premiership. Often in the literature there is not a clear distinction between the *individuals* who occupy the post of Prime Minister and the office. In this book, while there is discussion of particular prime ministers, it is from the perspective of their role as the leading figure within the premiership. The means used of distinguishing individual incumbents from the institution of which they are a part, set out in detail in Chapter Three, is through viewing the latter as a cluster of rights, functions and people performing them, centring on the former. In the following pages, the terms 'premiership', 'office of Prime Minister' and 'No.10'[22] are treated as interchangeable in referring to a widely-misunderstood institution, the development, nature and power of which we seek to reveal.

Blondel, *Political Leadership* (London: Sage, 1987); James MacGregor Burns, *Leadership* (New York: Harper and Row, 1978).

[22] Most prime ministers – including Walpole from 1735 – have operated out of 10 Downing Street

Chapter One

The Present Debate

In June 2007, after a decade as the British premier-in-waiting, Gordon Brown became Prime Minister. One who had waited so long to accede to the post might have been expected to be eager to wield the new authorities, instruments and personnel attached to No.10. But he displayed more interest in moving some of them away from the office he had just inherited. On taking up the job, he enacted or announced the intention to introduce a number of potentially decentralising changes. They included:

- More frequent, longer Cabinet meetings, allowing more time for the collective discussion of policy.[1]
- The attachment to No.10 of fewer special advisers – temporary officials, appointed on the patronage of the Prime Minister or minister they serve – than in the Tony Blair era.
- Revoking the 1997 measure issued under Order in Council that had provided a firmer legal basis for up to three No. 10 special advisers to exercise management functions over career staff; and issue instructions to officials anywhere in Whitehall.[2]
- Shifting what had been the Prime Minister's Delivery Unit, a team of approximately 35–40 staff, primarily concerned with the setting, monitoring and implementing of

[1] See eg: Andrew Rawnsley, 'The new Prime Minister is master of his universe', *Observer*, 1 July 2007.

[2] See: *The Civil Service (Amendment) (No.2) Order in Council 2007*, revoking Paragraph (3) of Article 3 of the *Civil Service Order in Council 1995* (the so called 'Principal Order' providing the legal basis for the Civil Service), as inserted by Article 1 of the *Civil Service (Amendment) Order in Council 1997*.

public service performance targets, more clearly into the organisational remit of the Treasury and away from the premiership.
- Making the *Ministerial Code* more focused and effective, arguably enhancing the autonomy of this set of rules for government members, and reducing the discretion of the premiership over its application (though the Prime Minister retained ultimate responsibility for drawing up the *Code* in conjunction with the Cabinet Secretary; and interpreting it in particular cases).[3]
- Introducing the *Governance of Britain* constitutional reform package, conceived initially as the flagship programme of the Brown premiership. It contained proposals to grant Parliament a new or increased part in activities in which No.10 played a primary or important role, such as entry into armed combat, treaty ratification, public appointments, intelligence and security, regulation and management of the Civil Service; and dissolutions and recalls of Parliament. There was to be a reduction in the involvement of the office of Prime Minister in church appointments as well.[4]

On the surface Brown appeared to be overseeing the dismantling of parts of the office to which he had long sought to move, some of which had been associated with it since the time it first emerged. Why should he do so? In part he was acting on a desire and political imperative for No.10 to operate – and to be seen to operate – differently from the way it had under his immediate predecessor, Blair.

In July 2002 Blair had told the House of Commons Liaison Committee his view:

> I make no apology about having a stronger centre. I think you need a stronger centre ... The real world is that with the Prime Minister the buck stops with you; that is the top job and that is how it should be. While the Departments ... are charged with policy ... the reality is for any modern Prime Minister you

[3] House of Commons Public Administration Select Committee (PASC), *Investigating the conduct of ministers*, HC381 (London: The Stationery Office, 2008).

[4] See: *The Governance of Britain*, CM 7170 (London: Ministry of Justice, July 2007).

> want to know what is happening in your own Government, to be trying to drive forward the agenda of change on which you were elected.[5]

The advent of a premier holding such an outlook and the actions carried out in pursuit of it helped generate much interest in the office of Prime Minister, within academia and beyond (although – as is shown in the next chapter – intensive scrutiny of this sort existed in earlier times as well). A particular focus was upon the role of the premiership in the controversial decision to participate in the US-led invasion of Iraq in 2003.[6] It was often argued that malign developments were underway – indeed this impression of the Blair period was so pervasive as to influence Brown to act in the way described above.

This chapter considers the interpretations of the premiership that have been advanced since Labour took office in 1997. It presents accounts and arguments that appeared between 1997 and 2010, and includes recollections provided by practitioners as well as secondary interpretations. Of necessity it is selective, with the emphasis on setting out the span of different arguments, across disciplines and made by differing kinds of observer. It describes how assessments of the premiership have widely portrayed it as a changing institution. Consideration is given to important themes within interpretations of the office of Prime Minister, including the roles of central government, Parliament, the Cabinet, local government, the No.10 staff, the Civil Service and the media. There is an examination of various conceptions of the nature of the premiership, including the idea of the appearance of a British presidency; and assessments of the power wielded by No.10. It reviews alleged constitutional defects associated

---

[5] House of Commons Liaison Committee (HCLC), Minutes of Evidence, 16 July 2002, Question 8.

[6] See eg: Andrew Blick, *How to go to War: A handbook for democratic leaders* (London: Politico's, 2005); Eoin O'Malley, 'Setting Choices, Controlling Outcomes: The Operation of Prime Ministerial Influence and The UK's Decision to Invade Iraq', *BJPIR*: 2007, Vol. 9; *Review of Intelligence on Weapons of Mass Destruction: Report of a Committee of Privy Counsellors*, HC898 (London: The Stationery Office, 2004); Clare Short, *An Honourable Deception? New Labour, Iraq, and the Misuse of Power* (London: Free Press, 2004).

with the role of the premiership and the remedies that have been proposed.

Theories of a developing institution

Nearly all theses of the premiership proposed since 1997 have contended that in various ways it was, or had recently been, changing. Dennis Kavanagh was one of a number of writers who set out a litany of difference when describing the key characteristics of Blair's 'leadership as Prime Minister'. There was 'a stronger political direction from No.10, substantially increasing the size, and influence of the political office, policy unit and press office' with the 'number of political appointees' growing from 8 to 28. Blair created 'new units' to serve him, 'focusing more on driving through No 10's agenda and less on acting as a broker between departments and overseeing the smooth working of the cabinet system'. He established a 'larger and much stronger media apparatus'[7]; and displayed a proclivity for 'listening to voters rather than the party'[8].

A key issue to be addressed following the conclusion that change occurred from 1997 is the extent to which it began with the Labour period of office, or was in motion before then. There has often been discussion of how far Blair's aggrandising tenure at No.10 represented something new.[9] In 2006 the Power Inquiry, an assessment of supposed democratic malaise in the UK, attributed a number of trends, including rising power wielded by the office of Prime Minister, to 'the last two decades', not emphasising the advent of the Labour government or the Blair ascendancy.[10] Conversely Peter Oborne and Simon Walters, in their biography of Blair's aide, Alastair Campbell, created the impression of a complete break with the past, with 1997 as a year zero, in their description of

---

[7] Dennis Kavanagh, 'The Blair premiership' in Anthony Seldon, *Blair's Britain* (Cambridge: Cambridge University Press, 2007), p.6.

[8] *Ibid*, p.7.

[9] See for instance: Martin Burch and Ian Holliday, 'The Blair Government and the Core Executive', *Government and Opposition*, 2004, pp.1–21; Richard Heffernan, 'Exploring (and Explaining) the British Prime Minister', *British Journal of Politics and International Relations*, 2005 Vol. 7, pp.605–620; R.A.W. Rhodes, 'The court politics of the Blair presidency', Senate Occasional Lecture, Parliament House, 27 June 2005.

[10] *Power to the People: the report of power* (York: Power Inquiry, 2006), p.125.

Blair's 'attempt to govern Britain in an entirely new and different way'.[11]

The most common view of the Blair premiership was as inheritor of certain processes, which it then accentuated and advanced. As the political scientists Martin Burch and Ian Holliday wrote: 'the Blair reforms ... represent an acceleration of pre-existing trends'.[12] The Conservative Democracy Task Force (CDTF), which reported to the party leader and would-be premier David Cameron, argued, 'The rise in the power of the Prime Minister at the expense of the Cabinet did not begin in 1997', noting that such a phenomenon had already been observed more than four decades beforehand; then went on: 'Nonetheless, the process has clearly accelerated in the last decade'. The Task Force concluded: 'the period since 1997 has seen an unprecedented further concentration of power'.[13] The political scientist Michael Foley wrote that 'Recent leaders have experienced pressures to become progressively differentiated from their organisational bases in terms of media attention, public recognition and political identity'. Foley labelled this phenomenon 'leadership stretch'. While arguing it pre-dated Blair, he insisted 'The level of expectations and the scale of outreach associated with Blair, however, have advanced the stretch effect to an unprecedented degree'.[14]

Alongside the issue of continuity and contrast between the pre- and post-May 1997 periods, the possibility of precedents from earlier eras was considered. In 2002 Blair to some extent placed his approach to the premiership in an historical tradition, when he remarked to the House of Commons Liaison Committee: 'If you go back in politics I think Prime Ministers fit into two categories: those that are supposed to have a strong centre are accused of being dictatorial; and those that do not are accused of being weak. You pays your money and you takes your choice really'.[15] The CDTF noted:

---

[11] Peter Oborne and Simon Walters, *Alastair Campbell*, p.358.
[12] Burch and Holliday, 'The Blair Government and the Core Executive', p.2.
[13] Roger Gough, *An End to Sofa Government: Better working of Prime Minister and Cabinet* (London: Conservative Democracy Task Force, 2007), p.2.
[14] Michael Foley, 'Presidential Attribution as an Agency of Prime Ministerial Critique in a Parliamentary Democracy: The Case of Tony Blair', *British Journal of Politics and International Relations*, 2004, Vol. 6, p.293.
[15] HCLC, Minutes of Evidence, 16 July 2002, Question 5.

'Both Harold Wilson – like Mr. Blair, another leader obsessed with media management – and Edward Heath were seen in their time as "presidential" leaders'. Margaret Thatcher too, the CDTF recalled, took steps 'to assert her priorities against departmental ministers, and moved discussion away from full Cabinet'.[16] Christopher Foster, the former academic and government adviser, claimed that while many premiers, including Lord Palmerston, Benjamin Disraeli, William Gladstone, Lord Salisbury, David Lloyd George, Winston Churchill, Harold Wilson, Edward Heath and Margaret Thatcher dominated their cabinets, some being criticised by contemporary ministers for their dictatorial nature, Blair was different. His 'unique contribution was to take [Cabinet's] executive supremacy away by no longer letting it be a decision-making body'.[17]

Describing a dilemma created by a focus on the characteristics of the premiership under Blair, the contemporary historian Peter Hennessy remarked:

> the big question ... is whether the years since 1997 have cumulatively amounted to a sea-change or merely a protracted squall: will the Blair style turn out to have been *sui generis*, intriguing and turbulent but essentially transient, or has my and others' fascination with what one of his Cabinet calls the "Tony wants" phenomenon distracted us from detecting deeper and more permanent changes in the way our government now works?[18]

Three related questions arise from this comment, and were explored by others. The first was: how lasting were the changes to the premiership that occurred during the Blair era likely to be? Oborne and Walters claimed the departure of Campbell in 2003 'marked the end of an experiment in government', with earlier less centralised practices reviving.[19] But Foster argued: 'Blair's replacement of Cabinet by prime ministerial government' was not properly reversed even after 'the collapse in Blair's

[16] Gough, *An End to Sofa Government*, p.2.
[17] Christopher Foster, *British Government in Crisis, or the Third English Revolution*, p.252.
[18] Peter Hennessy, 'Rulers and Servants of the State: The Blair Style of Government 1997–2004', p.6.
[19] Oborne and Walters, *Alastair Campbell*, p.361.

prestige at the end of 2003'.[20] Late in the Blair incumbency, the CDTF (to which Foster was an adviser) concluded: 'While the system's pathologies are to a certain extent a reflection of the current Prime Minister's preoccupations and working style, this does not provide a full explanation of what has happened, nor would a change of leadership alone be enough to resolve them'.[21] Discussing with the Liaison Committee in 2002 various administrative alterations he had affected, Blair said: 'Future Prime Ministers may decide to do it differently' but that he had 'a kind of hunch that most Prime Ministers will want to keep that strength in the centre'.[22]

The second question raised by Hennessy's observation was: to what extent was there a distinction between the particular premier and the institution they headed? Richard Heffernan cautioned, 'We too often allow the style of the individual Prime Minister to influence our understanding of the substance of the prime ministerial office'.[23] Graham Allen, a former Labour whip and backbench MP, stressed that the particular characteristics of those who arrive at No.10 should not distract from the nature of the role, since 'however "unpresidential" they may at first appear to be – perhaps a John Major or an Iain Duncan-Smith…[they] are presented with an *inventory of Prime Ministerial power which is awesome* [emphasis in original]'.[24] In their historical study of No.10 staff, Dennis Kavanagh and Anthony Seldon emphasised that in any consideration of the premiership there were people other than the particular holder to be taken into account. The authors asked 'How does the Prime Minister manage?' and answered that individual premiers do not make all their own decisions. They argued that prime ministers, at least since William Gladstone, had relied on 'an official who often became much more important than a mere confidential aide'. The authors went on: 'The position has now changed again.

[20] Foster, *British Government in Crisis*, p.174.
[21] Gough, *An End to Sofa Government*, p.3.
[22] HCLC, Minutes of Evidence, 16 July 2002, Question 8.
[23] Richard Heffernan, 'Why the Prime Minister cannot be a President: Comparing Institutional Imperatives in Britain and America', *Parliamentary Affairs*, Vol. 58, No.1, 2005, p.55.
[24] See eg: Graham Allen, *The Last Prime Minister: Being Honest About the UK Presidency* (London: Graham Allen, 2001), p.17.

No longer does the premier rely on just one or two key figures for advice: the prime ministership is now an office'.[25]

Finally, Hennessy suggested that types of change needed to be differentiated, but into what? The political scientist Martin Smith suggested a distinction between operating within existing structures and the 'reconstruction of the rules' themselves.[26] In a discussion of the relationship between the premiership and Parliament from a long-term historical perspective, Paul Langford stated: 'Change is undeniable. The question is whether it signifies a shift in the working of these august institutions, or merely fluctuations within an older pattern'.[27] Considering the history of the office as a whole, Kavanagh and Seldon argued, 'New roles have appeared' such as that of party leader in the nineteenth century, 'while other roles have declined relatively', including 'the importance of the relations with the monarch and the patronage role'. They saw the 'complexity of the job, and the speed of response demanded' as having 'changed out of all recognition'. But 'The nature of the Prime Minister's job has not changed fundamentally since the days of Walpole.[28]

Themes

Within this broad consensus that change of some kind had occurred to the premiership since 1997 a number of themes were explored.

The tasks of central government

There was often a consideration of the activities performed by government as a whole, and within it the tasks executed by the office of Prime Minister. In his account of what he defined as the emergence of an informal UK presidency Allen wrote,

> from the second half of the nineteenth century onwards, central government has taken on more and more responsibilities,

[25] Dennis Kavanagh and Anthony Seldon, *The Powers Behind the Prime Minister: The Hidden Influence of Number Ten* (London: HarperCollins, 2000), pp. xi–xii.
[26] Martin J. Smith, *The Core Executive in Britain*, p.80.
[27] Paul Langford, 'Prime Ministers and Parliament: The Long View, Walpole to Blair', p.383.
[28] Kavanagh and Seldon, *The Powers Behind the Prime Minister*, p.xi.

> particularly during the two world wars which required the total mobilisation of the British state. This has produced a massive rise in executive power.[29]

The process Allen described contributed in his view to a dominant premiership. Smith observed a similar trend, but did not see it as leading to the same outcome. Charting 'the growth of the state', Smith described how in the nineteenth century expansion took place 'to deal with the problems of urbanisation and industrialisation'; while in the 1920s and 1940s it was 'a response to war, and in the post-war period it was the result of class pressure, social change and economic crisis'. This process 'had a significant impact on the key institutions within the state – the core executive'. Departments appeared that were difficult to coordinate from the centre – presumably amounting to a constraint upon the office of Prime Minister in achieving an impact within government.[30]

As well as the 'state' or central government in general, No.10 was portrayed as having accumulated more tasks. In his work on the premiership and individual prime ministers since 1945 Hennessy depicted a series of 'historical accretions' to the office which, after the initial emergence of the role in the early eighteenth century, 'came in a cluster in the early 1780s and in spurts thereafter',[31] and he recorded what he described as a 'considerable waxing of functions over a fifty year period,' from the late 1940s.[32] Once again there was disagreement over whether such accruals should be viewed as a source of strength or weakness. Allen saw the office of Prime Minister as having accumulated a 'massive political arsenal with rack upon rack of power, authority and influence'.[33] But in the view of Michael Barber, Head of the Prime Minister's Delivery Unit from 2001–5, growing responsibilities undermined No.10. He observed a process of increasing strains upon the premiership 'which have accelerated since the 1960s'.[34] Barber

[29] Allen, *The Last Prime Minister*, p.9.
[30] Smith, *The Core Executive in Britain*, p.70.
[31] Peter Hennessy, *The Prime Minister: The Office and its Holders Since 1945*, p.45.
[32] *Ibid*, p.59.
[33] See eg: Allen, *The Last Prime Minister*, p.17.
[34] Michael Barber, *Instruction to Deliver: Tony Blair, Public Services and the Challenge of Achieving Targets* (London: Politico's, 2007), p.297.

argued, 'The demands of the role come in part from the lack of constitutional definition, which means that the limits are ill defined, and in part from the nature of the modern world'. Trends he identified as fitting into the latter set of causes included the requirements of the media; a rising volume of business; and a faster 'pace of decision-making'.[35]

Blair's testimony to the Liaison Committee in July 2002 suggested that his creation of what he described as a 'strong centre' was driven by a desire to ensure certain government functions were performed effectively. He described how he needed to respond to a quantity of mail that was more than double the amount received by his predecessor, John Major – seemingly making a broader point about being a greater focus for public attention. More significantly he referred to two prevailing concerns – over security, prompted by the rise of international terrorism; and his programme to improve public services – necessitating the introduction of new staff and functions around the Prime Minister. He concluded,

> I am not disputing the fact that we have strengthened the centre considerably; but I say that is the right thing to do; it is necessary if we are wanting to deliver the public service reform that is essential for us and given the totally changed foreign policy and security situation.[36]

For Foster, the supplanting of collective government by No.10 that he observed was prompted by the desire for an effective government response to crises of the post-Second World War period. Growing economic and social problems had created 'gridlock', with 'apparently endless wrangling in Cabinet over the best way forward'; and in turn 'overload', that is the subjection of the administrative system and personnel to greater burdens of work than could be effectively executed. Consequently the malaise of the 1970s, including substantial industrial unrest, 'tested to incipient destruction a system of government which had evolved to meet changing circumstances

[35] *Ibid*, p.300.
[36] HCLC, Minutes of Evidence, 16 July 2002, Question 7.

for almost two hundred years'.[37] Such circumstances, Foster argued, led Thatcher and later Blair, to draw the conclusion 'that successful politics now required prime-ministerial, or quasi-presidential, government, replacing Cabinet Government'. But in Foster's view it was a flawed approach that did not succeed.[38]

While the idea of the occurrence of a long-term growth in the functions of central government and often the premiership was generally accepted, Langford recorded certain reservations. He noted that while in present times there was 'activity, in the economy, in education, health and social welfare generally ... the implied historical contrast can be overdone'. As far back as the eighteenth century 'governments accepted considerable responsibility for social policy' and 'Walpole himself acknowledged his ministerial responsibility for the "wealth of the nation"'. Langford went on 'It is also worth recalling that the state at that time had religious functions unthinkable today. Some oversight of souls was its business well into the era of parliamentary government'.[39] He described how, before the mid-nineteenth century, the premiership normally directly controlled the Treasury[40]; whereas subsequently a loose principle had emerged that it was a non-departmental office. He concluded 'Contrary to the conventional wisdom, where executive authority is concerned, modern premiers seem less rather than more potent'.[41]

Parliament

A common subject of interest was the relative status of the premiership and Parliament. The CDTF argued: 'Parliament has been expected to be the Prime Minister's poodle';[42] while the writer Michael Dobbs believed 'the House of Commons has been neutered'.[43] The Power Inquiry thesis of aggrandisement by No.10 rested in part on the claim that over

[37] Foster, *British Government in Crisis*, p.85.
[38] *Ibid*, p.84.
[39] Langford, 'Prime Ministers and Parliament: The Long View, Walpole to Blair', p.383.
[40] *Ibid*, p.385.
[41] *Ibid*, p.388.
[42] Gough, *An End to Sofa Government*, p.1.
[43] Michael Dobbs, 'Brown's house of cards', *The Express on Sunday*, 5 November 2006.

the previous two decades 'The Executive has become more powerful at the expense of MPs in the House of Commons'.[44] It identified a number of tendencies as contributing to this shift. They included a growth in the number of MPs who were members of the government and were bound to vote with it; whips being more ruthless in enforcing party discipline; the possession of personal mandates by premiers; a more cramped legislative timetable; the weakening of the convention of ministerial responsibility; and the rise of the premiership as a monopolistic political force.[45] Foley referred to the existence of 'the belief that parliament is becoming marginalised as a political institution in contemporary British government'. He wrote that 'Political, constitutional and international dynamics are disrupting parliament's centrality to the British system'.[46]

The academic, Richard Rose, distinguished between three historic groups of prime ministers: the 'old school' who entered Parliament between 1900 and 1931; a 'transition generation', namely Harold Wilson, Edward Heath and James Callaghan; and the 'new school', that began with Margaret Thatcher. Those from the final group lived 'in a television age that can create celebrities overnight ... For the new-style Prime Minister, the box that counts is the television, rather than the despatch box, next to the Mace in the House of Commons. What is said on television matches or surpasses in importance what is said in Westminster'.[47] Simon Jenkins, a journalist, called the BBC 'Britain's parliament by default'.[48]

Another journalist, Peter Riddell, dissented from those who tended to portray Parliament as barely relevant. He acknowledged there were 'now ... many other ways of announcing decisions and communicating with the public – and more direct sources of political authority and legitimacy'. But:

---

[44] *Power to the People: the report of power*, p.125.

[45] *Ibid*, p.133.

[46] Michael Foley, *The British presidency: Tony Blair and the politics of public leadership* (Manchester: Manchester University Press, 2000) p.309.

[47] Richard Rose, *The Prime Minister in a Shrinking World* (Cambridge: Polity, 2001), p.6.

[48] Simon Jenkins, 'Blair wants history to judge him, but the police are first in line', *The Sunday Times*, 4 February 2007.

> Prime Ministers still have to govern through Parliament ... the House of Commons remains central both to the power and accountability of Prime Ministers. They are, and can continue, in office only because they can command a majority in the House of Commons. Prime Ministers cannot afford to ignore Parliament, and particularly the opinion and interests of their own party's backbench MPs.[49]

Cabinet

Another institution often portrayed as a loser in the face of a dominant premiership was the Cabinet. Oborne and Walters wrote that 'Tony Blair could not see the point of cabinets. He governed as a benevolent dictator, tempered by character assassination'.[50] Robin, Lord Butler, the former Cabinet Secretary and Head of the Home Civil Service (and, like Foster, an adviser to the CDTF), stated while in retirement in an interview with the journalist and Conservative politician Boris Johnson: 'The Cabinet now and I don't think there is any secret about this doesn't make decisions'.[51] Allen claimed, 'No one today other than the most self deluding Cabinet Minister or frustrated Permanent Secretary pretends that the Cabinet is an important policy forum'.[52] According to Foster, under Blair Cabinet 'became a briefing group'.[53] Foster went on 'When his iron grip over ministers and backbenchers weakened in 2003, what returned was not Cabinet, or rather not a Cabinet system, but a talking shop reminiscent of 18th and 19th century Cabinets, though with far more to do'.[54]

The Power Inquiry claimed to have identified a widely-held perception that

> the Prime Minister makes decisions and brings them to the Cabinet simply for endorsement. Indeed, there is much evidence in the public domain to support this view. *The political conventions of British government – that the Prime Minister is the first amongst equals and that policy is the product of discussion and*

[49] Peter Riddell, 'Prime Ministers and Parliament', *Parliamentary Affairs*, Vol. 57, No.4, 2004, p.814.
[50] Oborne and Walters, *Alastair Campbell*, p.359.
[51] Boris Johnson, 'How not to run a country', *Spectator*, 11 December 2004.
[52] Allen, *The Last Prime Minister*, p.25.
[53] Foster, *British Government in Crisis*, p.175.
[54] Foster, *Ibid.* p.159.

> *negotiation within Cabinet – are now seriously eroded* [emphasis in original].[55]

A further feature of Cabinet government said to have suffered was that of collective loyalty. Jenkins wrote that 'Cabinet government has collapsed, as ministers campaign against each other's policies (as on hospitals) or discard responsibility for the doings of their predecessors (as in the Home Office)'.[56]

Ideas of a diminished or extinguished Cabinet were often linked with Blair's supposed pursuit of an informal style of government, taking decisions in small, unofficial inner groupings. The CDTF – claiming that 'Cabinet government has been all but destroyed'[57] – referred to 'traditional cabinet government having atrophied in favour of the celebrated "denocracy" [a reference to the premier's 'den', a room in No.10] or "sofa government"'.[58] Clare Short was, as Secretary of State for International Development, a Cabinet member during the Iraq War. She later resigned, complaining that the body had been usurped. There was, she said, 'no real collective responsibility because there is no collective'.[59] She argued that during the lead-up to the conflict, 'Tony Blair and his entourage were running the policy in a very informal and personal way and wanted to keep knowledge to themselves in order to keep control'.[60] While the subject of Iraq was addressed at full Cabinet, 'there were no ... papers' to form the basis of discussion; and 'the Defence and Overseas Policy Committee never met'. The minutes produced of Cabinet discussions were 'lean ... They are very limited'.[61]

In 2004 an official inquiry, under the chairmanship of Butler, investigating the apparently flawed intelligence on the presence of weapons of mass destruction in Iraq, reported. It noted it had 'received evidence from two former Cabinet members, one of the present and one of a previous administration, who

---

[55] *Power to the People*, p.134.
[56] Jenkins, 'Blair wants history to judge him, but the police are first in line'.
[57] Gough, *An End to Sofa Government*, p.1.
[58] *Ibid*, p.2.
[59] Hansard, House of Commons Debates, 12 May 2003, col.38.
[60] Clare Short, *An Honourable Deception? New Labour, Iraq, and the Misuse of Power*, pp.146–7.
[61] House of Commons Foreign Affairs Committee (FAC), Minutes of Evidence, 17 June 2003, Questions 100, 72, 136.

expressed their concern about the informal nature of much of the Government's decision-making process, and the relative lack of use of established Cabinet Committee machinery'.[62] The Review Team described how, while the Cabinet discussed Iraq frequently, 'The Ministerial Committee on Defence and Overseas Policy did not meet'. Yet 'over the period from April 2002 to the start of military action, some 25 meetings attended by the small number of key Ministers, officials and military officers most closely involved, provided the framework of discussion and decision-making within Government'. The 'inescapable consequence ... was to limit wider collective discussion and consideration by the Cabinet to the frequent but unscripted occasions when the Prime Minister, Foreign Secretary and Defence Secretary briefed the Cabinet orally'. While 'Excellent quality papers were written by officials' they 'were not discussed in Cabinet or in Cabinet Committee'. The lack of 'papers circulated in advance' made it 'much more difficult for members of the Cabinet, outside the small circle directly involved, to bring their political judgement and experience to bear on the major decisions, for which the Cabinet as a whole must carry responsibility'.[63] The Review Team concluded by expressing concern 'that the informality and circumscribed character of the Government's procedures which we saw in the context of policy-making towards Iraq, risks reducing the scope for informed collective political judgement'.[64]

Cabinet members were said to have been weakened not only as a group, but also individually. The CDTF referred to 'the reduced independence of ministers, who have seen their objectives set at personal meetings with the Prime Minister. The most recent reshuffle saw Prime Ministerial letters giving new ministers detailed instructions as to their tasks'.[65] But Blair insisted:

> I simply do not recognise this notion that policy is not made in departments ... Now of course it is a product of a whole series of influences that come to them from within their own department,

[62] *Review of Intelligence on Weapons of Mass Destruction*, pp.146–7.
[63] *Ibid*, pp.147–8.
[64] *Ibid*, p.148.
[65] Gough, *An End to Sofa Government*, p.3.

> from outside their own department, but if you wanted to know who the best person is to talk to you about any of these policies, it would be the Ministers themselves.[66]

The Cabinet Secretary and Head of the Home Civil Service from 1998–2002, Richard Wilson, emphasised that in law and public accounting the traditional position remained, stating in 2000 'the legal power of action rests with Secretaries of State and the financial resources are voted by Parliament to Secretaries of State'.[67]

Other institutions

A number of other bodies were portrayed as suffering from reduced autonomy as a consequence of a dominant premiership. They included local government and political parties. One feature of Foster's theory of a growing role for No.10, was the idea that 'Local authorities no longer have the freedom they had to adjust their policies to reflect the wishes of their electorates'.[68] Allen wrote: 'Not for Britain the foreign concepts of States' Rights as in the USA or powerful regional Lander as in Germany or the Departments and Mayoralities of France. In the UK our power is unitary – a single track to the door of No 10 Downing Street'.[69] Allen stated: 'Party members and structures are now being reshaped by the consequences of the Presidency … one person or a key group can seize control of a Party, or have the Party gifted to them in order to recapture electoral success'.[70] Blair, Allen argued, 'knows that in the modern Presidential era, distance from the Party is actually an electoral asset'.[71] The commentator Keith Sutherland portrayed parties as both having lost autonomy and contributing to a dominant premiership:

> Political parties used to have much of the character of aristocratic clubs, containing most of the people without whom a leader could not govern. After 1945 this characteristic has more or

[66] HCLC, Minutes of Evidence, 16 July 2002, Question 17.
[67] House of Commons Select Committee on Public Administration, Minutes of Evidence, 9 February 2000, Question 50.
[68] Foster, *British Government in Crisis*, p.291.
[69] Allen, *The Last Prime Minister*, p.17.
[70] *Ibid*, pp.32–3.
[71] *Ibid*, p.36.

> less vanished – parties have become bands of standardized professionals who, having chosen a leader, are then obliged to fall in line behind him/her.[72]

Prime-ministerial aides and Whitehall

There was interest in the role of No.10 aides, who were often portrayed as possessing pronounced importance. In her account of the build-up to the Iraq War Short referred to the existence of a 'close entourage' of staff around Blair, comprising Alastair Campbell, Jonathan Powell, Sally, Baroness Morgan and David Manning. 'That was the team, they were the ones who moved together all the time ... That was the in group, that was the group that was in charge of policy'.[73] A member of this supposed clique, Campbell, responded by stating 'I was at a huge number of meetings with the Prime Minister during the Iraq conflict, and before and since'. He stated that courses of action regarding such issues as media appearances or the detail of diary commitments might be selected without ministers present, but 'If you are talking about a decision about whether the Prime Minister was going to commit British forces into action, the idea something like that is going to be taken without full consultation of his ministerial colleagues in the Cabinet is nonsense'.[74]

One focus was on the enlarged contingent of partisan staff at No.10, many of whom were employed as temporary civil servants, categorised as special advisers. Richard Rose wrote, 'Blair has made significant and irreversible alterations in the new-style Prime Ministership. First, Number Ten now has a far larger political staff than ever before, and the political staff has more authority over civil servants'.[75] Allen argued, 'One area where the current Prime Minister took the Presidency in the UK further was that in May 1997 he walked into No 10 with *the first Presidential transition team in UK history* [emphasis in original]'.[76] The Power Inquiry described how 'Prime Ministers have increasingly drawn a coterie of appointed advisers around

---

[72] Keith Sutherland, *A People's Parliament* (Exeter: Imprint Academic, 2008), p.42.
[73] FAC, Minutes of Evidence, 17 June 2003, Question 98.
[74] *Ibid*, 25 June 2003. "Questions 1115–7."
[75] Rose, *The Prime Minister in a Shrinking World*, p.234.
[76] Allen, *The Last Prime Minister*, p.29.

themselves who not only owe their positions to their boss, but are also only answerable to him or her'.[77] Individual partisan aides were singled out as important – in particular Campbell. Oborne and Walters described him as 'Blair's vizier or grand chamberlain'. Possessed of 'such complete authority he was greatly feared by Cabinet ministers, capable of poisoning or favouring their careers. Though technically no more than a press adviser he carried more mystique and authority than they did'.[78]

Special advisers across government and especially at No. 10 became a subject of much attention and controversy.[79] The journalist Martin Wolf drew a comparison with Ancient China, when emperors of the T'ang dynasty came to rely on eunuchs in preference to members of the established bureaucracy, since the former were clearly attached and loyal to the ruler.[80] There was interest in the engagement by special advisers in public relations activities. The CDTF claimed:

> Alongside an excessive expansion of policy advisers, the biggest growth has been in media management operations, which have been concentrated around the Prime Minister and the No. 10 Strategic Communications Unit ... Though there were changes at the top and a less intrusive style after Alastair Campbell's departure in 2003, the strong presentational focus has remained'.[81]

Interest in the media-related activities of special advisers continued under Brown. In 2009 the No.10 media aide Damian McBride, a special adviser, was exposed as having been involved in discussions about the possible spreading of malicious gossip about opposition politicians. McBride was forced to resign amidst widespread public criticism.

A new authority created for senior No.10 partisan aides was remarked upon. The journalist Nicholas Jones referred to the 'unprecedented executive powers' granted by Blair

[77] *Power to the People*, p.134.
[78] Oborne and Walters, *Alastair Campbell*, p.359.
[79] See: Andrew Blick, *People Who Live in the Dark: the history of the special adviser in British politics* (London: Politico's, 2004).
[80] Martin Wolf, 'The castration of British government', *Financial Times*, 12 May 2006.
[81] Gough, *An End to Sofa Government*, p.3.

to his two senior special advisers, Campbell and Jonathan Powell.[82] The CDTF noted how 'On the first weekend of the new government, an Order in Council unprecedentedly gave two special advisers – Jonathan Powell and Alastair Campbell – formal authority to manage civil servants'.[83] The former Cabinet Secretary, Robert, Lord Armstrong, judged that career officials 'should not be responsible or accountable to Special Advisers, and Special Advisers should not be given responsibility for managing or giving instructions to civil servants'. He felt the change brought about by the Order in Council 'was unwise' since a suspicion – whether correct or not – that it was exercised in pursuit of 'party political considerations' was likely.[84]

The issue of this provision for Campbell and Powell was linked to broader concern about the undermining of the status of the permanent Civil Service and traditional Whitehall values. Sir Robin Mountfield, a former Permanent Secretary at the Cabinet Office, told the Committee on Standards in Public Life, 'In the centre' – by which he meant primarily at No.10 – 'there is this very large number of special advisers, a critical mass, one might almost say'. The outsiders had between them created 'a sort of inner clique that has become ... very often the primary source of advice, with the civil service advice being seen as secondary'.[85] Foster wrote 'civil servants around Blair were kept at a greater distance than before. With few exceptions, they never got to know him as well as his [party political] aides did'.[86] There was a suggestion that permanent officials were downgraded to simply being responsible for implementing decisions in which they were not involved, but at the same time were targeted for criticism when failures occurred. In a discussion of 'political appointees in Number Ten' the CDTF complained 'Presentation has led policy. The

[82] Nicholas Jones, *The Control Freaks: How New Labour Gets its Own Way* (London: Politico's, 2001), p.239.
[83] Gough, *An End to Sofa Government*, p.3.
[84] 'Ministers, Special Advisers and the Permanent Civil Service', Memorandum by Lord Armstrong of Ilminster to the Committee on Standards in Public Life, 11 July 2002.
[85] The Committee on Standards in Public Life, Transcripts of Oral Evidence, 27 June 2002 (Afternoon Session).
[86] Foster, *British Government in Crisis*, p.161.

Civil Service has been left to carry the blame for policies that have proved impossible to implement'.[87]

Oborne and Walters claimed that during the Blair premiership there was a 'collapse of traditional dividing lines between civil servant and politician', affecting the Intelligence and Security Agencies as well as mainstream Whitehall.[88] They stated that Campbell was 'impatient with the proprieties, decencies and neutrality of the old civil service. He wanted to turn government into an election fighting machine';[89] and they portrayed the Blair regime as lacking respect for 'an independent civil service motivated by a disinterested ethic of public service rather than a feverish loyalty to the government of the day'.[90] Continuing the theme of an undermining of Whitehall impartiality, Nicholas Jones claimed that as a consequence of the approach to presentation taken under Blair, 'undue pressure has been placed on civil servants working for the government information and communication service'.[91]

There was discussion of whether No.10 support structures had undergone a qualitative change. The CDTF observed 'a blurring of roles between the No. 10 staff, serving the Prime Minister, and the Cabinet Office, serving the entire Cabinet – unsurprisingly, to the disadvantage of the latter'.[92] Jones claimed that Blair 'succeeded in turning the Prime Minister's office into a separate department in all but name'.[93] Foster argued a similar development had taken place, but rather than No.10, he claimed, the Cabinet Office 'Though not in name ... became a Prime Minister's Department in fact'.[94] Barber had a different outlook. Rather than emphasising growth at the centre he argued Blair:

> carries a far heavier burden than any of his Cabinet colleagues. Yet, ironically, he is the only one who does not have a department or a ministerial team to share his burden. Instead he has the

[87] Gough, *An End to Sofa Government*, p.1.
[88] Oborne and Walters, *Alastair Campbell*, p.360.
[89] *Ibid*, p.153.
[90] *Ibid*, p.359.
[91] Jones, *The Control Freaks*, p.241.
[92] Gough, *An End to Sofa Government*, p.3.
[93] Jones, *The Control Freaks*, p.238.
[94] Foster, *British Government in Crisis*, p.170.

> No.10 operation and a less-than-coherent collection of units and functions in the Cabinet Office.[95]

In 2002 Blair told the Liaison Committee that the view that a Prime Minister's Department was emerging was not 'constitutionally or practically correct'. He noted: 'my Number 10 office has roughly the same or perhaps even fewer people working for it than the Irish Taoiseach's. To put this in context, there are far fewer people than either the French Prime Minister, never mind the Elysee and the Prime Minister combined, or the German Chancellor'.[96]

One facet of a possible blurring of roles between No.10 and the Cabinet Office was explored by the Butler Review Team. It noted that in 2001 'two key posts at the top of the Cabinet Secretariat, those of Head of the Defence and Overseas Secretariat and Head of the European Affairs Secretariat, were combined with the posts of the Prime Minister's advisers on Foreign Affairs and on European Affairs respectively'. The impact of this reconfiguration was 'to weight their responsibility to the Prime Minister more heavily than their responsibility through the Cabinet Secretary to the Cabinet as a whole'. It was 'a shift which acts to concentrate detailed knowledge and effective decision-making in fewer minds at the top'[97]; and it had lessened 'the support of the machinery of government for the collective responsibility of the Cabinet in the vital matter of war and peace'.[98]

The media and 'personalised' politics

There was interest in the relationship between the office of Prime Minister and the media; and the importance of a public focus on the personality of the premier, as opposed to various institutions or collective structures. Paul Langford referred to the emergence of claims that 'the prime minister increasingly depends on a public beyond parliament, exploiting not merely the power of party, but the persuasiveness of the modern media'.[99] According to Oborne and Walters, Campbell,

[95] Barber, *Instruction to Deliver*, p.307.
[96] HCLC, Minutes of Evidence, 16 July 2002, Question 5.
[97] *Review of Intelligence on Weapons of Mass Destruction*, p.147.
[98] *Ibid*, p.148.
[99] Langford, 'Prime Ministers and Parliament', p.383.

on behalf of Blair, 'invented ... a form of manipulative populism, bypassing parliament and Cabinet in an attempt to communicate directly with the voters'.[100] Foster wrote that 'Many factors have long made Prime Ministers more than first among equals in gaining public attention' but 'modern Prime Ministers since Churchill – and television – must dominate election campaigns and, once elected, be visible every day, utter an opinion on every event'.[101] Allen wrote, 'As much as any other factor, it is the emergence of minute-to-minute political coverage which has allowed the Prime Ministership to make the quantum leap to a British Presidency in recent years'.[102] He went on: 'today's media demand one talking head that speaks for the whole of the Party and Government ... *If Britain did not have a President the media would need to invent one* [emphasis in original]'.[103] Allen concluded: 'The weakening of ideology and the improvement of communications means that the style of modern politics has become much more personal, aiding the decline of Cabinet Government and the rise of the UK Presidency'.[104] Michael Foley described how Blair:

> has achieved a ubiquitous presence in the coverage of news events and in the portrayal of political developments. He is constantly seen and heard as the authoritative voice of government intentions and reactions. Just as the Prime Minister dominates news agendas and political commentary, so in turn the media increasingly gravitate towards him as the chief source of news and explanation. The inflation of personal projection and the intensity of public consumption have the effect of displacing cabinet ministers into relative obscurity and of marginalising other political institutions to the periphery of public attention.[105]

Even those who did not endorse theses of presidency or dominance by No.10 often accepted that the nature of media coverage of the premiership was becoming more intense; and

[100] Oborne and Walters, *Alastair Campbell*, p.359.
[101] Foster, *British Government in Crisis*, pp.177–8.
[102] See eg: Allen, *The Last Prime Minister*, p.20.
[103] See eg: *Ibid*, p.21.
[104] *Ibid*, p.36.
[105] Michael Foley, 'Presidential Attribution as an Agency of Prime Ministerial Critique in a Parliamentary Democracy', p.293.

that there was a heightened concentration on individuals. Barber referred to 'the relentless, ever-growing demands of what Alastair Campbell calls the 24-hour media churn'; and argued 'The voracious appetite of the media, driven by technology, competition and globalisation, presents a huge challenge'.[106] Richard Heffernan referred to an international contemporary tendency for 'focus on individual leaders resulting from the ongoing and deepening personalisation of politics'.[107] But the political scientist Anthony King struck a dissenting note when arguing that 'there is no reason to think that today's prime ministers are more likely to be celebrities than yesterday's. Even allowing for today's phenomenon of super-celebrities, many prime ministers were tremendous celebrities in years gone by'.[108]

Presidential, prime-ministerial, monarchical and Napoleonic government

Concepts of presidential, and to a less extent prime-ministerial, monarchical and even Napoleonic government, were frequently advanced. Foley wrote that the term 'presidential' was 'increasingly employed to portray the position of the prime minister'.[109] The Power Inquiry quoted Shirley, Baroness Williams, the Liberal Democrat Peer and former Labour Cabinet minister, telling it about:

> the growth of the concept of presidential Prime Ministers which, I think, is deeply unsympathetic to the process of parliamentary government. In other words, a President doesn't fit into parliamentary government and in order to make it fit into parliamentary government, it requires the reduction of the Cabinet to essentially something of a sounding board, and of Parliament to not much more than a rubber stamp. All that has happened since 1980/81.[110]

[106] Barber, *Instruction to Deliver*, p.301.
[107] Heffernan, 'Why the Prime Minister cannot be a President', p.54.
[108] Anthony King, *The British Constitution* (Oxford: Oxford University Press, 2007), p.320.
[109] Foley, 'Presidential Attribution as an Agency of Prime Ministerial Critique in a Parliamentary Democracy', p.292.
[110] *Power to the People*, pp. 128–9.

The CDTF referred to the negative impact upon government of 'the demands of a hyperactive Presidential-style leadership from No.10, obsessed with the need for "eye-catching initiatives" that will dominate the short-term media cycle'.[111] Jones wrote that Blair 'has reinforced the steady shift towards a presidential style of government'.[112] Short claimed 'we have the powers of a presidential-type system with the automatic majority of a parliamentary system'.[113]

Foley, though he had his own 'presidential' thesis, argued the label was in large part a term of abuse. It was 'almost invariably used, and seen, as both an implicit and explicit indictment of prime ministerial behaviour'.[114] The purpose of such methods of attack was 'to delegitimise the Blair premiership and, in doing so, to reduce the reach of its influence'.[115] He grouped the use of the 'presidential critique in relationship to Tony Blair' into seven 'strands'. They were: personal hostility; excessive power; dysfunctional government; international intoxication – that is, an excessive involvement in foreign affairs; constitutional imbalance; 'Americanised' politics; and political pathology – that is a metaphor for weakness rather than strength.[116]

The two most detailed presidential theses were those of Allen and Foley. Central to Allen's analysis of the premiership was the theory that '*unplanned and imperfect as it is, we are for all intents and purposes ruled by a hidden Presidency* [emphasis in original]'.[117] But unlike observers such as Williams he argued that the development was desirable. Allen noted that 'While many learned works ... have been written about the end of Cabinet government in the UK and a few have alluded to the development of a Presidency in the UK, those which have talked about a Presidency have done so in negative or at best, neutral terms. I disagree. My view may be a more original one: *not only does the UK have a Presidency, but it is a*

[111] Gough, *An End to Sofa Government*, p.2.
[112] Jones, *The Control Freaks*, p.238.
[113] Hansard HC Debates, 12 May 2003, col.38.
[114] Foley, 'Presidential Attribution as an Agency of Prime Ministerial Critique in a Parliamentary Democracy', p.292.
[115] *Ibid*, p.307.
[116] *Ibid*, pp. 292–311.
[117] Allen, *The Last Prime Minister*, p.4.

welcome and necessary development for the UK in the modern world [emphasis in original]'.[118]

Foley accepted that 'in strict formal terms, a British prime minister possesses a different constitutional position to that of a president in terms of institutional independence, electoral authority and executive resources'.[119] He stated, 'the office of the prime minister is not, and can never be, the same as that of the American presidency ... the presidential analogy is often used in this country in exaggerated and polemical ways to make political capital'.[120] But 'The British prime minister has evolved, and is evolving rapidly away from what a prime minister used to be ... it is no exaggeration to declare that the British premiership has to all intents and purposes turned, not into a British version of the American presidency, but into an authentic British presidency'.[121]

In a critical assessment of such approaches Riddell argued that 'the Prime Minister as president thesis cannot be dismissed out of hand'. In the postwar period, he believed, the '"presidential" aspects of the premiership have grown – and not just since 1997'. Riddell noted that prime ministers engaged far more in international diplomatic activities; and he observed a greater media focus on 'the Prime Minister as the leader, who is seen as controlling the government and taking all key decisions' – though it was an image which was 'a caricature in view of the shared nature of power at the top of any government'. Riddell stressed that the 'projection of the leader as apart from the rest of the Cabinet is hardly novel', citing Gladstone, Lloyd George and Churchill as earlier cases of premiers characterised by this kind of distinction. But the perception existed and was 'reinforced by the growth of the "centre", both the Prime Minister's Office and of the Cabinet Office as at least a quasi-Prime Minister's Department'. Riddell's conclusion was that 'while the reality has varied, the image has unquestionably, and deliberately, been more "presidential"'.[122]

---

[118] *Ibid*, p.40.
[119] Foley, 'Presidential Attribution as an Agency of Prime Ministerial Critique in a Parliamentary Democracy', p.292.
[120] Foley, *The British presidency*, p.24.
[121] *Ibid*, p.26.
[122] Riddell, 'Prime Ministers and Parliament', p.816.

Some analysts were more hostile towards presidential analogies. Heffernan stressed the 'key institutional differences' between the British premiership and the US presidency.[123] He noted that the US state was federal, unlike the UK, and the executive was more limited; the US President, unlike the UK Prime Minister, was directly elected; there was a separation of branches of state absent from the UK; and that 'Prime Ministers, whether stronger or weaker, reflect the imperatives of parliamentary, not presidential politics'.[124] Heffernan concluded:

> Prime Ministers have to share a degree of power with other executive actors, but provided their political capital is in credit not debt, because they are better resourced in terms of their functions and executive-legislative arrangements, they are more authoritative than any President. As well as being institutionally incapably [sic] of becoming a President, then, a strong British Prime Minister has absolutely no need to be one.[125]

Some sought a term to convey that the premiership was not conforming to constitutional norms, but preferred not to use 'presidential'. The journalist and author Anthony Sampson considered the 'recurring complaint over forty years that the prime minister was turning into a president, or head of state, on the American pattern'. He concluded 'In some ways Blair was behaving more like a monarch than an American president – a monarch in the days before parliamentary controls and cabinet government had grown up to act as restraints'.[126] Jenkins similarly argued that 'When critics charge British government with being presidential, they misunderstand the word. Presidencies have checks and balances. Britain under Blair has been not presidential but courtly, a place of jesters, spinners, flattery, feuds and favouritism'. Because of an off-the-record comment made by Powell shortly before Blair took office, Napoleonic metaphors abounded as well.[127] Foster

[123] Heffernan, 'Why the Prime Minister cannot be a President', p.54.
[124] *Ibid*, pp.53–70.
[125] *Ibid*, p.69.
[126] Anthony Sampson, *Who Runs This Place? The Anatomy of Britain in the 21st Century* (London: John Murray, 2004), p.86.
[127] Jenkins, 'Blair wants history to judge him, but the police are first in line'.

seemed to regard such terms as interchangeable. He referred to 'Blair's replacement of Cabinet by prime ministerial government'[128]; called a chapter in his book 'Blair's Cabinet: Monarchy Returns'[129]; and described the Blair premiership as a 'try at presidential government'.[130]

Power

Another subject of interest was the power exercised by the premiership. The CDTF described a 'rise in the power of the Prime Minister at the expense of the Cabinet' over a number of decades; with 'an unprecedented further concentration of power' around No.10 since 1997.[131] The Power Inquiry argued that over twenty years:

> the Prime Minister's Office and whoever the PM decides to gather around him or her, has become the most powerful political institution in British politics. Of course, this power is subject to the balance of political forces in the Cabinet and in Parliament and to the standing of the Prime Minister amongst the wider public. However, when those political forces are running in the Prime Minister's favour, the influence of *No.10 may well be greater than it has ever been* [emphasis in original].[132]

Short warned the Commons of 'the centralisation of power into the hands of the Prime Minister and an increasingly small number of advisers who make decisions in private without proper discussion'.[133] Foster wrote that there were 'superficial swings between presidential and Cabinet Government'.[134] But over roughly the last twenty five years 'Power has drained from Parliament, Cabinet and Civil Service into the PM and those around him'. Local authorities were undermined as well and only 'The courts have made some ground as a check on executive power'.[135]

---

[128] Foster, *British Government in Crisis*, p.174.
[129] *Ibid*, pp.159–75.
[130] *Ibid*, p.259.
[131] Gough, *An End to Sofa Government*, p.2.
[132] *Power to the People*, p.125.
[133] Hansard HC Debates, 12 May 2003, col.38.
[134] Foster, *British Government in Crisis*, p.290.
[135] *Ibid*, p.291.

It was acknowledged that significant rivals to the Prime Minister within government could restrict dominance by the premiership. During the Blair era his Chancellor of the Exchequer, Brown, was seen as such a constraining figure. In the words of the CDTF 'the only effective counterweight to No.10 has been found next door'.[136] Some used the status of Brown to challenge theories of the 'presidential' sort. Kavanagh wrote that:

> For such a so-called presidential figure, Blair was blocked in key areas. The Chancellor carved out a measure of autonomy hardly ever achieved by a minister. Certain departments were regarded as Brown preserves, certain ministers regarded as Brownites, and No.10 staff complained that on occasions there was almost a separate whipping operation. Across much domestic policy Blair shared power with Gordon Brown. Brown unilaterally took control of entry to the euro ... In domestic policy the Treasury and No.10 were often at odds after 2001.[137]

At the outset of the Brown premiership the journalist Andrew Rawnsley emphasised the restraints placed on the premiership by Blair Cabinet members when claiming that Brown began 'his time at No.10 in an exceptionally powerful position ... Gordon Brown will not have to deal with a John Reid, a David Blunkett, a John Prescott or a Charles Clarke. Most of all he will not have to contend with a Gordon Brown, an alternative Prime Minister running a rival government from the Treasury'. But Rawnsley cautioned: 'Every big beast starts life as a small beast. Some of the younger cabinet members will grow in reputation to become substantial figures in their own right'.[138]

Other limitations were identified. The historian Vernon Bogdanor argued there was an important link between particular circumstances and the power of the premiership. He wrote:

> 'It is doubtful ... whether the twentieth century showed any trend towards increasing prime ministerial power as opposed to an

---

[136] Gough, *An End to Sofa Government*, p.2.
[137] Kavanagh, 'The Blair premiership', pp.7–8.
[138] Andrew Rawnsley, 'The new Prime Minister is master of his universe' .

ebb and flow of power determined by political vicissitudes'.[139]

Richard Rose noted that while

'The growth of education, health and social security programmes has increased Westminster's influence on British society ... the influence on Downing Street of the world beyond Dover has grown enormously ... If the Prime Minister takes credit when a world economic boom increases British prosperity, he or she cannot avoid blame when there is a world recession'.[140]

Rose went on:

There is not world enough and time enough for anyone to be informed about all that is done in the name of Her Majesty's Government, let alone influence all its activities. When the Prime Minister spends time on one problem, there is less time to spend on other activities of government. In "time-sharing" burdens with Cabinet ministers, a Prime Minister is necessarily engaged in power-sharing'.[141]

Anthony King referred to the existence of a belief 'that the British prime ministership has become a sort of super presidency, an office endowed with plenipotentiary and almost preternatural powers'. He argued that 'There is very little evidence to support the view that the probability of a prime minister's being able to dominate his or her government is greater today than it was in previous generations'. This mistake, King felt, came about partly because of a failure to consider properly the fuller historical perspective. 'People's long-term thinking tends to be overly influenced by the short-term feel of the time in which they live'. He added that there was a further error in assuming that the possession of celebrity by a Prime Minister such as Blair added to their power.[142]

Some emphasised weakness rather than strength. Michael Barber asked: 'suppose the real problem is not the extent of power the Prime Minister wields, but the lack of it? Suppose the problem is not the strength of the prime ministerial role,

[139] Vernon Bogdanor (ed.), *The British Constitution in the Twentieth Century* (Oxford: The British Academcy/Oxford University Press, 2003), p.10.
[140] Rose, *The Prime Minister in a Shrinking World*, p.7.
[141] *Ibid*, p.154.
[142] King, *The British Constitution*, pp.318–21.

but its weakness?'[143] Kavanagh and Seldon wrote that 'Since 1945 the powers of successive Prime Ministers have probably shrunk'. Causes of the tendency they identified were 'Britain's loss of Empire'; diminished control of the economy and utilities following privatisations; and 'the loss of powers to the EU and the Scottish parliament' entailing a 'hollowing out' of the state. Between them they 'reduced the standing of the Prime Minister outside the Westminster village'.[144]

Political scientists espousing the 'core-executive' thesis attempted to re-cast the debate about the power wielded by the premiership. Their approach had been developed before 1997[145], but a comprehensive statement of it was made in 1999 by Martin Smith in his book, *The Core Executive in Britain*. He described the 'core executive' as 'the heart of British government' containing 'the key institutions and actors concerned with developing policy, coordinating government activity and providing the necessary resources for delivering public goods'. Within this framework all actors possessed resources such as 'information, authority, finance and control of an organisation' which they exchanged with each other in order to secure their goals. None had a monopoly and they depended upon each other to achieve objectives.[146] The particular resources possessed by the premiership included 'powers of appointment; control, to some extent, of the cabinet agenda; appointment of the chairs and membership of cabinet committees; and the Prime Minister's office'. There were less formal potential sources of strength as well, 'an overview of government, the ability to intervene in any policy area, and authority'.[147]

The core-executive outlook challenged conventional discussions about the strength or weakness of the office of Prime Minister, setting out to undermine the notion that any one office or body could be held to have attained dominance within government – 'power cannot be conceived as an object that belongs to the Prime Minister or the cabinet'. Smith held

[143] Barber, *Instruction to Deliver*, p.297.
[144] Kavanagh and Seldon, *The Powers Behind the Prime Minister*, p.xv.
[145] See eg: R.A.W. Rhodes and Patrick Dunleavy (eds.), *Prime Minister, Cabinet and Core Executive* (London: Macmillan, 1995).
[146] Smith, *The Core Executive in Britain*, p.1.
[147] *Ibid*, p.76.

that in a sense 'power is everywhere'[148], not within a particular institution such as the premiership; and that 'Notions of prime-ministerial government, cabinet government or presidentialism are irrelevant, because power within the core executive is based on dependency not command'. Generalisations were unsatisfactory, he argued, since at any one time and in connection with a given issue the impact of the premiership could vary. As Smith put it, 'The degree of dependency that actors have on one another varies according to the context'.[149] Unusually for a journalist Riddell showed an awareness of this school, arguing that 'While the resources available to a Prime Minister have grown, the resulting power has varied depending on the political circumstances of the time and the personal position of the Prime Minister'.[150]

The core-executive concept has been criticised, including for the way it has been applied to the premiership. Kevin Theakston argued 'The core-executive model emphasizes institutions, structure and context. It allows some limited and variable scope for the agency of individual actors and their choices and strategies ... but structural/institutional factors are given much more explanatory weight'.[151] Theakston detected this neglect of the individual premier not only within core-executive studies, but across political-science as a whole. While not advocating 'Focusing on prime ministerial personality alone' he held that 'prime ministers [should not] be conceived of as nameless, faceless, institutionally-determined actors'.[152]

Another challenge to the core-executive interpretation of the premiership emerged with the theory of 'prime-ministerial predominance'. Heffernan argued that 'Power is relational between actors, but it is also locational. It is dependent on where actors are to be found within the core executive, and whether they are at the centre or the periphery of key core executive networks. Depending on the properties of actors and the nature of the network, domination of some actors

[148] *Ibid*, p.1.
[149] *Ibid*, p.2.
[150] Riddell, 'Prime Ministers and Parliament', p.816.
[151] Kevin Theakston, 'Political Skills and Context in Prime Minsiterial Leadership in Britain', p.284.
[152] *Ibid*, p.286.

by others can, at times, be as important as dependency'.[153] Heffernan stated that 'While no prime minister ever has absolute, *unconditional* power, he or she can have significant *conditional* power'.[154] The premiership could have a substantial impact upon outcomes through the effective deployment of a variety of personal and institutional resources. The former had to be accumulated, the latter could be accessed by virtue of the central position of No.10 within the executive. They had to be 'married'; and deployed 'wisely and well'.[155]

Arguing along similar lines to Heffernan, Eoin O'Malley used the successful imposition by No.10 of the decision to participate in the US-led invasion of Iraq in 2003 as a case study for an assessment of the power of the premiership. He noted that according to core-executive analysis 'The inability of the UK prime minister to set policy unilaterally' meant that 'prime ministers would need to use resources to achieve policy gains'. Consequently 'where a prime minister achieves his or her policy goals and appears dominant, network scholars [associated with the core-executive school] would expect either policy compromise to ensue or control of policy to be ceded in other areas'. But in the case of Iraq such a trade-off 'does not seem to have happened'. O'Malley argued, 'it is not clear that the policy network approach is more than a descriptive model; it does not show why one actor dominates another'. He proposed 'a theory of prime ministerial power which ... contends that prime ministers can achieve policy dominance by defining the alternatives from which other actors in the policy-making process must choose'.[156]

Pathology and cure

Observations of tendencies in the premiership were often accompanied by the conclusion that something was wrong and in need of rectification. A frequently advanced argument was that the effectiveness of government had been undermined. Lord [Richard] Wilson suggested the sometimes

[153] Richard Heffernan, 'Prime ministerial predominance? Core executive politics in the UK', *British Journal of Politics and International Relations*, Vol. 5, No. 3, August 2003, p.348.

[154] *Ibid*, p.350.

[155] *Ibid*.

[156] O'Malley, 'Setting Choices, Controlling Outcomes', p.2

casual procedural approach taken under Blair could lead to problems. He noted, 'Formal meetings and minute-taking may seem bureaucratic and not "modern"; but good minutes make sure that everyone knows what has been decided. The official machine responds well to a decision which is properly recorded by a No.10 private secretary or the Cabinet Office. I believe there is a connection between proper processes and good government'. While 'there is no "right" way of running a Government' there was a 'risk ... that informality can slide into something more fluid and unstructured, where advice and dissent may either not always be offered or else not be heard'.[157]

Foster argued the Blair premiership saw 'a succession of spun ministerial statements, ill-argued and often opaque public documents, and poorly drafted bills'.[158] He concluded:

> Prime-ministerial overload, and the intensity of his preoccupation with the media, seemed to prevent Blair gripping many problems, as it had not with Thatcher; though both Thatcher and Blair suffered from another flaw inherent in presidential systems, the ability, even certainty of making bad mistakes, hers the poll-tax, his most serious, but not the only one, being Iraq.

At the same time there was a problem with 'Britain's increasing ungovernability'[159] meaning that 'while the government tries to control everything as if from one railway box, many levers pulled do not work. Nothing much happens. Or what does, is seldom what was intended. Certainly the promised improvements in public services are slow to arrive'.[160]

Short complained of the replacement of collective government by 'diktats in favour of increasingly badly thought through policy initiatives that come from on high'.[161] In describing Blair's handling of the lead-up to the Iraq War she complained of 'a collapse of normal British procedures for decision-making' associated with bad policy-formation. She

[157] W. G. Runciman (ed.), *Hutton and Butler: Lifting the Lid on the Workings of Power* (Oxford: The British Academy/Oxford University Press, 2004), p.85.
[158] Foster, *British Government in Crisis*, p.175.
[159] *Ibid*, p.291.
[160] *Ibid*, pp. 291–2.
[161] Hansard HC Debates, 12 May 2003, col.38.

claimed, 'the decision-making was sucked out of the Foreign Office which I think is a great pity because there is enormous expertise about the Middle East in the Foreign Office'.[162]

Others felt that democratic principles were undermined by the nature of the office of Prime Minister. In observing the development of the premiership, Allen argued, 'An awful democratic dysfunction lay at the heart of British politics'.[163] A central conclusion of the Power Inquiry, which identified the power of the premiership as part of a broader problem, was that 'Popular engagement with the formal processes and institutions of democracy has been in long-term decline since the 1960s'.[164]

The CDTF made a connection between both these strands of criticism. It argued 'the combination of an overpowerful premiership and the dominance of news management within policy-making have been very damaging to both effective and accountable government'.[165] There was, the CDTF argued, 'a sense of malaise and decay surrounding British government and British democracy, reflected in widespread public cynicism, a fall in turnout and clear polling evidence of loss of faith in both the intentions and competence of politicians'. It saw the existence of 'something wrong with the central machinery of government' as contributing to this 'Public disenchantment'[166] through 'the sheer ineffectiveness of government – the torrent of poor quality legislation, the failure to deliver on some of its very basic requirements'.[167]

Finally, the idea that the premiership was operating in a way that was morally or legally wrong was sometimes either implied or directly stated. Such portrayals noted activities including the supposed use by No.10 of off-the-record press briefing to undermine personally particular individuals, both during the Blair era and under Brown, particularly in the wake of the McBride scandal.[168] Following the invasion

[162] FAC, Minutes of Evidence, 17 June 2003, Question 114.
[163] See eg: Allen, *The Last Prime Minister*, p.10.
[164] *Power to the People*, p.27.
[165] Gough, *An End to Sofa Government*, p.1.
[166] *Ibid*, p.1.
[167] *Ibid*, pp. 1–2.
[168] See eg: Stephen Glover, 'What low, despicable, barely human creatures they are to smear a man who's risked his life for his country', *Daily Mail*, 20 August 2009.

of Iraq there was a doomed attempt within Parliament to revive a practice that had fallen into disuse since the early eighteenth century, and impeach Blair.[169] Late on during the Blair tenure a criminal investigation into alleged corruption in the conferral of Peerages (ultimately leading to no-one being charged) involved some No.10 aides being questioned under caution by the police (and Blair himself being interviewed, but not under caution). Media coverage focused to a considerable extent on the lines of inquiry that led to No.10, although activities elsewhere were being probed as well.[170]

A variety of prescriptions were developed for reforms designed to counteract the various problems supposedly associated with the premiership; some of which found their way into Brown's constitutional programme embarked upon shortly after he moved to No.10. Foster set out fourteen principles to be adhered to and in the absence of which 'representative democracy must be something of a sham, deceiving the electorate'.[171] The CDTF made recommendations including 'A system ... to entrench a process of collective cabinet government'. [172] It argued further that 'Decisions to go to war or to commit troops to areas of conflict should require Parliamentary approval. Decisions on war-making should no longer rest solely on the unfettered use of the Royal Prerogative by the Prime Minister'.[173] The Power Inquiry made proposals which took in the drawing up of a 'Concordat ... between Executive and Parliament indicating where key powers lie and providing significant powers of scrutiny and initiation for Parliament'. Select committees, it was argued, should have more autonomy, power and resources; 'Limits should be placed on the power of the whips'; Parliament should be made more able to initiate legislation, instigate public inquiries and act on public petitions; and 70 per cent of the House of Lords should be elected.[174] Speaking to Boris Johnson, Butler complained that 'the government reaches conclusions in rather small groups of people who are not necessarily representative of all the groups of interests in government, and there is insufficient

[169] See: Blick, *How to go to War*, p.61.
[170] For an account of this episode see: PASC, *Propriety and Peerages*, HC 153 (London: Stationery Office, 2007).
[171] Foster, *British Government in Crisis*, p.298.
[172] Gough, *An End to Sofa Government*, p.1.
[173] *Ibid.*
[174] *Power to the People*, p.21.

opportunity for other people to debate dissent and modify'. He urged Blair to 'restore open debate in government at all levels up to the Cabinet'.[175]

Some called for changes more radical than the re-establishment of the supposedly undermined traditional Cabinet and parliamentary system. Allen called for the informal presidency he observed to be accepted and properly institutionalised, making the office directly elected, affecting a separation of executive, legislature and judiciary, with devolved government to nations, regions and localities and clearly defined human rights. The new settlement would be 'set out for all to see in a written constitution'.[176] Allen argued, 'there is a need to end the pretence that the UK Chief Executive can or should run a major Western democracy out of a few rooms in No 10 and to confront the need to *build a Prime Minister's department* on a par with a Presidential staff in order to see through the responsibilities of the office'.[177] Barber took the view that the premiership was too weak. He called for 'a clearer, sharper, more effective prime ministerial function' to 'enhance the power of the holder of the office to successfully do a job which is becoming steadily more demanding' and at the same time provide efficient constraints upon it. He argued that, to this end, 'Blair's successor, should, immediately on becoming Prime Minister, learn a lesson from the Australian government and establish a Department of the Prime Minister and the Cabinet, incorporating No. 10 and the Cabinet Office'.[178] At the other end of the spectrum from Allen and Barber, Sutherland argued there was no absolute need for the premiership to exist. He called for a set of constitutional changes that would make it 'perfectly possible for a monarch with an active interest in public affairs to dispense with the services of a "prime" minister'.[179]

Conclusion

The many theories of the office of Prime Minister advanced since 1997, differed over a number of its features, including the nature of its development and its power and over what steps should be taken in future. A degree of disagreement in such

[175] Johnson, 'How not to run a country'.
[176] Allen, *The Last Prime Minister*, p.76.
[177] *Ibid*, p.45.
[178] Barber, *Instruction to Deliver*, p.315.
[179] Sutherland, *A People's Parliament*, p.130.

areas is inevitable and indeed healthy. But the debate around the premiership was flawed, with lacunae and weaknesses in the literature.

Though the importance of distinguishing the individual occupant from the institution was noted, there was no method offered for doing so. Nor was a clear means suggested for differentiating types of change associated with the office, and of weighing their significance. The ample consideration of the idea of alteration to the premiership was not balanced by sufficient assessment of whether it had a constant, underlying nature and, if so, what it was. Those who claimed the existence of certain trends – such as the increasing 'personalisation' of politics – did not offer a satisfactory means by which the trend could be identified and measured. When two or more associated tendencies or events were identified, such as the rise of the premiership accompanied by the decline of Cabinet, the chain of causality between them – that is, the extent to which each caused the other – was not always clearly depicted. The use of certain phrases – in particular 'presidency' or 'presidential' – tended to beg a number of questions. Did they refer to a stylistic development, or a substantive shift? If the latter, had it already occurred – and if so, when; was it taking place at that moment – and if so, how long might it last; or was it approaching?

While the concept of power was often invoked in discussion of the premiership, it was rarely defined. The debate between exponents of the core-executive and prime-ministerial predominance marked the beginning of an attempt to fill this gap, but there remained scope for further exploration, and the work that has been carried out has been largely ignored outside the political-science discipline. Frequently the power of the premiership was assessed as its ability to secure the adoption of particular courses of action by government. While the idea that a policy option, once secured, might prove unsuccessful in some way was acknowledged, an explicit link between this kind of ineffectiveness and power was generally lacking. It could be asked, how strong was a premiership that could achieve the pursuit of particular approaches, if they did not in turn bring about the outcomes they were intended to produce by those who supported them, or triggered unwanted consequences?

Another common way of presenting the power of the office of Prime Minister was as something exercised over or at the expense of other institutions, especially the Cabinet, as well as Parliament, the Civil Service, different tiers of government; and political parties. Scant consideration was given to the possibility that the premiership could achieve objectives better by working through or with these supposed rival organisations. Rawnsley touched on this idea when he argued that Brown's supposed intention to enhance Cabinet and Parliament 'may sound like a dilution of his power – it may well be presented as just that – but it is actually a way of further strengthening his hand'. As Rawnsley put it 'A Prime Minister with a solid majority has much more command over and authority in Parliament than he has in the … media. Gordon Brown will raise Parliament in order to put the media down'. Similarly 'It suits Gordon Brown to increase the status of the cabinet because he will be so powerful within it'.[180]

Claims were often made about the development of the premiership over time – yet few were founded in assessments of the entire historical sweep of the office of Prime Minister which might be seen to be necessary to support such stances. There were some exceptions. For Hennessy and Langford the use of such a perspective was the essence of their shared profession. Langford explicitly considered the premiership from Walpole to Blair, 'not to challenge' existing claims about the role 'so much as to set them in historical context'.[181] Barber, Foster, King, Allen and Sutherland took longer views as well. But few others made detailed reference to the past; and, if they did, they tended to ignore the eighteenth and nineteenth centuries. Nor was there sufficient consideration of how the office has been perceived and analysed over time.

One purpose of the remainder of this work is to make good the omissions and faults, both evidential and theoretical, in recent discussion of the premiership, putting forward a more satisfactory interpretation of the office than any currently on offer. The ideas present in the literature as discussed in this chapter will be verified; refuted; placed in revealing perspective; and reconciled with other concepts that may at first glance seem to contradict them.

---

[180] Rawnsley, 'The new Prime Minister is master of his universe'.
[181] Langford, 'Prime Ministers and Parliament', p.383.

Chapter Two
Recurring Errors

Jonathan Swift's satirical fantasy, *Gulliver's Travels*, first published in 1726, begins with the hero Captain Gulliver travelling to the land of Lilliput, whose inhabitants are less than six inches high. Swift describes a rope-dancing game played by 'Persons, who are candidates for great Employments, and high Favour, at Court'. When a 'great Office' becomes vacant five or six candidates entertain the Emperor of Lilliput and his court by dancing on a rope two feet long and twelve inches from the ground. The one who 'jumps the highest without falling, succeeds in the Office'. Established ministers are often commanded to perform as well, 'to convince the Emperor they have not lost their Faculty'. Fatal accidents occur regularly.

Swift's was an oblique account of the rivalry and insecurity of high-level politics of his time. One of the dancers – the Treasurer, Flimnap – is able to leap 'at least an inch higher than any other Lord in the whole Empire' and perform several somersaults together.[1] Flimnap was a caricature of Robert Walpole[2], commonly regarded as the first British Prime Minister.[3]

Exactly two-and-a-half centuries after Swift, Harold Wilson reproduced on the back endpaper of his book *The Governance of Britain*,[4] another satirical portrait of the premiership. Appearing in *The Sun* newspaper during his second and final tenure at

[1] Jonathan Swift, *Gulliver's Travels* (Oxford: Oxford University Press, 1998), pp.25–6.

[2] See eg: Edward Pearce, *The Great Man: Scoundrel, Genius and Britain's First Prime Minister* (London: Jonathan Cape, 2007), p.194.

[3] For a dissection of the validity of this perception of Walpole, see: A.J.P. Taylor, *British Prime Ministers and Other Essays* (London: Allen Lane, 1999), pp.6–14.

[4] Harold Wilson, *The Governance of Britain* (London: Weidenfeld and Nicolson and Michael Joseph, 1976).

No.10 of 1974–6, it was a cartoon by the artist 'Franklin' entitled 'The Greatest Show on Earth'. It depicts Wilson performing in front of a transfixed big-top audience a variety of precarious circus acts, each representing his engagement with one of the difficulties faced by his government. He simultaneously rides three horses labelled 'labour right', 'labour centre' and 'labour left' while juggling skittles; places his head in the mouth of a tiger with a fur pattern which reads 'oil'; has knives – one of which has 'strikes' written on it – thrown at him; pedals a unicycle on a high-wire representing the 'social contract' package for conciliating the trades-union movement; performs a trapeze routine signifying his 'election double' success of February and October 1974; and in the form of a seal, recognisable because it has his trademark pipe in his mouth, balances a globe on his nose, with 'Europe' marked on it. At the centre of the show is Wilson as ringmaster with top hat, pipe again, jodhpurs, riding boots and giant whip.

The similarity between these two representations is striking. Both could be taken as emphasising the importance of the premiership. Flimnap/Walpole is depicted as 'higher than any other'; while Wilson is both the ringmaster and all the circus acts – his Cabinet members play no part. Yet despite this prominence another inference might be drawn from the two scenarios about the ability to achieve objectives associated with the office: that it is not guaranteed but dependent upon the successful execution of spectacular acts that could end in disaster. Benjamin Disraeli created a similar impression when, upon attaining the premiership, he said he had 'climbed to the top of the greasy pole at last'[5] – suggesting that the level he had reached was the highest in politics, but there was a considerable hazard of sliding down again. Swift conveyed an environment in which there were multiple actors in competition with each other – the court rope dancers – rather than a single dominant force. Emerging from the imagery of Swift and Franklin is the importance of balance – the reconciliation of conflicting forces – either when dancing on a rope for Flimnap/Walpole or, for Wilson, riding on a high-wire or horses, or keeping a globe on his nose. The idea of a connection between the

[5] Lord Blake, *The Office of Prime Minister* (London: Oxford University Press, 1975), p.2.

premiership and show-business is conveyed as well. It was not enough just to perform effectively – it was necessary to be seen to do so by an audience. Again a comment by Disraeli underlines this point. Upon first meeting at a country house in 1865 the man who would become his most trusted aide at No.10, Montagu Corry, Disraeli told him 'I think you must be my impresario'.[6] Finally, the scenes from 1726 and 1976 both demonstrate there existed a personalised media focus on the office of Prime Minister long before 1997.

Issues raised by comparative analysis of these two images of the premiership are echoed by some of those emerging from the literature review conducted in the previous chapter. This recurrence suggests that consideration of the history of the office of Prime Minister, and portrayals of it over time, can provide revealing perspectives on assessments of the premiership that have appeared since 1997. The purpose of this chapter is to provide such an approach. First, consideration is given to key features of the office in its emergent form under Walpole and how it was perceived at the time. Second, is a discussion of differing contemporary portrayals of the institution in subsequent periods. Finally, the series of themes identified as central to theories advanced from 1997 onwards are considered from the perspective of the history of the office of Prime Minister.

Sir Robert Walpole: 'sole and prime minister'

Walpole was First Lord of the Treasury continuously from 1721–42. During this time he became so prominent a political figure as to be widely labelled 'Prime Minister'. At this time no such post existed officially. It had begun to be applied to an individual judged dominant within the king or queen's government, probably from around the early eighteenth century. It was initially a term of abuse used against Queen Anne's successive favourites, Sidney Godolphin and Robert Harley. The raising of one subject above all others had long been seen as improper; and there was a tradition that all ministers were equal in their direct responsibility for their departments to the King. The term was adopted from the

[6] George Earle Buckle, *The Life of Benjamin Disraeli, Earl of Beaconsfield*, Vol. IV, *1855-1868* (London: John Murray, 1916), p.420.

French 'Premier Ministre', showing that such ascendancy was regarded as alien and by implication inappropriate. In more recent times the presidential analogy has been deployed to similar effect, used to suggest the accrual of excessive power to one particular office at the expense of more collegiate government; and the idea of inaptly adopting foreign – usually US – methods. So negative were the connotations of the title that one of the charges against Harley when he was impeached in 1715 was being a Prime Minister.[7]

Given the implications of the term, Walpole publicly rejected the allegation he was a Premier, telling the Commons in 1741 'I unequivocally deny that I am sole and prime minister'.[8] Yet the long Walpole ascendancy came to be regarded as the crucial initial stage in the development of the premiership, leading A.J.P. Taylor to remark that Walpole was 'as much the first modern Prime Minister we should recognize as Adam was the first man'.[9] A consideration of the emergent institution during Walpole's period of tenure reveals it shares many features with the premiership since 1997, which have been singled out as exceptional in the latter period.

There are key differences. Handling the monarchy is not the central task it was. Cabinet has developed in various ways. The office of Prime Minister is no longer directly attached to the Treasury, which Walpole – who was simultaneously First Lord of the Treasury and Chancellor of the Exchequer – used to build control over patronage and as a means of ranging across government policy. But, the similarities are numerous and significant enough to prompt reconsideration of any temptation to believe that various characteristics of the premiership noted in more recent times are peculiar.

The position Walpole established for himself was dependent upon the mutually reinforcing confidences of the monarchy and Parliament – in particular the Commons.[10] Being able to carry crown business through the legislature ensured

---

[7] Betty Kemp, *Sir Robert Walpole* (London: Weidenfeld and Nicolson, 1976), pp.3–5.

[8] *Cobbett's Parliamentary History of England*, Vol. XI (London: 1812), col. 1296.

[9] 'Introduction', Kemp, *Robert Walpole*, ix.

[10] Sir Lewis Namier, *Crossroads of Power: Essays on Eighteenth-Century England* (London: Hamish Hamilton, 1962), p.113.

the backing of the king, which in turn enabled Walpole to influence the bestowal of royal patronage, securing approval for the appointments he wished to make and access to money to disburse, both of which could be traded for parliamentary support. Even the Commons Speaker, Arthur Onslow, though he made a show of his supposed independence, was on the payroll. Walpole was served by assistants who were in part prototypical whips. In the Commons MPs such as Henry Pelham, Thomas Winnington, Thomas Brereton, and Walpole's brother, Horatio, were deployed to inform, communicate with and coax backbenchers[11]; while in the Lords, the Bishop of London, Edmund Gibson – widely known as 'Walpole's Pope' – helped secure the votes of the bloc of 26 bishops.

Under Walpole the premiership operated in an un-collegiate fashion. The principle that senior politicians should deliberate as a collective had yet to develop. There existed at the time a full Cabinet of around a dozen and an inner body of about five. The origins of the first body can be traced to the 1660s, the second – which developed into Cabinet as it later came to be understood – to the 1690s.[12] Walpole preferred to use the latter, smaller group for serious business, otherwise working with two or three colleagues he selected himself, or alone.[13] As J.H. Plumb noted 'A great deal which nowadays would demand the attention of the cabinet, was settled out of hand by Walpole himself'. When he took personal policy initiatives Walpole could have been seen as encroaching upon the territory of others: foreign affairs might be regarded as more properly the remit of the Secretary of State. But given his Treasury role he could, if need be, justify such activity on the grounds he had to find the funds to pay for policies.[14]

---

[11] H.T. Dickinson, *Walpole and the Whig Supremacy* (London: The English Universities Press, 1973), p.78.

[12] John Mackintosh, *The British Cabinet* (London: Methuen, 1968), pp. 37,42. See as well: Andrew Browning, 'Parties and Party Organisation in the Reign of Charles II', *Transactions of the Royal Historical Society*, 4th Series, Vol. XXX, pp.21–36.

[13] Brian W. Hill, *Sir Robert Walpole: 'Sole and Prime Minister'* (London: Hamish Hamilton, 1989), p.3.

[14] J. H. Plumb, *Sir Robert Walpole: The Making of a Statesman* (London: The Cresset Press, 1956), p.77.

Aides were integral to Walpole's term of office. Though not officially categorised as staff to the Prime Minister (since no such post formally existed) it is possible to identify a number of assistants attached to the developing premiership. Walpole had, as First Lord of the Treasury, his own 'department' to support him, the Treasury, by far the largest in government at the time; and he received further help from a variety of other individuals, including Gibson. Many staff helping Walpole had one foot in the administrative world of Whitehall and another in the party political environment of Westminster. John Scrope, who served as Secretary to the Treasury in the Walpole period, performed some tasks that would now be associated with senior civil servants, but he sat in the Commons and was able to vote for the same financial measures he had devised. Scrope and similar aides can be seen as precursors to the No.10 special advisers who attracted so much interest from 1997, combining official and party political roles.

The emerging premiership attracted personalised coverage. Few politicians have endured concerted attacks of the high literary quality launched against Walpole by associates of the 'Scriblerus Club' – a collection of Tory authors of talent unsurpassed in any era – excluded from office and favour by Whig hegemony. Parodies and criticisms of Walpole are contained in works as illustrious as *Gulliver's Travels* by Swift, Alexander Pope's *Dunciad* and John Gay's *The Beggar's Opera.* In them Walpole the person was treated as synonymous with his government, with an assault on the former serving as an attack on the latter. In *The Beggar's Opera* the famous couplet 'How happy could I be with either, Were t'other dear charmer away'[15] was understood at the time as a depiction of the triangular relationship between Walpole, Lady Walpole and Walpole's mistress, Maria Skerret. Swift made similar insinuations in *Gulliver's Travels*[16]; and in a poetic tirade of 1738 Pope stated: 'Sir ROBERT'S mighty dull, Has never made a friend in private life, And was, besides, a tyrant to his wife'.[17]

---

[15] John Gay, *The Beggar's Opera* (London: Penguin, 1986), p.91.
[16] Swift, *Gulliver's Travels*, p.53.
[17] Alexander Pope, *Selected Poetry* (Oxford: Oxford University Press, 1994), p.124.

Walpole responded to this onslaught by constructing a political communications operation to rival that of any subsequent Prime Minister. At first the methods were defensive. Control of the postal service was used to prevent the distribution of critical works; and writers were bribed not to author them. There then began a campaign on a grand scale, involving the production, printing and circulation of newspapers, journals and poems praising Walpole and attacking his enemies.[18] Walpole had two chief managers in this enterprise. Nicholas Paxton, the Treasury Solicitor, advised on whether to attempt prosecutions for sedition and arranged payments for the authors of pro-government work. Thomas Gordon, a political pamphleteer, was more concerned with the content of the written material.

Walpole's media campaign became the subject of vehement criticism. Of 'rather sinister reputation'[19], Paxton was referred to in *Manners*, a poem by the opposition poet Paul Whitehead, as 'yon fell Harpy hovr'ring o'er the Press'.[20] In 'Dialogue II' from *Epistle to the Satires* Pope remarked on Paxton's role as purchaser of favourable coverage with the lines 'each spur-galled hackney of the day, When Paxton gives him double pots and pay, Or each new-pensioned sycophant'.[21] Pope attacked the writer William Arnall, who assisted the Walpole media operation, in the same work, exclaiming: 'Spirit of Arnall! aid me while I lie'.[22]

In his development of the premiership, Walpole was widely regarded as using morally and legally inappropriate methods. He was often portrayed as a purveyor of corruption. A central theme of *The Beggar's Opera* is that of the moral equivalency between common criminals and leading figures in society. The depiction of society as debased by dishonesty from the top was central to the Scriblerian narrative. One character, Robin of Bagshot, a member of the highwayman Macheath's gang, has aliases including 'Bob Booty' – a nickname which stuck to

[18] Tone Sundt Urstad, *Sir Robert Walpole's Poets: The Use of Literature as Pro-Government Propaganda, 1721-1742* (London: Associated University Presses, 1999), p.38.

[19] *Ibid*, p.86.

[20] Paul Whitehead, *Satires* (Los Angeles: The Augustan Reprint Society, 1984), p.14.

[21] Pope, *Selected Poetry*, p.124.

[22] *Ibid*.

Walpole for the rest of his career, chiming with his reputation. After Walpole's fall there was an attempt to impeach him for his supposedly improper use of funds. A Committee of Secrecy was established by Parliament and began investigating electoral irregularities. It found evidence of Paxton dispensing immense sums of money officially set aside for secret service purposes to purchase seats for selected individuals. But he refused to give evidence that might incriminate himself and despite a spell in prison still would not talk. There were difficulties in obtaining the testimony of other Walpole aides. Scrope brandished a letter from King George II excusing him from disclosing information about the Secret Service funds. The Committee could not construct a satisfactory case against the former premier.

The office that Walpole shaped was often presented as politically dominant. Fellow ministers were regarded as tools. Walpole's ally John, Lord Hervey, later wrote of Walpole that 'he did everything alone ... whilst those ciphers of the Cabinet signed everything he dictated ... without the least share of honour or power'.[23] The supposed immense strength of the premiership under Walpole was portrayed as inappropriate. In 1741 Samuel Sandys told the Commons that 'According to our constitution we can have no sole and prime minister'. There should instead, he argued, be several senior ministers, each with his 'own proper department'; none of whom 'ought to meddle in the affairs belonging to the department of another'. But it was 'publicly known, that this minister, having obtained a sole influence over all our public counsels, has not only assumed the sole direction of all public affairs, but has got every officer of state removed that would not follow his direction, even in the affairs belonging to his own proper department'. Such practices amounted to 'a most heinous offence against our constitution'. They were compounded by the use of the monopoly of 'all the favours of the crown' in order to bring about 'a blind submission to [Walpole's] direction at elections and in parliament'. Sandys asserted 'This is so notoriously known, that it can stand in need of no proof'.[24]

[23] E.N. Williams, *The Eighteenth Century Constitution: Documents and Commentary* (Cambridge: Cambridge University Press, 1960), p.126.

[24] *Cobbett's Parliamentary History of England*, Vol. XI, col. 1232.

But some evidence undermines the view that the office of Prime Minister in the Walpole period achieved what Sandys called 'the sole direction of all public affairs', obedience from ministers and 'blind submission' amongst parliamentarians and in elections. Until 1730 and the resignation of Charles Townshend, the Secretary of State, Walpole had an arguable ministerial equal. Even with the departure of Townshend there remained other constraints upon the early premiership, including the complexity of the tasks involved and its dependency upon the cooperation of others. The advice Walpole provided while in retirement to his protégé, Henry Pelham, demonstrated both. In October 1743 he discussed methods of securing the support of the monarch, which was an essential but difficult-to-achieve objective. One suggestion he offered was 'the more you can make any thing appear to be his own ... the better you will be heard'.[25] In the same month Walpole counselled the Duke of Newcastle on the making of ministerial appointments. Walpole conveyed the need to satisfy different groups of potential supporters, along with the difficulty of doing so. He captured a perennial dilemma with the question 'how can you bring in two new Setts of men, wthout [sic] removing some that are in ...?'[26]

The office Walpole developed did not have guaranteed dominance attached to it. Rather, contingencies such as, shifting political alignments played an important part, as when Walpole felt obliged to resign after losing support in the Commons in 1742. The previous year, in the Commons debate quoted above, Walpole had responded to those who, 'having first invested me with a kind of mock dignity, and styled me a prime minister' then 'impute to me an unpardonable abuse of that chimerical authority which they only have created and conferred'. Walpole asked rhetorically whether his critics had:

> produced one instance of this exorbitant power, of the influence which I extend to all parts of the nation, of the tyranny with which I oppress those I oppose, and the liberality with which I

[25] Lord Orford (Walpole) to Henry Pelham, 20 October 1743, reproduced in Williams, *The Eighteenth Century Constitution*, p.81.

[26] Orford to Duke of Newcastle, October 1743, reproduced in Williams, *The Eighteenth Century Constitution*, p.107.

> reward those who support me? ... What is this unbounded sole power which is imputed to me? How has it discovered itself, or how has it been proved?

Walpole insisted 'the crown has made no encroachments ... all supplies have been granted by parliament ... all questions have been debated with the same freedom as before the fatal period in which my counsels are said to have gained the ascendancy'. Why then were these claims made? Walpole felt they signified dishonesty in pursuit of an agenda rather than simple mistakes. He was 'far from believing that [his critics] feel those apprehensions which they so earnestly labour to communicate to others'. Walpole concluded 'even in their own judgement, they are complaining of grievances that they do not suffer, and promoting rather their private interests than that of the public'.[27]

Conflicting accounts

Since the fall of Walpole many assessments of the premiership have in various combinations dwelt on its power, a supposed association with alterations to constitutional practice, the idea of change and developments that are new or accelerating, and the notion that something has gone wrong.

Sometimes the focus has been upon a particular incumbency. In 1806 the incoming premier, Lord Grenville, described his predecessor, Pitt the Younger, as having led in his second, final period of office 'a Cabinet of cyphers and a government of one man alone', which he felt was a 'wretched system'.[28] During his premiership of 1828–30 the Duke of Wellington was described by an ally as 'sole Minister and decidedly superior to all'.[29] Some saw in Wellington an undesirable military import into politics. One critic said his ministers 'dare not have an opinion, but must move either to the right or the left as this Dictator may think proper'.[30] Charles Greville referred to the premier's 'ministerial despotism'; and Lord Lyndhurst, critical of Wellington's failure to consult with others, reportedly called

[27] *Cobbett's Parliamentary History of England*, Vol. XI, cols 1295–6.
[28] A. Aspinall, *The Cabinet Council: 1783–1835*, The Raleigh Lecture on History (1952: British Academy, London), p.203.
[29] *Ibid*, p.207.
[30] Duke of Cumberland to Eldon, 21 February 1830, cited in *ibid*.

the government 'the poorest Administration which England has ever seen'.[31]

The 1916–22 Lloyd George premiership, characterised by a domineering approach and institutional change, was associated with widespread speculation that substantial constitutional change was afoot. In an article for the *Nation* that appeared in October 1920[32] Harold Laski argued: 'Since the accession of Mr. Lloyd George to supreme power, a notable change has come over the office that he holds'. Previously the premier was more 'the chairman of a board who knows that his power depends upon the careful weighing of his colleagues' judgements, than an American President who ... may follow his own decision in defiance of his Cabinet'. But this 'system' had 'completely disappeared'. The Prime Minister had become 'virtually the President of a State'. He was 'his own Foreign Secretary' and 'the deciding factor in Labor policy'. Other members of the Cabinet became 'not colleagues who can weigh decisions, but subordinates who can accept them'. A casualty of this arrangement was 'coherent policy'. Conflicting approaches could simultaneously be promoted though the press, and 'by a careful scrutiny of the papers the policy upon which the greater degree of eulogy is bestowed may be selected as the most likely to succeed'. Laski believed that 'at bottom, the system implies ... personal government'. Party loyalty was not important to it and Parliament was now 'not merely a cumbrous mechanism, but ... in danger of becoming an engine of corruption'. The absence of principle meant that the 'essentially vocational nature' of Parliament 'reasserts itself' with 'its groups of particular interests either ... promoting their private end, or preventing concessions which may decrease their power'. This change in the legislature had led to 'direct action' on the part of those outside Parliament who sought to pursue particular causes. Laski concluded 'the method by which we are governed leads, by its inherent nature, either to the violence of civil disruption or the inertia which its defeat exacts from despair'.

[31] *Ibid*, pp.207–8.
[32] Harold Laski, 'Mr. George and the constitution', *Nation*, 23 October 1920, pp.124–6.

Lloyd George was not the only premier to be criticised through the use of presidential analogies. George Brown resigned as Foreign Secretary in 1968 because, in his account, the premier Harold Wilson was 'introducing a "presidential" system into the running of the Government that is wholly alien to the British constitutional system' and was taking decisions 'over the heads and without the knowledge of Ministers'.[33]

A comparison of these claims about particular terms of office prompts certain critical observations. Some of them lack credibility because of their resort to hyperbole – such as Grenville's assertion that Pitt the Younger ran 'a government of one man alone'.[34] In each individual account the impression is created of exceptionality in the case under consideration – yet the similarities between the various descriptions cited above undermines any such notion. Finally it was held by some that the mode of operation during a particular prime-ministerial tenure was, as Brown put it, 'wholly alien to the British constitutional system'[35]. But the repeated appearance of analogous claims over time could lead to the conclusion that at least some of the conduct that encouraged them was – rather than involving the extension into new territory – within an existing broad framework which allowed for substantial variance in the way the office of Prime Minister operated.

At the early stages of its emergence under Walpole there were complaints that this institution represented the excessive accrual of power in one place, posed a threat to Parliament and the status of other ministers and relied on manipulation of the media to disseminate misleading information and undermine opponents. In other words, the institution that Walpole helped to establish, contained within it from the outset, the potential to be used in a way that prompted or formed the basis for such criticism. Allegations about rupture with constitutional norms made during the tenures of some of his successors at No.10 ,were partly responses to the exploitation of characteristics inherent in the premiership, rather than the transformation of arrangements for governance that they were claimed to be.

[33] George Brown, *In My Way* (Harmondsworth: Penguin, 1972), p.161. For Brown's resignation speech see: Hansard, House of Commons Debates, 18 March 1968, cols 55–7.

[34] Aspinall, *The Cabinet Council*, p.203.

[35] George Brown, *In My Way*, p. 161.

Further consideration is given to the occurrence of sometimes dramatic stylistic fluctuations in the exercise of the premiership in the next chapter.

At other times trends in the office that stretched across individual tenures were detected. Theories of this sort became increasingly common after the premiership had become a more clearly entrenched and accepted feature of UK governance (a development that had taken hold by the mid-nineteenth century), encouraging some observers to consider it an established institution with its own dynamics, rather than merely analysing the supposed efforts of individuals to subvert the constitution. Writing in the early twentieth century, Sidney Low argued that the prominence of No.10 had for a time been expanding. As he put it in 1904 in his book *The Governance of England,* for 'the greater part of the past half century ... The office of Premier has become more than ever like that of an elective President'[36]; and in a 1914 edition of the same work: the 'Prime Minister's influence and importance are growing'.[37] He judged that 'Much of the authority of the Cabinet has insensibly passed over to that of the Premier'. One source of strength for the Prime Minister – Low argued – was that he was 'the really "responsible" minister, the person who answers to the Sovereign and who answers to the nation'. Premiers drew authority from being 'nominated by the choice of the people, as expressed at a general election'; and as leaders of their parties.[38] In 1914 Low cited as further evidence for his thesis the formal recognition of the post of Prime Minister by Royal Proclamation in 1905;[39] and stated that 'the Premier is acquiring the attributes of an Imperial Chancellor'.[40]

A little over thirty years after his individual focus on Lloyd George as 'virtually the President of a State', Laski identified a general tendency in the office of Prime Minister which was not associated with any one holder. He held that 'if we compare 1850 with 1950, or even 1900 with 1950, the

[36] Sidney Low, *The Governance of England* (London: T. Fisher Unwin, 1904), p.158.
[37] Sidney Low, *The Governance of England* (London: T. Fisher Unwin, 1914), p.xx.
[38] Low, *The Governance of England,* 1904 edition, p.156.
[39] Low, *The Governance of England,* 1914 edition, p.xx.
[40] *Ibid,* p.xxii.

centralisation of power in the Prime Minister's hands has proceeded at a swift pace, and ... its judicious use is mainly dependent upon his own self-restraint'. Laski believed that 'This centralisation ... is only part of a similar process that is taking place in all areas of governmental authority' including most severely 'in the passage of important local functions to the central government'.[41] Laski attributed the development in the premiership partly to its separation from the post of Leader of the House of Commons, increasing the impact of the fewer appearances that were made in the Chamber by the Prime Minister; and to 'the occasional broadcasts he delivers ... as ... under the King ... head of the nation'.[42] He considered possibilities including that 'the Prime Minister has excessive power in proportion to that of other Cabinet Ministers, and ... in relation to the Cabinet as a whole'; and that 'Cabinet has come to acquiesce in the right of the Prime Minister to play ... an independent role over a wide range of general policy'. A potential means of 'limitation of the Prime Minister's functions', Laski felt, lay 'in the area of his relations with his Party, both in and outside the House of Commons'.[43]

The following decade saw a wave of interest in the strength of the premiership. Amongst others, the Labour politicians John P. Mackintosh and Richard Crossman wrote on this subject. In *The British Cabinet*, a work that initially appeared in 1962 and was updated in 1968, Mackintosh argued 'The position and power of the Prime Minister has been the focal point of modern Cabinets'. Such a development was 'not due to the personality of any particular Premier or to the triumph of personal desires to arrogate power'. Rather there were at work a number of tendencies. The Prime Minister had 'a leading place in the eyes of the public and has increased his control of appointments and promotions within the Government'. Cabinet – 'loaded' as it was 'with business' – needed a 'chairman who can guide, summarise, and close the discussions'; and 'the forces of party loyalty and organisation naturally tend to support the individual who is most closely

[41] Harold J. Laski, *Reflections on the Constitution: the House of Commons, the Cabinet, the Civil Service* (Manchester: Manchester University Press, 1951), p.119.
[42] *Ibid*, p.117.
[43] *Ibid*, pp.118–9.

identified with the success of the party'.[44] Mackintosh argued that while

> British government in the latter half of the nineteenth century can be described simply as Cabinet government, such a description would be misleading today. Now the country is governed by the Prime Minister, who leads, co-ordinates and maintains a series of ministers all of whom are advised and backed by the Civil Service.[45]

The closing words of the 1968 edition of *The British Cabinet* were 'the politics of the 1960s have strengthened rather than weakened or altered the lines of development which have led contemporary British Government to be described as Prime Ministerial rather than Cabinet Government'.[46]

In 1963 Crossman wrote the introduction to a new edition of *The English Constitution* by the nineteenth century political journalist Walter Bagehot. Here Crossman claimed 'The postwar epoch has seen the final transformation of cabinet government into prime ministerial government'. Even before the time Bagehot wrote in 1867 prime ministers, according to Crossman, wielded 'near-presidential powers', arising from the ability to choose and remove Cabinet ministers, set its agenda, 'announce the decisions reached without taking a vote', and their 'control, through the chief whip, over patronage'. Since this time, Crossman held, their 'powers have ... steadily increased', with the 'centralisation of the party machine under [their] personal rule, and secondly by the growth of a centralised bureaucracy, so vast that it could no longer be managed by a cabinet behaving like the board of directors of an old-fashioned company'.[47] Crossman saw the 'coming of prime ministerial government' as entailing the Cabinet being consigned to join what he described, adapting a concept employed by Bagehot, as 'the "dignified" elements in the constitution'. Cabinet was now more an ornament than a functioning part of the political process, though it retained

[44] Mackintosh, *The British Cabinet*, p.428.
[45] *Ibid*, p.529.
[46] *Ibid*, p.627.
[47] R.H.S. Crossman, 'Introduction' to Walter Bagehot, *The English Constitution* (London: Collins/Fontana, 1963), pp.51–2.

'very real reserve powers which can on occasion be suddenly and dramatically used for good or for ill'. This development – which had been 'concealed from the public eye'[48] – was something Crossman seemingly regarded as undesirable. He argued that while during the Second World War the 'British people readily put their democratic Constitution into cold storage, and fought under a system of centralised autocracy' it was not as widely known that the 'institutions and the behaviour of voluntary totalitarianism' had been retained into peacetime. Crossman expressed his 'hope and belief' that 'the British people' would 'throw off its deferential attitude and reshape the political system, making the parties instruments of popular control, and even insisting that the House of Commons should once again provide the popular check on the executive'.[49]

The decades which followed the 1960s saw similar ideas continue to be promoted. In a lecture entitled *The Case for a Constitutional Premiership* given in Bristol in 1979, shortly after Labour was ousted from office, the former Labour Cabinet minister Tony Benn claimed that:

> the wide range of powers at present exercised by a British Prime Minister, both in that capacity, and as Party Leader, are now so great as to encroach upon the legitimate rights of the electorate, undermine the essential role of Parliament, usurp some of the functions of collective Cabinet decision-making, and neutralise much of the influence deriving from the internal democracy of the Party.

In Benn's view, 'the present centralisation of power into the hands of one person has gone too far and amounts to a system of personal rule in the very heart of our Parliamentary democracy'. He held that 'the powers of the Prime Minister, and Party Leader, must be made more accountable to those over whom they are exercised, so that we can develop a Constitutional Premiership in Britain'.[50]

[48] *Ibid*, p.54.
[49] *Ibid*, pp.56–7.
[50] Tony Benn, *The Case for a Constitutional Premiership* (Nottingham: Institute for Workers' Control, 1979), p.5.

Arguments that traditional forms of government have been, are in the process of being, or are about to be supplanted by, a dominant premiership have a long lineage. Because of this repetition across different eras, whatever similarities they may share, such theses inevitably contradict each other. If one period has seen the emergence of a presidential system or the ending of Cabinet government, then how can this process take place once again later on? One observer's time of No. 10 ascendancy can later be portrayed as a golden age for collegiality. Writing in 1904, Low argued that for 'the greater part of the past half century ... The office of Premier has become more than ever like that of an elective President'.[51] Yet from the vantage point of the 1960s Mackintosh claimed: 'British government in the latter half of the nineteenth century can be described simply as Cabinet government'; but that 'such a description would be misleading today'.[52] For Crossman an important stage in ascendancy of the premiership he detected came when, in 1945 'The wartime centralisation of power in the person of the premier was in no way reduced by Mr Attlee' who 'had no intention of becoming chairman of a large traditional Cabinet'.[53] But according to Christopher Foster, writing in 2005, under Attlee the Cabinet was in its 'second classic phase' in which, though Cabinet sub-committees were used, 'there was no less discussion between ministers than previously'.[54] In 1979 Benn claimed that 'the present centralisation of power into the hands of one person has gone too far and amounts to a system of personal rule in the very heart of our Parliamentary democracy'.[55] Similar claims were made by Shirley, Baroness Williams, who was quoted by the Power Inquiry in 2006 as describing the emergence of 'presidential Prime Ministers', requiring 'the reduction of Cabinet to essentially something of a sounding board, and of Parliament to not much more than a rubber stamp'. But she believed 'All that has happened since 1980/81'[56] – that is to say, one or two years after Benn

[51] Low, *The Governance of England*, 1904 edition, p.158.
[52] Mackintosh, *The British Cabinet*, p.529.
[53] R.H.S. Crossman, 'Introduction', p.49.
[54] Christopher Foster, *British Government in Crisis, or the Third English Revolution*, p.66.
[55] Benn, *The Case for a Constitutional Premiership*, p.5.
[56] *Power to the People: the report of power*, pp.128–9.

made his speech, including in it the announcement that the same tendencies to which Williams referred, had already taken hold.

Each individual who advances an interpretation of the tenure of an individual premier, or of the development of the office in general is, not responsible and cannot be condemned for the work of others. But where two theories disagree, the inescapable conclusion is that one or both must be wrong. When consideration is given to such theses as those of a 'presidential' or an increasingly dominant No.10 from 1997 onwards, it is important to bear in mind earlier similar proclamations. Accepting the more recent accounts entails rejecting the earlier incarnations, and vice versa. Agreeing with both is not an option – but dismissing each is.

Having established that at least most of the theories set out in the preceding pages must be wrong, it might be asked why they have been made so often. First, a possible reason is ignorance about debates of earlier times, partly produced by the gaps in the literature that the present work identifies and sets out to correct. Second, consideration should be given to the claim made by Walpole that those who made allegations about his 'exorbitant power'[57] did not believe they were true, and advanced them in pursuit of agendas other than that of honest constitutional analysis. Portrayals such as the assertion that Cabinet or Parliament has been devalued, may be seen as a means of political attack by anyone who wishes to erode the position of No.10 under a particular incumbent. Both Walpole and his enemies understood that a significant means of political attack was through the challenging of legitimacy: that is, casting doubt on whether a position had been acquired and was being exercised in accordance with 'justifiable rules, and with evidence of consent', as the political scientist David Beetham puts it.[58] Another cause of the attractiveness of the kind of assessments of the premiership set out here may be that they provide a dramatic – if simplistic – narrative. Images of unprecedented or accelerating developments occurring in the present and pointing only in one – possibly undesirable – direction might

[57] Reproduced in Williams, *The Eighteenth Century Constitution*, p.129.
[58] David Beetham, *The Legitimation of Power*, p.3.

be sensed as easier to convey in a compelling fashion than more nuanced accounts.

There is evidence to support the view that theses of an over-mighty premiership have at times been motivated primarily by political convenience or some other whim of the moment. Some who advanced them have been inconsistent in their outlook, possibly suggesting their views could be taken up or dropped as circumstances required. In the later years of the Walpole ascendancy, Samuel Johnson produced anti-government literature, including a version of the parliamentary debate described above in which Walpole was accused of being a Prime Minister.[59] Yet time changed his view of the Walpole tenure. In April 1775 Johnson complained to James Boswell that 'This [Lord North] ministry is neither stable nor grateful to their friends as Sir Robert Walpole was' – appearing to approve of the strength and use of patronage associated with the Walpole premiership.[60] Boswell recorded Johnson stating later in the same month that 'the great loss now was that government had too little power ... there was now no Prime Minister. Lord North was only the agent for Government in the House of Commons. He said we were governed by the Privy Council; but that there was no one head there, as in Sir Robert Walpole's time'.[61] Similar contradictions can be found in the views of Lord Lyndhurst, who, though on another occasion disparaging Wellington's supposed tendency to act on his own without consulting others, said the Duke was 'candid, reasonable, and ready to discuss fairly every subject'.[62]

While Laski criticised Lloyd George's attempts at strengthening the premiership, he was an advocate of not entirely dissimilar measures. He wrote of Lloyd George's Prime Minister's Secretariat that

[59] See: Benjamin Beard Hoover, *Samuel Johnson's Parliamentary Reporting: Debates in the Senate of Lilliput* (1953: University of California Press, Berkeley and Los Angeles).

[60] Charles Ryskamp (ed.), James Boswell, *Boswell: The Ominous Years, 1774–1776* (London: William Heinmann, 1963), diary entry for 7 April 1775, p.134.

[61] Ryskamp (ed.), James Boswell, *Boswell: The Ominous Years*, diary entry for 14 April 1775, pp.143–4.

[62] Aspinall, *The Cabinet Council*, p.208.

> In another form ... that department has been obviously wanting for a generation; for a much more thorough sifting was demanded of the material which eager colleagues with a zeal for their own office were anxious that the Prime Minister himself should investigate. But in the hands of Mr. Lloyd George the secretariat serves purposes unconnected with so simple an aim'.[63]

There are arguable tensions as well between the view Laski later espoused of a general tendency towards 'centralisation of power in the Prime Minister's hands' over a period of fifty or even a hundred years up to 1950, and his earlier concentration on Lloyd George as exceptional.

There are various problems of consistency in Crossman's views as expressed over time.[64] Most notably, as a member of Wilson's Cabinet from 1964–70, he developed a view diametrically opposed to his previous position that 'prime ministerial government' existed and was to be regretted, adopting the attitude that No.10 was not dominant, but should be. He pressed Wilson to affect measures, such as the establishment of an inner Cabinet designed to bolster the premiership[65]; and complained in his diary about:

> a complete absence of effective central control ... the whole of Whitehall has revolted against this idea of strong Prime Ministerial Government. Central coherent purpose was, after all, the main thing which Harold laid down as the characteristic which distinguished our method of government from the spasmodic drooling of the Tories; now we are drooling in a not very dissimilar way ... [Wilson] hasn't an idea how to construct the vital central machine of control. The strange thing is that the Cabinet would be entirely willing to accept central direction from No.10 because this will make the Cabinet system work and also because my colleagues want to survive and feel that they can't go on muddling through ... It's at the centre, where strong strategic purpose is essential, that the failure lies.[66]

---

[63] Laski, 'Mr. George and the constitution', pp.124–6.

[64] See eg: Kevin Theakston, 'Richard Crossman: The Diaries of a Cabinet Minister', *Public Policy and Administration* 2003; Vol. 18; No.4, Winter 2003, pp.31–4.

[65] Andrew Blick, *People Who Live in the Dark: the history of the special adviser in British politics*, p.87.

[66] Richard Crossman, *The Diaries of a Cabinet Minister*, Vol. II, *Lord President of the Council and Leader of the House of Commons, 1966–68* (London: Hamish

Views that diverged from, or at least suggested a need to qualify, theses of a dominant or 'presidential' premiership, or that it was increasingly taking on such characteristics, or that they were undesirable, have been frequently offered over time. In 1778 Lord North, recognising the lack of strength characterising his term in the premiership, recommended to George III that

> in critical times ... there should be one directing Minister, who should plan the whole of the operations of government, & controul [sic] all the other departments of administration so far as to make them co-operate zealously & actively with his designs even tho contrary to their own.[67]

During the 1807–9 tenure of the Duke of Portland as First Lord of the Treasury, No.10 was weak because he was in ill-health and faced a fractious group of ministers he could not control. Spencer Perceval, Portland's Chancellor of the Exchequer and a future Prime Minister, lamented the consequent lack of direction in a private letter. In a passage conveying the idea that the strength of the premiership was affected by political contingencies, in this instance involving the configuration of personalities, he remarked that because

> The present Government is so constituted with so many of equal or nearly equal pretensions with respect to personal weight in the Government, and importance to its continuance by the share of public opinion for talent and character which attach on such an individual's belonging to it may contribute to the whole, that Government, under whatever head, must to a great degree be and remain a Government of Departments.

Perceval argued that the appointment, in Portland, of an infirm First Lord was a product of this power balance, not the cause: 'It is not because the Duke of Portland is at our head that the Government is a Government of Departments, but it is because the Government is and must be essentially a

---

Hamilton and Jonathan Cape, 1976), diary entry for 25 September 1966, pp.50–1.

[67] Lord North to George III, 10 November 1778, reproduced in Williams, *The Eighteenth Century Constitution*, p.132.

Government of Departments that the Duke of Portland is at our head'. Suggesting that substantial power could be wielded in parts of government other than at No.10 and that the mere anticipation of its use could have a significant impact, Perceval noted:

> There are more than one among us who might, by saying, 'If you will not do so and so, I will resign,' bring the Government to very great difficulty if not nearly to an end – and while there is that power in several, provided there is a disposition to use it, it is impossible there can be in anyone [*firm prime-ministerial direction*].

Perceval saw prevailing circumstances as 'a great defect in the Government and a great misfortune to the country' and preferred the idea of 'a Government under an acknowledged head who would, upon the best view and judgement, select the best system and insist upon its being followed'.

The current position of Portland contrasted starkly with that of Pitt the Younger. Perceval described how the former premier

> must have felt, and his colleagues must have felt also, that he had such comprehensive talents and powers that he was himself essentially the Government in all its Departments – that he could form a Government almost of himself, and each of his colleagues must have felt that Mr. Pitt could do without him, though he could not do without Mr. Pitt.

Yet Perceval recognised that even when it enjoyed the relative strength within government that it did during the ascendancy of Pitt the Younger, there were limits upon what the premiership could achieve: 'even under these circumstances I have understood ... that Mr. Pitt himself could not in all Departments control expenditure as he wishes'.[68]

In his 1867 work *The English Constitution*, Bagehot suggested that the power afforded to the premiership could vary significantly according to circumstance.[69] He stressed the

[68] Spencer Perceval to Huskisson, 21 August 1809, cited in Aspinall, *The Cabinet Council*, pp.203–4.

[69] Bagehot, *The English Constitution*, pp.78–9.

limitations on the ability to exercise discretion in the conferral of patronage. When appointing Cabinet ministers 'Between the compulsory list whom he must take, and the impossible list whom he cannot take, a Prime Minister's independent choice ... is not very large; it extends rather to the division of the Cabinet offices than to the choice of Cabinet Ministers'. Bagehot – to a misleading extent – placed emphasis on the importance of the Cabinet and in turn Parliament above that of the office of Prime Minister. He called Cabinet 'a board of control chosen by the legislature, out of persons whom it trusts and knows, to rule the nation'.[70]

In an article first published in 1878, William Gladstone, then in the interregnum between the first and second of his four stints at No.10, portrayed the premiership as important, but at the same time lacking in formal status and authority and required to work with the Cabinet. As he put it: 'upon the whole, nowhere in the wide world does so great a substance cast so small a shadow; nowhere is there a man who has so much power, with so little to show for it in the way of formal title or prerogative'.[71] The premier was:

> Departmentally ... no more than the first named of five persons, by whom jointly the power of the Lord Treasureship are taken to be exercised; he is not their master, or, otherwise than by mere priority, their head: and he has no special function or prerogative under the formal constitution of the office. He has no official rank, except that of Privy Councillor. Eight members of the Cabinet, including five Secretaries of State, and several other members of the Government, take official precedence of him. His rights and duties as head of the Administration are nowhere recorded. He is almost, if not altogether, unknown to the Statute Law.[72]

While the post has acquired a more formal existence since Gladstone wrote these words, his general point about the absence of clear definition remains valid.[73] After noting that

[70] *Ibid*, p.67.
[71] W.E. Gladstone, 'Kin beyond sea', reproduced in: W.E. Gladstone, *Gleanings of Past Years*, vol. I, *The Throne, and the Prince Consort, the Cabinet, and Constitution* (London: John Murray, 1879), p.244.
[72] *Ibid*, p.240.
[73] See: Chapter Three.

being Leader of the House of Commons was an important source of strength, he went on to argue that 'The head of the British Government is not a Grand Vizier. He has no powers, properly so called, over his colleagues: on the rare occasions, when a Cabinet determines its course by the votes of its members, his vote counts only as one of theirs'; though their appointments and dismissals were made 'on his advice'. While premiers had the task of reporting to the Sovereign on the proceedings of Cabinet and had 'many audiences of the august occupant of the Throne' they were 'bound, in these reports and audiences, not to counterwork the Cabinet; not to divide it; not to undermine the position of any of [their] colleagues in Royal favour'. One device at the disposal of prime ministers was the ability, through resigning their post, to force the dissolution of a Cabinet, while the departure of another minister was substantially less likely to have the same effect. But Gladstone noted that: 'The Prime Minister has no title to override any one of his colleagues in any one of the departments. So far as he governs them, unless it is done by trick, which is not to be supposed, he governs them by influence only'.[74]

The Anthony Trollope novel *The Prime Minister* appeared in the same year as the article by Gladstone. Like Gladstone, and more than a hundred years in advance of the 'core-executive' school, Trollope stressed the inability to issue direct commands and emphasised in its place reliance on others. Trollope's character the Duke of Omnium returns home after being asked by the Queen to form a coalition government and finds his wife thrilled at the prospect of his elevation to the post of Prime Minister. But he tells her 'I never felt before that I had to lean so entirely on others as I do now'. His 'efficacy for my present tasks depends entirely on the co-operation of others, and unfortunately upon that of some others with whom I have no sympathy, nor have they with me'. Trollope conveyed, like Bagehot, the possible restrictions upon the exercise of choice in the appointment of ministers. The Duchess proposes a solution to the problem of the more problematic 'others', recommending he 'Leave them out'. But the Duke explains 'they are men who will

[74] *Ibid*, pp.242–4.

not be left out, and whose services the country has a right to expect'.[75]

In 1889 the Liberal politician and author John Morley produced a monograph on Walpole, in which he provided a depiction of the strength exercised by the premiership as potentially vast but conditional:

> The flexibility of the Cabinet system allows the Prime Minister in an emergency to take upon himself a power not inferior to that of a dictator, provided always that the House of Commons will stand by him. In ordinary circumstances he leaves the heads of departments to do their work in their own way.[76]

In the same year another Liberal politician, William Harcourt, in a commentary on Morley's depiction, stressed the need to avoid setting out 'the rules as to the position of the Prime Minister ... too absolutely. In practice the thing depends very much upon the character of the man. What was true of the Cabinet of Peel and Palmerston would not be true of other Ministers.' He doubted that 'Mr. Gladstone would agree in the position of autocracy'[77], seemingly referring to Morley's reference to a 'dictator'; although ironically the chapter in Morley's book which contained an account of the premiership was supposedly the work of Gladstone.[78]

Lord Rosebery was premier from 1894–5. A short while after he had moved to this post, having previously been Foreign Secretary, he told an old friend, the Treasury official Edward Hamilton, that 'he was not the least more reconciled to the Prime Ministership. He was sure that the Foreign Secretaryship was not only much more pleasant, but really more powerful'.[79] In an essay on Peel published in 1899, Rosebery provided a detailed analysis of the premiership

[75] Anthony Trollope, *The Prime Minister* (Oxford: Oxford University Press, 1999), Vol. I, pp.55–6.

[76] John Morley, *Walpole* (London: Macmillan, 1889), p.158.

[77] Memorandum by Sir William Harcourt on the Chapter on the Cabinet in Mr Morley's *Walpole*, 12 July 1889 in A. Gardiner, *The Life of Sir William Harcourt* (London: Constable, 1923), vol. II, Appendix II, pp.609–12.

[78] See: Earl of Oxford and Asquith, *Fifty Years in Parliament*, vol. 2, (London: Cassell, 1926), p.183, footnote 1.

[79] David Brooks (ed.), *The Destruction of Lord Rosebery: From the Diary of Sir Edward Hamilton, 1894–1895* (London: The Historians' Press, 1986), p.127, diary entry for 29 March 1894.

which expanded upon this feeling of impotence. He noted of the title 'Prime Minister' that to 'the ordinary apprehension it implies a dictator, the duration of whose power finds its only limit in the House of Commons ... But the reality is very different'.[80] While Peel 'kept a strict supervision over every department' and was 'master of the business of each and all of them' a little over half a century later it was 'more than doubtful, indeed, if it be possible in this generation, when the burdens of empire and of office have so incalculably grown, for any Prime Minister to discharge the duties of his high post with the same thoroughness or in the same spirit as Peel. To do so would demand more time and strength than any man has at his command'.[81] Rosebery stated that 'in these days of instant, continuous, and unrelenting pressure, the very tradition of such a minister [as Peel] has almost departed; indeed, it would be impossible to be so paternal and ubiquitous'.[82] He concluded that a 'Prime Minister who is the senior partner in every department as well as president of the whole, who deals with all the business of government, who inspires and vibrates through every part, is almost, if not quite, an impossibility'.[83] Rosebery added that an overweening premier might not be 'welcome to his colleagues'.[84]

A premier had to reckon with the Sovereign, Cabinet, Parliament and public opinion 'before he can have his way'. All were 'potent factors in their various kinds and degrees'.[85] Their compliance could not be demanded. Rosebery emphasised the need to work with Cabinet. While to the 'popular eye' the Prime Minister appeared to represent 'universal power', the truth was that a 'First Minister has only the influence with the Cabinet which is given him by his personal arguments, his personal qualities, and his personal weight'. Continually working to persuade ministers was 'a harassing, laborious, and ungracious task'.[86] The Cabinet had to be held together and any resignation from it was dangerous, a 'storm signal'.[87]

[80] Lord Rosebery, *Sir Robert Peel* (London: Cassell and Company, 1899), p.33.
[81] *Ibid*, p.27.
[82] *Ibid*, p.29.
[83] *Ibid*, p.30.
[84] *Ibid*, p.29.
[85] *Ibid*, p.34.
[86] *Ibid*, p.34.
[87] *Ibid*, p.35.

Rosebery described the challenge faced by the premier as that of the operator of 'a "machinery" liable to so many grains of sand' who needed 'all the skill and vigilance of the best conceivable engineer'.[88]

One of the present authors first entered the debate about the premiership in 1965 in response to theses such as those being advanced by Crossman and Mackintosh. In an article entitled 'The Prime Minister's Power' G.W. Jones argued these theories 'neglect many factors which restrain the prime minister in the exercise of his power. His actual position is not as predominant as has been presented'.[89] After challenging a variety of propositions contained in the then contemporary literature Jones concluded:

> Cabinet government and collective responsibility are not defunct notions. Shared responsibility is still meaningful, for a prime minister has to gain the support of the bulk of his cabinet to carry out his policies ... The prime minister is the leading figure in the cabinet whose voice carries most weight. But he is not the all-powerful individual which many have recently claimed him to be. His office has great potentialities, but the use made of them depends on many variables, the personality, temperament, and ability of the prime minister, what he wants to achieve and the methods he uses ... A prime minister who can carry his colleagues with him can be in a very powerful position, but he is only as strong as they let him be.[90]

In 1976 another former Prime Minister, Harold Wilson, engaged in detail with the nature of the premiership. Referring to the claims of Crossman about the supposed decline of collective government Wilson stated that 'the classical refutation of this 1963 assertion was Richard Crossman as a minister, and his unfailing, frequently argumentative, role from 1964 to 1970 in ruthlessly examining every proposal, policy or projection put before Cabinet by departmental ministers – or by the prime minister'.[91]

[88] *Ibid*, p.35.
[89] Reproduced in Anthony King (ed.), *The British Prime Minister* (Basingstoke: Macmillan, 1985), p.203.
[90] *Ibid*, p.216.
[91] Wilson, *The Governance of Britain*, p.4.

While rejecting the Crossman thesis, Wilson felt prime ministers were able to exercise increasing amounts of power, because of a growth in the 'power and influence' of governments in which the premier shared 'and almost certainly has increased his share'. He argued that in his time the expansion of the No.10 'share' came about because of increasing demands for action from the premiership over crises; and because of 'the overriding power of television and, to only a slightly smaller extent, of radio'. Prime ministers were required to make broadcasts and were 'constantly in the news'. In 'emergency situations such as world wars' prime ministers were 'invariably accorded emergency powers, but these are limited in duration' and dependent upon retaining parliamentary confidence. Yet 'the power of government and to that extent of the prime minister never reverts to the *status quo ante bellum*'.[92]

Few prime ministers 'except in wartime and rarely then, could dictate to their Cabinets'. While Wilson believed there had been 'a steady accretion to the power of the prime minister' in selecting ministers and allocating portfolios, it was subject to 'strict limitations'. Since parties contained within them a variety of different viewpoints, Cabinet had to as well. Premiers who have 'refused to appoint anyone who has opposed their views or in any way given offence, and have instituted "government by crony", have invariably paid the price'. Reshuffles were 'anything but set-piece movements on a chess board'.[93] In a passage reminiscent of Walpole's complex advice to Pelham on appointments, Wilson described how 'A re-disposition affecting a substantial number of ministers at all levels is like a nightmarish multidimensional jigsaw puzzle, with an almost unlimited number of possible permutations and combinations'.[94]

Another flaw in the 'prime ministerial theorem' was the 'unrealistic assumption that everything is static'. In favourable circumstances, such as 'after a successful government election' action might be contemplated that a premier would hesitate to undertake 'if things were going badly for him in Parliament'.[95]

[92] *Ibid*, p.31.
[93] *Ibid*, p.10.
[94] *Ibid*, p.34.
[95] *Ibid*, p.11.

There was considerable variability in circumstances according to the personalities involved.[96] Finally Wilson referred to the emergence of 'new checks and balances qualifying the power of the prime minister' including 'the greater power of Cabinet committees' and parliamentary select committees.[97]

In 1980, prefiguring Michael Barber's arguments of a quarter of a century later[98], Sir Kenneth Berrill gave a Stamp Memorial Lecture for the University of London entitled *Strength at the Centre – The Case for a Prime Minister's Department*. In it he emphasised the relative weakness of the institutional support provided for the premiership. He began by conceding that, 'The power of a Prime Minister to intervene in any field at any time is clear enough (and prime ministerial intervention is a significant force indeed)'.[99] This involvement was driven by a number of pressures. First there was the need to ensure the government pursued a coherent strategy. Second was 'the tendency of the media and the public to hold the Government responsible for virtually any problem that arises in both the public and the private sectors and to identify the Government's reaction to the problem with the persona of the Prime Minister': there was, he held, an 'increased personalisation of government which ... stems mainly from television and Parliament'.[100] Third was 'the growth in personal contact between heads of government'.[101] In order to cope with these demands Berrill argued in favour of the establishment of 'An across the board support system for a Prime Minister'. He concluded: 'The role of a Prime Minister at the centre has increased, is still increasing, and will not be diminished. We will be foolish if we do not face up to that fact and structure our arrangements adequately'.[102]

---

[96] *Ibid*, p.9.
[97] *Ibid*, p.11.
[98] See: Michael Barber, *Instruction to Deliver: Tony Blair, Public Services and the Challenge of Achieving Targets*.
[99] Sir Kenneth Berrill, *Strength at the Centre – The Case for a Prime Minister's Department* (London: University of London, 1980), p.4.
[100] *Ibid*, p.6.
[101] *Ibid*, p.7.
[102] *Ibid*, p.15. A similar argument was expressed in P. Weller, 'Do Prime Ministers' departments really cause problems?' in *Public Administration*, vol. 61, pp.59-78, 1985, and contradicted by G.W. Jones, 'Prime Minister's departments really do cause problems' in the same volume of *Public Administration*, at pp.195–220.

The paragraphs above show that there has always been dissent from theses such as those which allege the appearance of a presidency. But a consideration of the contrary viewpoints – and those akin to them from 1997 onwards – throws up certain difficulties, some of which are similar to those associated with the interpretations to which they are opposed. Rosebery argued in 1899 that during the period since Peel 'the burdens of empire and of office have so incalculably grown'[103] as to inhibit the relative impact that could be achieved by the premiership. Writing in 2007 Barber described how the 'ever-increasing demands of the job suggest the task is becoming more difficult to do'. For Barber the lives of prime ministers in the eighteenth, nineteenth and part of the twentieth centuries were relatively tranquil.[104] Once again we are confronted with difficulties in reconciling two theories – those of Rosebery and Barber – and may be led to conclude that one or both are wrong.

The remainder of this chapter provides an historical perspective on the themes identified as central to the literature emerging from 1997. This exercise makes it possible to draw out observations about the premiership and interpretations of it that have been advanced, in particular in the Blair/Brown era as well as from earlier periods. A key focus is upon the idea of the office changing.

Functions of the 'state', central government and the premiership

Certain interpretations of the premiership refer to some kind of expansion affecting the 'state'. The state is a loose concept, hard to define beyond the totality of the institutions of government, including local and central. When the functions the state has performed over time are examined, it is difficult to detect continuous, one-way, linear development. In economic policy the period between 1945 and the 1990s experienced numerous shifts of approach[105]: attempts variously at demand management, indicative planning, and monetarism; the

[103] Rosebery, *Sir Robert Peel*, p.27.
[104] Barber, *Instruction to Deliver*, p.298.
[105] For an account of economic policy during this period see eg: Alec Cairncross, *The British Economy since 1945* (Oxford: Blackwell, 1992).

abandonment of fixed exchange rates and the introduction of the full convertibility of sterling; and programmes of nationalisation and privatisation. The particular state agencies involved and their roles have fluctuated, including central government; regional and local bodies; nationalised industries and utilities; regulators; and the Monetary Policy Committee of the Bank of England. Though they are complex, trends are possible to discern and it should not be claimed such developments are unconnected with the office of Prime Minister. But it is difficult to conclude that churn of this kind, or in other areas of state activity, could somehow contribute to the continuous development of the premiership in one particular direction.

Examination of the development of central government and its implications for the office of Prime Minister, reveals another complicated picture. There is evidence that the tasks it performs are more numerous than they were in the time of Walpole. If the number of what came to be termed civil servants is taken as a proxy for activity, there was considerable expansion from the nineteenth century, prompted to a significant extent by economic growth. This increase continued until the 1980s, followed by a fall and rise again after 1997. From 1945 enhancements to central government took place to a large extent at the expense of local authorities. But there has been a parallel process by which central government has been forced to abandon responsibilities to, or share them, with a range of institutions, including supranational organisations (such as what is now termed the European Union; and the North Atlantic Treaty Organisation); regulators; bodies such as the Information Commissioner; and a judiciary increasingly engaged in areas of political controversy. To describe the tasks of central government simply as expanding or contracting, amounts to a misleading simplification. Consequently, the changes that have occurred are unlikely to encourage straightforward developments in the premiership. Even when the state in general and central government in particular acquire new functions, they are not necessarily exercised by the office of Prime Minister. Numerous Whitehall departments since the nineteenth century have appeared and grown outside the immediate remit of No.10. In addition to this tendency, various functions have on the one hand moved towards or been created within the remit of the office of Prime Minister, and on the other hand have been moved away from its ambit, or having been close to it, abolished altogether. These processes are described here as 'administrative fusion and fission'.[106] Their incidence means it is impossible to chart a simple process of expansion or contraction over the history of the office of Prime Minister.

Associated with the theme of the tasks performed by No.10, the workload to which prime ministers are subject has been of interest to observers of the premiership, and it has been claimed to be rising. But any attraction held by the idea that operation of the premiership has ever been a leisurely occupation, either for prime ministers or their aides, should be resisted. Barber drew attention in 2007 to Pitt the Younger's fighting of a duel as evidence he was not stretched in the way premiers over the last four decades have been. But observers from a future time may take Blair's providing a voiceover for an episode of *The Simpsons* or commentary by Brown about the tribulations of reality television stars as evidence that those within No.10 were not overtaxed in the present era. Referring to Pitt the Younger is not an effective way of showing that individuals attached to the premiership have become more heavily burdened over time. Some of his tasks amounted to manual labour. Like other prime ministers of his era he was obliged to spend considerable time handwriting letters to eminent persons who expected to receive communications in his own hand.[107] His correspondence with his Secretary to the Treasury, George Rose, shows the extent to which Pitt the Younger was engaged in the minute detail of financial policy.[108] Overwork was widely believed to have contributed to his premature death. As a later premier, Peel, put it to the Commons in 1834 'Mr. Pitt ... was cut off in the prime of life ... by the labours and anxieties of office'.[109]

[106] See: Chapter Three.
[107] See eg: John Ehrman, *The Younger Pitt: The Years of Acclaim* (London: Constable, 1969), p.582.
[108] See: George Rose, *The diaries and correspondence of the Right Hon. George Rose* (London: Bentley, 1860), 2 vols.
[109] House of Commons Debates, 5 May 1834, Col. 566.

Others were similarly stretched at No.10. Lord Arden, concerned about his brother, the premier Perceval, described in 1812 'the labour, fatigue and anxiety of his situation'.[110] In a letter written shortly after the end of his second and final 1841–6 term of office, Peel described how 'So far from regretting the expulsion from office, I rejoice in it as the greatest relief from an intolerable burden'.[111] He wrote: 'To have your own way, and to be for five years the Minister of this country in the House of Commons, is quite enough for any man's strength'. The tasks involved having to 'incur the deepest responsibility, to bear the heaviest toil, to reconcile colleagues with conflicting opinions to a common course of action, to keep together in harmony the Sovereign, the Lords and the Commons'. A further difficulty he noted came from a parliamentary party seeking to impose courses of action upon the premiership.[112] At around the same time Peel imparted to a future premier, Gladstone, his view of the stress which the post brought with it. Gladstone recorded in July 1846 that Peel told him:

> he had been twice prime minister, and nothing should induce him again to take part in the formation of a government; the labour and anxiety were too great; and he repeated more than once emphatically with regard to the work of his post, 'No one in the least degree knows what it is'.[113]

On this occasion, according to Gladstone, the main complaints Peel made were about the requirement to conduct correspondence with notables 'in my own hand ... the sitting seven or eight hours a day to listen in the House of Commons' and the need to 'have my mind in the principal subjects connected with the various departments ... and all the reading connected with them'. Finally there was 'the difficulty that you have in conducting such questions on account of your

[110] Denis Gray, *Spencer Perceval: The Evangelical Prime Minister, 1762–1812* (Manchester: Manchester University Press, 1963), p.428.

[111] Charles Stuart Parker (ed), *Sir Robert Peel: from his private papers*, vol. III (London: John Murray, 1899), Peel to Lord Hardinge, 24 September 1846, p.473.

[112] *Ibid*, pp.473–4.

[113] John Morley, *The Life of William Ewart Gladstone* (London: Macmillan and Co., 1903), p.297.

colleague whom they concern' – in other words, dealing with those in the Cabinet within whose remit a particular issue fell.[114] While Rosebery would later claim there had been a vast growth in government work since Peel, the latter had observed in his own time, as he told Gladstone, 'the immense multiplication of details in public business'.[115] There were physical consequences. Peel 'had suffered dreadfully in his head on the left side' following a shooting accident in earlier life. 'Since then he had always had a noise on that side, and when he had the work of office upon him, this and the pain became scarcely bearable at times'.[116] That Gladstone – having heard this description of the post and its impact upon someone who occupied it – should nevertheless seek to emulate Peel in reaching No.10 can perhaps be seen as a manifestation of his masochistic tendencies.

Similar points can be made about excessive stress levels for other premiers and various No.10 staff over the centuries. Kavanagh and Seldon claim that 'Britain may have been at the heart of a great worldwide empire under Gladstone and Benjamin Disraeli, but there was little evidence of Number Ten appearing to be overloaded'.[117] Yet Gladstone worked himself to or beyond the point of breakdown more than once. During the passage of the Bill for the Disestablishment of the Church of Ireland in 1869, his secretary Algernon West described how after a 'terrible crisis of anxiety' at the prospect of its being rejected the premier was 'fairly laid up' and unable to inform the Queen that it had passed.[118] In what was presumably a case of understatement, George Leveson-Gower, another secretary to Gladstone, complained in a letter of August 1880 how the weight of business was leaving him feeling 'regularly seedy'.[119] In 1893 West produced a description of the working day of the by-then octogenarian Gladstone that leaves the

[114] *Ibid*, p.298.
[115] *Ibid*, p.299.
[116] *Ibid*, p.300.
[117] Dennis Kavanagh and Anthony Seldon, *The Powers Behind the Prime Minister: the hidden influence of Number Ten* (London: HarperCollins, 2000), p.34.
[118] Sir Algernon West, *Recollections: 1832 to 1886*, Vol. I (Smith, Elder, & Co., London, 1899), p.350.
[119] Sir George Granville Leveson-Gower, *Years of Content: 1858–1886* (John Murray, London, 1940), p.153.

reader exhausted.[120] During the tenures of Disraeli at No.10 similar strains manifested themselves, perhaps less on the part of the premier than the person upon whom he delegated many important tasks. Early in 1878 Disraeli informed Queen Victoria that his senior private secretary, Montagu Corry, had 'broken down from overwork and over-anxiety. His nervous system has given way ... Mr. Corry will have to travel abroad'.[121]

These accounts of the pressures which existed during the tenures of Pitt the Younger, Peel, Gladstone and Disraeli undermine the various claims that have been made about rising individual burdens and the premiership. So too does the description James Callaghan, Prime Minister from 1976–9, provided of his time in the post. He held all the great offices of state in the course of his career and concluded: 'In my experience the work-load was greater both as Chancellor and as Foreign Secretary'[122] than it was as premier. The difference between the accounts provided by Callaghan and Peel confirms there has been no simple transition from a smaller to a greater burden of work for those inside No.10 over time. Particularly since the mid-nineteenth century[123] the premiership has been characterised by a combination of a lack of specific duties and at the same time the potential for much activity. As West put it: 'The Prime Minister has nothing to do. The Prime Minister has everything to do. These statements are contradictory; yet both are true'.[124] Precisely how much work is undertaken can be determined by external contingencies, including exceptional circumstances such as the occurrence of war, potentially prompting an increase in the load. The personal approach of individuals within No.10, in particular the Prime Minister, is important also. In the words of Callaghan 'To a large extent the Prime Minister makes his own pace. It is the Prime Minister himself who takes the initiatives, who pokes about

[120] Algernon West, 'The Prime Minister', part I of a series entitled 'A Cabinet Minister's Day', reproduced in Horace G. Hutchinson (ed), *Private Diaries of the Rt. Hon. Sir Algernon West, G.C.B.* (London: John Murray, 1922), pp.128–35.

[121] George Earle Buckle, *The Life of Benjamin Disraeli, Earl of Beaconsfield*, Vol. VI, *1855–1868* (John Murray, London, 1916), pp.237–8.

[122] James Callaghan, *Time and Chance* (London: Collins, 1987), p.403.

[123] See: Chapter Three.

[124] West, 'The Prime Minister'.

where he chooses and creates his own waves'.[125] Gladstone had 'everything to do', to use West's phrase, partly because he chose to operate in this way, as did Pitt the Younger and Peel. Callaghan did not.

Parliament

The notion of a straightforward historical shift in the relations between Parliament and premiership is also not sustained by the evidence. The basic principle that statute law, including finance bills, requires parliamentary assent has remained unchanged throughout. Initially the office of Prime Minister emerged to a large extent because the monarchy needed the support of the legislature – and in particular the House of Commons – for its policies; and during the course of the eighteenth century a practice developed for the crown to rely on an individual parliamentary figure to deliver the required majorities, who was usually the First Lord of the Treasury. In this sense the premiership has always been dominant within Parliament, rather than having acquired such a feature lately. By the same token no individual Prime Minister can be sustained in office in the face of continual defeats in the legislature. Indeed the possibility of being propped up for a time by a supportive monarch despite the objections of a majority in the Commons, as Pitt the Younger was by George III in 1784, passed away in the nineteenth century.

Though they have become more specialised, mechanisms for the enforcement of party discipline have existed throughout the history of the office of Prime Minister: the term 'whip' has its origins in the eighteenth century as an adaptation of hunting terminology – a 'whipper-in' of humans rather than hounds. The rise of the mass party organised within and without Parliament in the era after the 1832 Great Reform Act, meant that the premiership could rely on a firmer base of parliamentary support. But just as the body of those loyal to the government solidified, so too did the opposition, who were more likely to vote against government proposals on a regular basis. More cohesive parliamentary groups were better able to combine to seek to impose specific courses of action upon the premiership. Peel, whose terms at No.10

[125] Callaghan, *Time and Chance*, p.403.

occurred during a time when the mass party was developing substantially, did not view this entity as enhancing the power of the office of Prime Minister. In 1846, shortly after leaving No.10, he wrote: 'There is too much truth in the saying "The head of a party must be directed by the tail." As heads see, and tails are blind, I think heads are the best judges as to the course to be taken'. Peel described the idea, intolerable to him, of a premier becoming 'the tool of a party' adopting 'the opinions of men who have not access to your knowledge, and could not profit by it if they had, who spend their time in eating and drinking, and hunting, shooting, gambling, horse-racing, and so forth'. He would 'take care ... not again to burn my fingers by organising a party'.[126]

During the Blair period, which in some accounts saw an increasing marginalisation of Parliament, government MPs became increasingly prone to rebelling, suggesting that whips did not enjoy the authority sometimes attributed to them. Philip Cowley has found that during the 2001–5 Parliament 'Labour backbenchers rebelled in 20.8 per cent of votes, a higher rate of rebellion than in any other parliament since 1945'. Contrary to suggestions of an increasingly supine Commons, Cowley found evidence of a trend in the opposite direction. 'Backbench cohesion was at its peak in the 1950s and early 1960s ... There were two sessions in the 1950s – two whole years – in which not a single Conservative MP defied their party whip even once'.[127]

But there was a bloc within the Commons – ministers – who could not rebel against the government if they wished to retain their positions. Langford noted in 2006 that:

> In the nineteenth century the size of this élite corps diminished steadily, but in the twentieth century it grew again, from 42 office-holding M.P.s in 1900 to 95 in 1945 and 115 in 1970 ... Tony Blair has 129 such jobs at his personal disposal, more even than the 124 that Walpole had at the height of his power before his fall, in 1742.[128]

---

[126] *Ibid*, p.474.

[127] Philip Cowley, *The Rebels: How Blair mislaid his majority* (London: Politico's, 2005), pp.6, 2.

[128] Langford, 'Prime Ministers and Parliament', p.388.

There exist many other means of measuring the strength of Parliament relative to that of the executive in general and the premiership in particular. But broadly speaking for every indicator suggesting one trend, it seems possible to furnish another pointing in the opposite direction, and the same trend may be open to contradictory interpretations. In the case of statistics on the attendance of prime ministers in the Commons and their participation in the proceedings of the House[129], frequent presence and involvement may mean the premiership is a dominating force in the Commons or that it is weak and needs to be constantly wooing it. Low attendance and participation may mean that the office of Prime Minister feels secure enough to ignore the Commons or is so feeble it fears facing critics.

Cabinet

There have frequently been suggestions that the premiership was supplanting the Cabinet. A discussion of this idea must begin with a simple chronological point. The office of Prime Minister developed roughly in tandem with Cabinet. Consequently any idea that the premiership usurped Cabinet must be qualified. Indeed the abolition of collective government alongside the retention of the office of Prime Minister could be seen to some extent as restoring circumstances prevailing in the time of Walpole.

The precise nature of the British Cabinet has always been subject to vagaries. Gladstone wrote in 1878 that 'It lives and acts simply by understanding, without a single line of written law or constitution to determine its relations to the Monarch, or to the Parliament, or to the nation; or the relations of its members to each other, or to their head'.[130] While during the twentieth century there developed some codification of Cabinet (but not in law), uncertainty persisted. Consequently, a degree of caution should be exercised when proclaiming the demise of Cabinet: if we do not know exactly what it was

[129] See: Patrick Dunleavy and G.W. Jones with June Burnham, Robert Elgie and Peter Fysh, 'Leaders, Politics and Institutional Change: The Decline of Prime Ministerial Accountability to the House of Commons, 1868-1990' in R. A. W. Rhodes and Patrick Dunleavy (eds) *Prime Minister, Cabinet and Core Executive.*

[130] Gladstone, 'Kin beyond sea', p.241.

in the first place, how do we know it is no longer with us? And since, as will be shown, it has changed in its nature over time[131], it may be that what appears to be the undermining or destruction of Cabinet government is, in fact, simply another stage in its development.

Cabinet can be viewed in a number of interrelated ways. Beginning as an *event*, a regular meeting of senior ministers, it became increasingly established during the course of the eighteenth century, to be accepted in the nineteenth as the *supreme committee of government*.[132] It acted as a *means* to achieve certain ends – a cohesive government in which opposing opinions could be reconciled and policy was made that was politically sensitive and effective thanks to its thorough consideration from different viewpoints. In the nineteenth century Cabinet increasingly became associated with a *principle* as well. Known as collective responsibility, it meant that Cabinet members, who stood or fell together politically, were involved together in important deliberations and united publicly around the decisions that were made, with their personal views remaining confidential.[133] Within such a model the Prime Minister came to be known as *primus inter pares*, first among equals, an expression that seems to have denoted that while premiers chaired Cabinet, they had no formal right to command its members in the exercise of their responsibilities. Those who bemoan the supposed demise of Cabinet, often seem to have the *principle* of collective responsibility foremost in their minds, in particular the idea of group involvement. Increasingly – especially following the emergence of the Cabinet Office out of the First World War period – Cabinet became an *institution* consisting of the main committee, a constellation of sub-bodies and a support staff, operating according to certain *procedures* that constituted a system of Cabinet governance.

---

[131] For a consideration of this process of transmutation in the twentieth century, see: Anthony Seldon, 'The Cabinet System', in Vernon Bogdanor (ed.), *The British Constitution in the Twentieth Century*, pp.97–137.

[132] For an account of this manifestation of Cabinet see: G.W. Jones, 'Development of the Cabinet' in W. Thornhill (ed.), *The Modernisation of British Government* (London: Pitman, 1975), and G.W. Jones, 'Cabinet Government since Bagehot' in Robert Blackburn (ed.), *Constitutional Studies: Contemporary Issues and Controversies* (London: Mansell, 1992).

[133] See eg: Sir Ivor Jennings, *Cabinet Government*, Third Edition, (Cambridge: Cambridge University Press, 1959), pp.277–89.

The development and acceptance of the *principle* of Cabinet were gradual. The initial employment in *The Times* of the term *primus inter pares* in describing the premier came in 1880, in an article suggesting that Pitt the Younger had presented himself in such a light.[134] (This article predates by nine years the most famous attachment of this label to the Prime Minister, by Morley in 1889[135], suggesting a need to revise the view that he originated it[136]). The first occurrence in *The Times* of the phrase 'collective Cabinet responsibility' was in 1903 (with parliamentary deployment beginning the following decade). It came in the quotation of a statement issued by a free trade pressure group. The organisation, the Free Trade Union, was claiming that 'The old theories of collective Cabinet responsibility have been ... completely shattered'.[137] In both cases the inaugural uses of these terms presented them as being long-established. But while they must have already been in circulation for some time, and the concepts they referred to could have been expressed using different words, their prior absence from *The Times* suggests a need for caution about backdating their pervasiveness excessively.

The engagement by the premiership with the *principle* of Cabinet – in particular the idea of group decisions – has varied significantly. During certain premierships – such as those of Peel, Gladstone and Lloyd George – there was a pronounced tendency to lead from the front; while in others – including those of Lord Liverpool, Asquith and Attlee – No.10 was less assertive. This fluctuation is a manifestation of the phenomenon labelled here 'zigzag'.[138] The manner in which the office operates may vary within individual terms as well, according to the issue and circumstances concerned. When No.10 is more forceful the consequence can be that the group involvement part of the *principle* of Cabinet is adhered to less. When the premiership is less interventionist, one of two outcomes can come about. Either the commitment to the *principle* of group decisions is boosted because the collective

[134] Editorials/Leaders, *The Times*, 20 April 1880.
[135] Morley, *Walpole*, p.157.
[136] Anthony King (ed.), *The British Prime Minister*, Second Edition (Basingstoke: Macmillan, 1985), p.11.
[137] 'Fiscal Policy', *The Times*, 17 September 1903.
[138] See: Chapter Three.

plays a larger role, or undermined, because individual ministers are given greater freedom to act without reference to either the collective or the premiership.

It could be concluded that all that occurred from 1997 was one more in a long line of oscillations in the behaviour of No.10. Blair was open about his personal proclivity for meetings with individual secretaries of state rather than group discussions within the formal remit of Cabinet, noting: 'I do probably place a lot more emphasis on bilateral stock-takes'.[139] Yet there is ample precedent for direct dealings between No.10 and other parts of government and it is hard to establish absolutely whether the premiership relies on this technique more at one time than another. Gladstone told Peel shortly after his fall in 1846 that 'Your government has not been carried on by a cabinet, but by the heads of departments each in communication with you', a proposition to which Peel, Gladstone recorded, assented.[140] When he became premier the correspondence between Gladstone and his Foreign Secretary Lord Granville[141] shows bilateralism in action again.

But it is possible that, rather than just being adhered to less for a time, the *principle* of collective government had undergone from 1997 a more serious decline. Collective responsibility has a relatively informal existence, being referred to, but not comprehensively described, in the non-legally binding *Ministerial Code* (before 1997 known as *Questions of Procedure for Ministers*).[142] Consequently its persistence depends to a large extent upon some degree of commitment to it amongst those responsible for the operation of government. At least one senior aide to Blair has rejected it. In evidence to an inquiry into the Cabinet Office by the House of Lords Constitution Committee in 2009, Jonathan Powell, Chief of Staff throughout the Blair premiership, wrote:

---

[139] House of Commons Liaison Committee, Minutes of Evidence, 16 July 2002, Question 4.

[140] Morley, *The Life of William Ewart Gladstone*, p.298.

[141] Agatha Ramm (ed.), *The Political Correspondence of Mr. Gladstone and Lord Granville: 1868–1876* (London: Offices of the Royal Historical Society, 1952).

[142] For the history of the *Code* see Amy Baker, *Prime Ministers and the Rule Book* (London: Politico's, 2000).

> Cabinet is not the right body in which to attempt to make difficult decisions. It has too many members for a proper debate. Many of those who are there will not necessarily be well briefed on the subjects under discussion unless they come directly within the remit of their departments. And many individuals whose input is necessary for well informed decisions, eg the military chiefs of staff, are not present.

Powell favoured the use of Cabinet committees which he saw as:

> an essential instrument of government decision making: all the relevant people can be there (and not the irrelevant), they are focussed on particular decisions, properly prepared and they have as much time as they need to reach a decision. In my view therefore rather than arguing about the death of Cabinet government, when it in fact died a long time ago, we should spend more effort reinforcing the Cabinet Committees and their supporting infrastructure as a key part of government decision making.[143]

Traditionally Cabinet committees are regarded as a means of supporting full Cabinet, including helping it better to fulfil the *principle* of Cabinet. But here Powell appeared to advocate their use to bypass full Cabinet, because members of it could be classed as 'irrelevant' to decisions that did not 'come directly within the remit of their departments'. Yet the more orthodox understanding is that anyone in Cabinet, regardless of their specific portfolio, can potentially take part in discussions of any given issue. While others in the past may have had similar views to those expressed by Powell, if his outlook was or came to be shared by a substantial number of officials and politicians, who in turn transmitted it on to their successors in later generations, then the *principle* of Cabinet would have been undermined in a more fundamental and lasting sense.[144]

Cabinet began serious development as an *institution* when Lloyd George attached to the War Cabinet he established

[143] 'House of Lords Constitution Committee Inquiry: Written evidence from Jonathan Powell, former Chief of Staff to Tony Blair', 11 June 2009.

[144] A similar erosion of Cabinet has often been expressed by John Prescott who felt the role of ministers is to be consulted by and give advice to the Prime Minister who then decides: ministers advise; prime ministers decide.

upon acceding to the premiership late in 1916 a secretariat, which went on to become the Cabinet Office. As will be shown in the next chapter, during the Labour term of office beginning in 1997, Cabinet as an *institution* was diminished through the drafting and re-drafting of the terms of reference of the Cabinet Office and associated administrative change. The approach taken to Cabinet *procedures* favoured by No.10 from 1997 had some precedents. Commenting on the existence of an inclination to avoid the discussion of papers in formal meetings of Cabinet and its subcommittees, the Cabinet Secretary and Head of the Home Civil Service Richard Wilson noted in 2000:

> it has always been the case that around the edge of government – indeed not just at the edge – there have been other ways of taking decisions than having a formal discussion on the basis of a piece of paper in the Cabinet or a Cabinet Committee.[145]

But the role that circulated policy documents have played in Cabinet should not be underestimated. Their production and distribution is one of the longest established Cabinet procedures, pre-dating the appearance of the Cabinet Office from 1916. The practice gained ground from the early nineteenth century, although there was no central machinery for organising it and consequently no single record of materials sent around. In the National Archives/Public Record Office CAB 37 class there are more than 5,000 papers circulated to Cabinet from the period 1880–1916 alone, and even this set is not complete.

There is evidence of a recent trend away from discussion of documents at full Cabinet, but one which began before Blair took office. Cabinet Secretary and Head of the Home Civil Service Andrew Turnbull told the House of Commons Public Administration Select Committee (PASC) in 2005:

> I do not think the way Cabinet has worked has changed dramatically ... Back in the mid-1980s, they were meeting about 40 times a year and only taking 10 or 15 papers. That was a pattern which had been established late in Mrs Thatcher's time, through Mr Major's time and continues to this day ... The role

[145] House of Commons Select Committee on Public Administration (PASC), Minutes of Evidence, 9 February 2000, Question 52.

> of Cabinet, whereby it is not the forum for detailed decision making, is something which has been around for at least 20 years.[146]

Clare Short complained after leaving the Cabinet that the minutes of its discussions were 'lean'. Without access to the records of any meetings in the last thirty years it is impossible to verify whether there has been a substantial change in their quality during this period, and if there has the extent to which it preceded or occurred after Labour took office in 1997. But if minutes were in some way diminished as an expression within government of the collective will of senior ministers, then a procedure central to Cabinet since late 1916 – when a secretariat was attached to the War Cabinet newly formed under Lloyd George – would have been undermined.[147]

Table 1 details the occurrence of Cabinet as an *event*, detailing the number of full formal Cabinet meetings taking place by calendar year from 1916 (before which, without the existence of the secretariat, it is harder to trace their occurrence).

What trends can be read into these figures? The first is that war cabinets formed during the two world wars met more frequently than regular cabinets at other times. If the statistics are considered using an admittedly arbitrary division into decades, the figures for relatively peaceful times show that the 1950s saw a peak in frequency of meetings, with an average of 87.1 per year. In the 1960s there was a decline to 67.8; which was a return to earlier levels – the figure is precisely the same as that for the 1920s and close to that of the period 1930–8, 65.7. The decline of the 1960s continued into the 1970s. The average for the period 1970–6 was 61.9. The fall-off then accelerated. It is possible that the experience of the IMF crisis of 1976, which was handled in depth by full Cabinet, encouraged an unfavourable view of such meetings

[146] *Ibid*, 10 March 2005, Question 193.

[147] For an account provided by the first Cabinet Secretary, Maurice Hankey, of the historical precedent for his role as Cabinet minute-taker, see: Lord Hankey, *The Eleventh Haldane Memorial Lecture* (Birkbeck College: University of London, 1942), pp.9–14.

[148] John Morley, *The Life of William Ewart Gladstone*, p.300.

TABLE 1

War Cabinet/Cabinet meetings since 1916

1916*		1947	96	1978	44
1917	308	1948	82	1979	40
1918	204	1949	72	1980	45
1919**	121/18	1950	87	1981	41
1920	82	1951	82	1982	53
1921	93	1952	108	1983	38
1922	72	1953	81	1984	41
1923	59	1954	92	1985	37
1924	67	1955	75	1986	42
1925	61	1956	104	1987	37
1926	67	1957	90	1988	40
1927	64	1958	88	1989	39
1928	58	1959	64	1990	40
1929	55	1960	65	1991	38
1930	73	1961	71	1992	40
1931	93	1962	76	1993	40
1932	68	1963	74	1994	40
1933	70	1964	64	1995	40
1934	47	1965	73	1996	41
1935	56	1966	68	1997	36
1936	75	1967	74	1998	37
1937	49	1968	52	1999	35
1938	60	1969	61	2000	36
1939***	49/123	1970	72	2001	33
1940	312	1971	63	2002	38
1941	138	1972	59	2003	39
1942	174	1973	63	2004	38
1943	176	1974	63	2005	36
1944	176	1975	56	2006	37
1945****	17/48	1976	57	2007	42
1946	108	1977	41	2008	41

* Figure, which dates from establishment of War Cabinet in December 1916 onwards, amalgamated with 1917 total. War Cabinet sat from 1916–19.
** War Cabinet/full Cabinet figure.
*** Full Cabinet / War Cabinet figure. War Cabinet sat from 1939–45
**** War Cabinet/full Cabinet figure
Source: National Archive, Public Record Office CAB 65; CAB 128; Freedom of Information request.

amongst senior ministers, or officials, or both. It could be that there emerged a view similar to that expressed by Peel to Gladstone in 1846, that it had become 'impossible ... even to work the public business through the medium of cabinet, such is the pressure upon time'.[148] While the figure for 1976, 57, was not high when compared to previous counts, it fell by 16 the following year and has never been equalled since. Only once since 1976 has the annual total reached the 50s.

These figures show that Richard Wilson was technically correct to note in 2000 that 'It is public knowledge that the Cabinet meets less often now – and has done actually for a long time – than it did in the 1960s and 1970s'.[149] But it should not be concluded that there has been little change during this period. While the figure for 1977, 41, was the same as that for 2008, there have been noteworthy fluctuations since 1976. The peak annual figure came in 1982, when 53 full Cabinet meetings were held. This surge, compared with 41 in 1981 and 38 in 1983, is probably explained by the Falklands conflict which occurred that year. In 2003, when the invasion of Iraq took place (with a build-up to the action from 2002), there was no such spike (the total for 2003 is 39, compared with 38 for 2002 and 38 for 2004). Could it be that while a general tendency of decline in the number of meetings was already underway by 1982, there still existed a disposition inside government to utilise full meetings more extensively in grave circumstances that had disappeared by 2003?

The frequency of full Cabinet meetings did not alter significantly between the Thatcher and Major premierships. For 1980–9 (excluding 1982) the average was 40; while for 1991–6 it was 39.8. The average during 1998–2006 was 36.6, showing a small but perceptible drop under Blair, followed by an initial rise under Brown (41 for 2008). These minor shifts are suggestive of fluctuations under individual premiers within a broader framework determined across a time-frame overlapping a number of tenures, a theme explored further in the next chapter.

Another indicator of the nature of Cabinet as an event is the length of full meetings. From 1997, as no doubt in earlier

[148] John Morley, *The Life of William Ewart Gladstone*, p.300.
[149] PASC, Minutes of Evidence, 9 February 2000, Question 51.

eras, the time they took up was the product partly of political circumstance. As the Blair premiership progressed and his political stock declined their duration extended. Turnbull told PASC in 2004:

> In my time, Cabinet discussion has expanded rather than contracted. I have pushed the Prime Minister, advised the Prime Minister, to allow more time. The Cabinet now blocks out more time in the diary than it did before ... The pendulum has swung.[150]

When using indicators, such as the frequency and length of gatherings, as a means of understanding Cabinet, caution should be exercised. While a long-term decline in the number of full meetings is a significant tendency, it should not be equated directly with such supposed events as the supplanting of Cabinet government by the premiership. The potential danger of simplistic reading of the statistics is illustrated by consideration of figures from the 1920s. In the last full year of the Lloyd George premiership, 1921, there were 1,200 Cabinet memoranda, 93 full meetings of Cabinet and 220 of its sub-committees. In 1923, when Bonar Law and then Baldwin occupied No.10, there were 424 memoranda, 59 meetings of full Cabinet and 110 of its subcommittees. The combined staff of the Cabinet Office and Committee of Imperial Defence for the respective years numbered 143 and 39.[151] These shifts could be read as suggesting that the Lloyd George premiership was far more collegiate than those of Bonar Law and Baldwin, with the first of the three prime ministers more committed to the holding of meetings, circulating of papers and furnishing of staff to support collective processes. Yet first-hand accounts of government from the time suggest that in practice the No.10 of Lloyd George was more domineering than that of his two successors. Measurable indicators are important but cannot tell the whole story. The mere occurrence of a meeting, circulation of a paper or existence of a secretariat, do not reveal the quality or dynamics of the discussion that took place.

---

[150] *Ibid*, 4 March 2004.

[151] See: S. S. Wilson, *The Cabinet Office to 1945*, Public Record Office Handbooks No. 17 (London: HMSO, 1975), Annex 7(a), p.174.

Despite such qualifications there is clear evidence of a long-term decline in Cabinet as an event since the late 1950s. But was it still the *supreme committee of government*? Powell informed the House of Lords Constitution Committee that 'at least since the late 1970s the Cabinet has been used to ratify decisions rather than to take them'.[152] The tone of his account encouraged the inference that full Cabinet approval was a simple rubberstamping process, similar to the provision of Royal Assent to a Bill presented by Parliament. But there is other evidence that full Cabinet could still function as the final means of taking decisions over which there was disagreement. As Blair's political standing lowered, it became increasingly necessary to use Cabinet in this way. Hyman describes how:

> By the second term, partly through political necessity, Tony began to use Cabinet more seriously as a forum for discussion, as a way of briefing colleagues on the reform programme on public services – ministers would take it in turn to present their plans – and on occasions to air controversial issues where the outcome was genuinely in doubt, like whether to introduce identity cards.[153]

The use of Cabinet in this way suggests that, contrary to the statement by Powell, that it 'is not the right body in which to attempt to make difficult decisions'[154], it could be the perfect entity for such a purpose. If a particular issue was problematic, arguably a good way of resolving it was through a gathering of individuals who represented both the complete span of departmental interests, and a variety of different constituencies within the governing group in Parliament.

Policy was not habitually formed at the level of full Cabinet, a position that seems to have prevailed at least since the 1980s, but it remained possible for Cabinet members, if they chose, to force upon the premiership the discussion of a subject, leading to a decision not sought by No.10. Acting in a large enough group, which full Cabinet meetings gave them the opportunity

[152] 'House of Lords Constitution Committee Inquiry: Written evidence from Jonathan Powell, former Chief of Staff to Tony Blair', 11 June 2009.

[153] Peter Hyman, *1 Out of 10: From Downing Street Vision to Classroom Reality* (London: Vintage, 2005), p.86.

[154] 'House of Lords Constitution Committee Inquiry: Written evidence from Jonathan Powell, former Chief of Staff to Tony Blair', 11 June 2009.

to do, they could not be overwhelmed by the premiership. This possibility remained whether or not participants in government subscribed fully to the *principle* of Cabinet. It is the place where it could be said 'the buck finally stops'.

Another safeguard of the existence of Cabinet was its manifestation as a *means* to various ends. Regardless of whether they were committed to it as a *principle,* formal processes of collective government might be seen for a variety of reasons as useful or necessary within No.10 and across government. This issue is considered in more detail in Chapter Four.

Other institutions

During its existence the office of Prime Minister has dealt with various different bodies and groups, often of shifting levels of prominence. By the mid-nineteenth century the monarchy had become less important. William IV in 1834 was the last ruler to dismiss a government with a majority in the Commons. By the twentieth century the established church was not the social force it had been in the time of Walpole. During the twentieth century trades unions became increasingly significant, at least until the 1980s. Mass parties and local government became prominent during the nineteenth century, but by the end of the twentieth century their decline was evident. Generally as the significance of certain bodies lessens, others are becoming more noteworthy. Various entities appearing in the post-Second World War era could be seen as rivals to, or constraints on, No.10, including the European Union; devolved governance; a judiciary more likely to become involved in issues of political controversy such as human rights; and bodies like the Committee on Standards in Public Life and the Office of the Information Commissioner, which were capable of creating difficulties for the government.

Prime-ministerial aides and Whitehall

Though the Prime Minister is one individual politician, from the outset the premiership has been exercised by a group.[155] Prime ministers have always required help. Because official

[155] For the full history of aides to the Prime Minister, see: Andrew Blick and George Jones, *At Power's Elbow: the Prime Minister's People from before Walpole to the Present* (2011, forthcoming).

recognition of the premiership was slow to develop, the staff attached to it similarly lacked formal existence. But in practice aides were heavily deployed. Until the mid-nineteenth century prime ministers had a 'department'. Since they usually held the post of First Lord of the Treasury, and if they sat in the Commons they combined it with that of Chancellor of the Exchequer, they were directly responsible for the Treasury. Maurice Wright observes that up to the mid-nineteenth century 'the First Lord [was] intimately connected with Treasury business'.[156] Treasury officials during this period can be regarded as aides to the premier. Foremost amongst the Treasury team during the eighteenth century was the Secretary to the Treasury, who combined various roles on behalf of the emergent premiership, including recording decisions at meetings and ensuring they were put into effect; enforcing parliamentary discipline; advising on policy; organising election campaigns and predicting the outcomes; managing the distribution of patronage; and providing personal assistance to the premier. Control of the Treasury was ceded by No.10 from the mid-nineteenth century, representing a substantial reduction in the staff support attached to the premiership. In as far as institutional change from 1997 signified the establishment of a semi-official 'department of the Prime Minister', it partly amounted to a restoration of arrangements prevailing in an early part of the history of the office of Prime Minister.[157]

Another significant aide has been the secretary to the premier. It is possible to name someone who performed this role for every individual who is generally regarded as a Prime Minister apart from the first, Walpole. Like secretaries to the Treasury, secretaries to the premier were multi-taskers, performing a wide range of possible support functions from personal assistance to policy advice to public relations. The post of secretary to a Prime Minister was not always as alluring as it later became. Shortly after securing the post the young Edmund Burke wrote to a friend on 11 July 1765:

> I have got an employment of a kind humble enough; but which may be worked into some sort of consideration, or at least advantage; Private Secretary to Lord Rockingham,

[156] Maurice Wright, *Treasury Control of the Civil Service: 1854-1874* (Oxford: Oxford University Press, 1969), p.49.

[157] See: Chapter Three.

> who has the reputation of a man of honour and integrity; and with whom, they say, it is not difficult to live.[158]

But though their role has not always possessed the glamour it later acquired, secretaries have always been vital to the premiership, as recognised by Trollope a century later. In an exchange from *The Prime Minister* Omnium tells his friend and ally the Duke of St. Bungay he would like to remain alone at a country home with his family. St. Bungay replies 'I doubt whether such a life, even for a month, even for a week, is compatible with your duties. You would hardly find it possible. Could you do without your private secretaries?'[159]

As well as regularly using private secretaries and – until the mid-nineteenth century – the staff of the Treasury, the premiership has acquired other aides. Pitt the Younger drew on the advice of the political philosopher and demographer Richard Price when devising his Sinking Fund, intended to redeem the national debt. Francis Bonham helped Robert Peel in his handling of the Conservative Party within Parliament and nationally in the 1830s and 40s, a time when the mass party was an emergent phenomenon. John, Lord Acton, the eminent historian and liberal Catholic, helped Gladstone with various tasks, from developing his overall policy approach to liaising with Queen Victoria, with whom, unlike Gladstone, Acton was on good terms. Ever since the time of Walpole various aides have been deployed on media management. Alfred Austin, a pro-Conservative journalist, wrote anonymous articles in the press to help Lord Salisbury promote certain ideas, as well as providing him with political advice. In recognition of his efforts Austin was appointed Poet Laureate in 1896, despite being notorious for the poor quality of his verse, in which post he produced such efforts as the partisan 'Why England is Conservative'.[160]

Many of the kinds of tasks performed lately by No.10 staff have ample broad precedents. The shift has been more that

---

[158] Thomas W. Copeland, *The Correspondence of Edmund Burke*, Vol. 1, *April 1744–June 1768* (Cambridge at the University Press, 1958), Burke to Charles O'Hara, 11 July 1765, p.211.

[159] Trollope, *The Prime Minister*, Vol. I, p.163.

[160] Alfred Austin, *Songs of England* (London: Macmillan and Co., 1900), pp.43–5.

of formalisation, regularisation and specialisation than the taking on of wholly new categories of functions. In the early nineteenth century public funding was made available for one then two secretaries, who were previously reimbursed by various circuitous means. Then in the twentieth century many of the duties performed by the individuals described above became more institutionalised, with such innovations as Lloyd George's 'Garden Suburb' of policy aides; the creation of a No. 10 Press Secretary under Ramsay MacDonald; and the Policy Unit introduced under Harold Wilson. What changed was more the specific work undertaken rather than the general areas of operation, like media, policy or party politics.

Sometimes aides have facilitated initiatives in which the role of No.10 has been pre-eminent above the input of collective processes or ministers with interests in the policy areas concerned. Philip Kerr, foreign policy adviser to Lloyd George, was regarded by some as in effect supplanting the Foreign Office under the Foreign Secretary, Lord Curzon. Chamberlain's No.10 was supported in the pursuit of appeasement in the late 1930s by Horace Wilson, operating under the misleading title of 'Chief Industrial Adviser to H.M. Government'. The attempt at reflation of the economy under Heath in the early 1970s was assisted by the Head of the Home Civil Service, William Armstrong, with parts of government other than No.10 closed off from the project.

Much has been was made of the extensive use of partisan assistants and the supposed marginalisation of permanent officials under Blair. But given an overview of the history of the premiership as a whole, the period in which No.10 was dominated by career Whitehall appears as an aberration. There was no Civil Service as it came to be understood when the premiership first began to develop. Ministers, including premiers, received assistance from individuals known as 'men of business', who combined functions now associated with junior ministers with those that would today be attributed to bureaucratic staff. The party political and administrative fields began to be separated with such measures as the *Place Act* of 1742; and the process accelerated with the gradual implementation of ideas proposed by the Northcote-Trevelyan report of 1854. Not until the 1920s did there begin to develop a practice of the senior private secretary and most of the private office staff at No.10 being permanent officials. Nor did this approach last long. Outsiders were recruited to No.10 during the exceptional circumstances of the Second World War. From the 1960s the introduction of aides from beyond Whitehall, working alongside the career officials, began to be established as the norm.[161]

Finally, the idea present in the literature since 1997 that there is a principle of an 'independent' Civil Service (that was somehow eroded under Blair) is false. Rather than being autonomous the constitutional position has long been that permanent officials are impartial, offering frank views but implementing the ultimate decisions of all ministers with equal loyalty regardless of the party they represent. There is no clear evidence that this central quality was substantially compromised from 1997. There are more grounds for arguing that the overall importance of the career Civil Service was reduced through the increased reliance on outsiders, and that in some instances another constitutional principle – that ministers should give due consideration to the advice of permanent officials – was neglected.

The media and 'personalised' politics

West wrote in 1893: 'though unknown to the theory of constitution, the Prime Minister looms large in the eyes of the public'.[162] This popular focus on an individual figure has both prompted and been fed by the various media that have always displayed an interest in the person occupying the premiership. Discerning trends in this coverage, such as whether it is becoming more intense and at the expense of attention paid to institutions such as the Cabinet and Parliament, is difficult to carry out with precision. Technology and forms of presentation have changed. Photographic images meant that prime ministers were more easily recognisable to the public. In 1842 Peel escaped an assassination attempt because his would-be killer mistook his secretary, William Drummond, for the premier. Such an error would not have been conceivable in later times. Yet the physical appearance of prime ministers was always

[161] See: Blick, *People Who Live in the Dark*.
[162] Algernon West, 'The Prime Minister'.

important to public representations of them, including in caricatures by cartoonists. The length of Pitt the Younger's nose was used as a way of mocking him. While political coverage may be updated more regularly and channelled through different media, its disposition towards a personal focus in the portrayal of political events is not new. Equally there has always been an interest in political personalities other than the Prime Minister – in particular possible replacements for the existing premier. Even if there was a clearly identifiable trend towards a greater concentration on the premiership and the individual occupying it, such a tendency would not necessarily mean that the way in which the office operated had altered, and might be merely a perceptual development.

The office of Prime Minister has always sought to utilise the media in pursuit of its ends, often to portray its holder in a favourable light, or promote certain ideas and policies. The most important change in the relationship between government and media had already taken place before the Walpole ascendancy. Pre-publication censorship came to an end in 1695 when the Licensing Act lapsed. An effective means of official control was not found in its place and a growth in the appearance of political works followed. Though it possessed various means of harassment and intimidation, government could no longer control the media in the same way, and had to develop methods to influence their output, which could include financial inducements for writers and other forms of encouragement.[163] As the circulation of newspapers increased by the early nineteenth century, purchasing their support (or buying them outright) became more expensive (and parliamentary control on finance had tightened). Another problem associated with the financing of propaganda of this sort was that a transparently pro-government newspaper, whether specifically set up or acquired, was less likely to achieve a substantial readership.[164] Other methods of news management were then developed, including the use of favoured outlets for exclusive inside information, which could be regarded as a form of currency.

---

[163] Urstad, *Sir Robert Walpole's Poets*, p.27.
[164] A. Aspinall, *Politics and the Press: c.1780–1850* (Brighton: The Harvester Press, 1973), p.373.

As one journal noted in 1839:

> All Governments have occasionally given more or less of their confidence to a particular paper, but even this to a very limited extent, and never avowedly: indeed the prudence of Governments and the independence of editors have alike disclaimed any such co-partnership.[165]

As this remark suggests, if it was to be effective such an approach had to be pursued discreetly. One publication in particular has benefited from these methods over a long period. A letter to Gladstone written in 1870 suggests that the habit of No.10 staff informing *The Times* about certain developments before any other newspaper was already established by this time.[166]

Whatever techniques were used, at no point has it been possible completely to prevent public criticism from being voiced. Arthur Aspinall describes how during the early nineteenth century 'All governments ... irrespective of their composition and party labels, were conscious of a sense of failure, a feeling of helpless frustration, in seeking to influence the Press'.[167] The approach has been both to try to reduce the level of dissent and to ensure that the case of No.10 was advanced. Damian McBride, media aide to Gordon Brown, saw a challenge in Conservative-inclined bloggers of the twenty-first century that was the same as that posed for the Walpole premiership by the 'Scriblerus Club'. In both eras a similar possible solution was arrived at: to try and shift the balance of total coverage in a favourable direction. The difficulty lay in the execution.

In analysis of the premiership the idea that politics have somehow become more 'personalised' has been advanced. Foley's description of 'leadership stretch', that of prime ministers distancing themselves as individuals from institutions such as party, Cabinet and Parliament, is insightful. But it can be applied throughout the history of the premiership, and it is hard to establish that this phenomenon has over time, become more pronounced. In the eighteenth century, with looser

[165] *Quarterly Review*, December 1839, p.301.
[166] Ramm (ed.), *The Political Correspondence of Mr. Gladstone and Lord Granville*, Lord Granville to Mr. Gladstone, 11 October 1870, p.144.
[167] A. Aspinall, *Politics and the Press: c.1780–1850*, p.372.

party structures and less of a concept of ministers working collectively, it could be argued that leadership stretch was more pervasive than it later became. In the 1750s and 1760s the approach of Pitt the Elder/Chatham included cultivating 'out of doors' public popularity and distancing himself from factional allegiances. He was, in the words of the historian Jeremy Black, 'in many respects temperamentally a political outsider'.[168] Another fine example of leadership stretch came in the 1840s with No.10's pursuance of free trade under Peel, in defiance of much of his party and the social interests underpinning it.[169] In the Lloyd George era there was stretch between No.10 on the one hand and both Parliament and Cabinet on the other, since throughout his premiership he was part of a minority group within a coalition government. Prime ministers such as Gladstone and Churchill were distanced from party in the sense that over their careers, they switched their allegiances; more recent premiers did not move around in this way and are, in this sense, more closely aligned with their parties.

Conclusion

This chapter has challenged certain claims about the premiership that have been made across a long time span. It has identified two broad schools of literature, both of which can be detected in the pre- and post-May 1997 periods. In the first, can be found claims, including that the power of the office is growing at the expense of other institutions, and that it is morphing into a presidency. The second tends to emphasise the constraints upon No.10. This chapter has shown there is more to commend the arguments advanced in the latter group. But both sets of interpretations contain within them contradictions which, though not necessarily invalidating them all, certainly mean that most or at least some of the individuals advancing theories contained within them were wrong. Such are the discrepancies within the first school, that there is good cause to query the credibility of all the pronouncements made within it.

---

[168] See eg: Jeremy Black, *Pitt the Elder: The Great Commoner* (Stroud: Sutton Publishing, 1999), p.129.

[169] See: Douglas Hurd, *Robert Peel: A biography* (London: Weidenfeld & Nicolson, 2007), pp.333–70.

The problems do not end there. It is difficult to reconcile many of the claims made in both groups, in particular about change, with the historical record of the premiership. Tendencies identifiable from the Walpole period onwards call into question many of these theories of the office, exposing them variously as founded in false premises, such as an 'independent' Civil Service; creating the impression of trends that did not occur, such as a simple transition from relatively leisured to overstretched prime ministers and staff; making claims that are difficult to prove, such as an intensified public focus on the person who is premier as the embodiment of the government; or referring to processes that are more complex than their portrayal, possibly consisting of contradictory trends, such as in the ability of Parliament to restrain the premiership, or to some extent being cyclical rather than linear in nature, such as the rise of partisan aides at the expense of permanent civil servants. When the existence of a particular tendency – such as the rise of the mass party in the nineteenth century – is not in doubt, it is not always clear that it had the impact that is claimed for it.

This work does not deny the possibility of development in the premiership. Rather its intention is, through sifting evidence across the longest possible time-frame, to assess whether and when alteration has occurred and to differentiate between different kinds of development. A further objective of this book is to reconcile tendencies noted in the institution by observers, including Gladstone and Wilson that may initially appear contradictory. Both dwelt on the constraints applying to the operation of the office. Yet at the same time they portrayed it as associated with substantial power. Similarly, Morley (though possibly ghost-written by Gladstone) portrayed No.10 as potential dictator or non-intervener, depending on circumstance. Further examination is required of the varied ways in which the premiership functions and how it is able, within the framework of a wide variety of limitations, to work towards certain goals.

Chapter Three

Style and Substance

In 1974 Lord [Robert] Blake, Oxford academic and biographer of Disraeli, gave three British Academy lectures on the premiership. Later published as *The Office of Prime Minister*, they came to wield substantial influence on perceptions of the institution they described. Yet for all their merit they exemplified and helped encourage a gap in understanding of the development of the premiership, which continues to the present.

The problem came in the second lecture – 'The History' – in a passage where Blake identified three 'Turning points' for the premiership, while noting they were 'very hard to fix').[1] First came the advent during 1782–4 of a 'change ... from a monarch who was the real head of the executive, an active political force concerned with the day-to-day issues of government to a monarch with a veto – the right to dismiss the Prime Minister and so the right to prevent the implementation of policies he disliked' – though Blake stressed 'It was a power which always had to be exercised within limits'. The second change, 'and the greatest', Blake argued, was the shift 'from the King's government to party government', which became apparent in 1834–5. The third transition, which was 'less obvious at the time and less radical, though in the end not less significant, was from government by parties based on parliament to government by parties based on nation-wide organizations'. Its beginning, according to Blake, could be dated from the expansions in the franchise by the Reform Acts of 1867 and 1884.[2]

[1] Lord Blake, *The Office of Prime Minister*, Thank-Offering to Britain Fund Lectures (London: Oxford University Press, 1975), p.41.

[2] *Ibid*, pp. 41–2.

The developments Blake selected as pre-eminent were significant, but they referred to changes external to the premiership, although with substantial implications for the way it operated. Another shift, which Blake omitted from his group of 'Turning points', concerned the substance of the premiership. It can be illustrated by a description Pitt the Younger gave of the office in 1803 (in an account by Lord Melville). Blake cited part of this text, noting Pitt the Younger's statement that it was 'an absolute necessity ... that there should be an avowed and real Minister possessing the chief weight in the Council and the principal place in the confidence of the King'.[3] Blake ends the quotation there. He does not record Pitt going on to stipulate that this 'Minister ought ... to be the person at the head of the finances'.[4] The arrangement Pitt regarded as apt – that the Prime Minister should have direct responsibility for the Treasury, and the policy brief and patronage associated with it – was established practice in his time. It ceased to be so in the mid-nineteenth century, although an ability to confer favour was retained. The premiership had by this latter period relinquished its major Treasury role, changing significantly in the process.

Despite the import of this transformation, of all the works considered in Chapter One, only the article by Paul Langford fully acknowledged it. Such a serious lapse not only requires correction, but also exposes the present absence of a systematic method for assessing development in the office of Prime Minister. This chapter begins by depicting the underlying nature of the premiership throughout its existence. It then uses a new framework, providing a definition of change in the premiership to identify and distinguish different kinds of shifts; and determining their importance. This method ensures that core transitions that have not been properly appreciated are accorded their true significance. It facilitates both the division of the office of Prime Minister into key historical periods; and a new assessment of the premiership since 1997.

---

[3] *Ibid*, p.30.

[4] Lord Melville to Mr. Addington, 22 March 1803, reproduced in Earl Stanhope, *Life of the Right Honourable William Pitt*, Vol. IV (London: John Murray, 1862), p.24.

The underlying nature of the premiership

It is easier to discern and understand change once that which has remained constant has been identified. Throughout its existence the office of Prime Minister has been associated with an underlying role: the provision of public leadership. This task has always been more important to No.10 than any other responsibility, a primary duty to which all others are secondary. While imparting public leadership is a function carried out across the whole of Whitehall, nowhere other than in the office of Prime Minister is it the one overriding duty. After a transitional period during the eighteenth and up to the mid-nineteenth centuries the figure upon whom the premiership is centred, the Prime Minister, eclipsed the monarchy as in practice the most prominent individual provider of public leadership in the UK (subject to the emergent convention of collective Cabinet supremacy).

But what is public leadership? In a recent study[5] Paul 't Hart and John Uhr provide a useful working definition, describing it as 'a number of distinctive functions that need to be performed in order for a polity to govern itself effectively and democratically, but which are not performed spontaneously by a polity's public institutions, organisations and routines'. They argue that 'public leadership evolves as an adaptive response to the non-routine, strategic challenges in a society'. For 't Hart and Uhr

> However elaborate and complex the institutional fabric of government is and, however overwhelming the situational pressures and contextual ... constraints, at the end of the day it is down to individuals and groups taking up the strategic challenges and dilemmas of "managing the public's business" ... to give direction to governing'.

This task, the authors state, is accomplished by these individuals and groups 'devising, deliberating, interpreting, challenging and changing the institutional rules and practices of government.'

The reference to 'democratically' made by 't Hart and Uhr

[5] Paul 't Hart and John Uhr, *Public leadership: perspectives and practices*, p.3.

does not apply throughout the history of the office of Prime Minister. And there is an arguable tension inherent in the role of No.10 as an institution in part comprising organisations and routines engaged in providing public leadership, if this task is defined as carrying out functions 'which are not performed spontaneously by a polity's public institutions, organisations and routines'. But subject to these qualifications, the second of which is explored below, this description of public leadership fits well with the fundamental role of the office of Prime Minister throughout its history. The premiership – through functions it has assumed such as being the organiser of Cabinet – has had key responsibility for strategy and direction within government, Parliament and on the national stage, and has taken on a major part in ensuring effective responses to 'non-routine' events such as military emergencies. The means by which these duties were discharged involved special responsibilities for the 'institutional rules and practices of government' (to use 't Hart and Uhr's phrase) which have been attached to No.10, including the task of managing the Civil Service; and determining, interpreting and enforcing the contents of documents such as the *Ministerial Code*.

The historical development of the premiership can be seen as a series of variations upon this basic theme of public leadership. Such a perspective accords with the outlook of numerous analysts who stress there are many different ways and means by which leadership may be exercised.[6] Three processes considered here: 'zigzag' and 'administrative fusion and fission' are realisations over time of some of this range of possibilities.

The informal development of the office

As noted above 't Hart and Uhr emphasise public leadership as providing something more than can be obtained from 'institutions, organisations and routines' and entailing the efforts of 'individuals and groups'. Since the role of the office of Prime Minister involves filling in the cracks of government it has of necessity always been characterised by an 'elasticity' that permits significant variations of approach by the people,

[6] See eg: James MacGregor Burns, *Leadership*.

both prime ministers and staff, operating it.[7] This flexibility is associated with the fluid, informal development of the office.

In 1841 Prince Albert asked Queen Victoria to obtain information for him about the premiership and she turned to her mentor and former Prime Minister, Viscount Melbourne, for advice.[8] Melbourne struggled to provide meaningful detail. In a letter of 1st November he stated: 'How the power of Prime Ministry grew up into its present form it is difficult to trace precisely', and then hazily outlined the importance of Robert Walpole.[9] (An official file from the 1950s attempts to describe the origins of the office but it is no more successful.[10]) Melbourne wrote to Victoria again on 4th November 'with respect to the questions put to me by your Majesty at the desire of His Royal Highness'. He noted that 'points of this sort ... are very curious, very important, very worthy to be enquired into' but that 'accurate information is not easily to be found'. Commenting about the need to seek 'explanation and description ... in debates, protests, in letters, in memoirs, and wherever it can be picked up'[11], Melbourne proceeded once again to give an unhelpfully vague account of the evolution of the office of Prime Minister from the eighteenth century.[12] He was uncertain both as to how the premiership had come about and what it was. If a former Prime Minister and the person to whom the institution was formally answerable lacked this knowledge it is unlikely to have existed anywhere else.

This uncertainty can be traced to the beginning. Clear starting points for bodies such as the Home Office and Foreign Office can be identified (1782 for both); but not for the premiership. During the early stages of the office in the eighteenth century the legitimacy of such an entity – or, as

[7] See eg: G.W Jones, 'Cabinet Government since Bagehot', in Robert Blackburn (ed.), *Constitutional Studies: Contemporary Issues and Controversies* (London: Mansell, 1992), pp.26–7.

[8] See: Introduction

[9] Arthur Christopher Benson and Viscount Esher (eds), *The Letters of Queen Victoria*, 3 vols, Vol. 1, *1837–1843* (London: John Murray, 1908), Viscount Melbourne to Queen Victoria, 1 November 1841, p.356.

[10] For analysis of this document see: Peter Hennessy, *The Prime Minister: the office and its holders since 1945*, p.38.

[11] See: Introduction.

[12] Benson and Esher (eds), *The Letters of Queen Victoria*, 3 vols, Vol. 1, *1837–1843*, Viscount Melbourne to Queen Victoria, 1 November 1841, p.358.

it was perceived, of an individual who was premier – was challenged.[13] No-one would admit to being Prime Minister even if he obviously were. Though holding the post of First Lord of the Treasury could often be associated with being the most prominent figure in government, it was and is not always clear who the premier was in the decades after the fall of Walpole in 1742 – or if there were one at all. Various historians confirm this point. Lewis Namier described how in the mid-eighteenth century 'It is often difficult to say who ... was the Prime Minister or, to use the contemporary expression – *the* minister'.[14] Richard Pares stated 'The history of the Prime Minister before 1832 – and perhaps after it – is more like that of the Cheshire Cat: sometimes there is almost a whole cat, sometimes no more than a grin, and it is not always the same end that appears first'.[15] In the words of Betty Kemp 'For more than [a] half century after Walpole's death, there was only one question that Englishmen could ask about Prime Ministers – "Is there a Prime Minister?" The question "*Who* is the Prime Minister?" would not have made sense. It could not be asked until there always was one, and no one disputed that there should be'. Kemp noted that 'By the middle of the nineteenth century, this change had taken place'.[16]

Various signs of the emergence of the acceptance described by Kemp are scattered across the preceding decades. In 1764 George III insisted to his premier George Grenville that 'it was necessary to lodge the power of the government in one man alone'.[17] It seems there was some entrenchment in the era of Pitt the Younger. In the gap between his two terms in 1803 he described to Lord Melville the need for an 'avowed and real Minister'.[18] *The Times* was beginning to use the phrase 'Prime

[13] See: Chapter Two.

[14] Sir Lewis Namier, *Crossroads of Power: Essays on Eighteenth-Century England* (London: Hamish Hamilton, 1962), p.112.

[15] Richard Pares, *King George III and the Politicians: The Ford Lectures 1951–2* (Oxford: Clarendon Press, 1953), p.176.

[16] Betty Kemp, *Sir Robert Walpole* (London: Weidenfeld and Nicolson, 1976), pp.5–6.

[17] William James Smith (ed.), *The Grenville Papers*, Vol. II (London: John Murray, 1852), diary entry for 23 March 1764, p.500.

[18] Melville to Addington, 22 March 1803, reproduced in Stanhope, *Life of the Right Honourable William Pitt*, Vol. IV, p.24.

Minister' as descriptive of a British government post by 1805. Two articles of this year, from May and June, employed the term. The latter described William Pitt the Elder, later Chatham, as 'the father of the present Prime Minister', implying Pitt the Elder was a premier as well, and creating the impression that the post existed in the present and had a lineage.[19] By around this time the title 'Prime Minister' was beginning to be used in parliamentary debates as a description rather than term of abuse.[20]

References to an institution rather than simply a person who had risen to pre-eminence took longer to take hold. The term 'premiership', depending on the context, could be taken as denoting the former. In 1827, the year when it began being employed regularly in *The Times* in this way, an editorial in the journal discussing the possible accession of Canning opened by referring to: 'The affair of the Premiership, if we may use the word'.[21] Thomas Macaulay MP provided in 1832 its earliest utterance recorded in Hansard, and further uses came in 1835, 1848 (twice) and more regularly in the 1850s.

The first use of the phrase 'office of Prime Minister' in Parliament took place in 1822; and five years later it was used by Peel when notably referring to 'all the influence and power which belong (and I think properly) to the office of Prime Minister'.[22] Here Peel created an image of an entity which existed in its own right, to be captured by those who sought to utilise it (as he would in the decades that followed). Later in the same year the phrase 'office of Prime Minister' first began to appear in *The Times*.[23] It may be that the deployments of 'premiership' and 'office of Prime Minister' which took place in 1827 were the consequence of interest stimulated in the institution by the changeovers in this year, following the fifteen year tenure of Liverpool as premier, first to Canning then after his death to Goderich.

Despite the development of popular acknowledgement

---

[19] The two articles are: 'Public Virtue', *The Times*, 18 May 1805; and 'Duke of Athol's Claim', *The Times*, 8 July 1805.

[20] See eg: Hansard, House of Commons (HC) Debates, 29 April 1805, col. 495.

[21] Editorials/Leaders, *The Times*, 6 April 1827.

[22] (HC) Debates, 1 May 1827, col. 397.

[23] Editorials/Leaders, *The Times*, 25 December 1827.

by the mid-nineteenth century, there was as yet no official recognition of the post or office of Prime Minister. Famously the Treaty of Berlin of 1878, not a domestic UK document, described Disraeli as 'First Lord of Her Majesty's Treasury, Prime Minister of England'.[24] Three subsequent shifts have been neglected in accounts of the premiership.

The first involved the list of government members printed in Hansard, which can be read as an official statement in a way that terms employed in parliamentary debates are not. Use of the title 'Prime Minister' seems to have begun in this source to clarify that Salisbury – who had a practice of not holding the title 'First Lord of the Treasury' – was the premier. In July 1885 Salisbury was tentatively described as 'Secretary of State for Foreign Affairs (Prime Minister)'. Eventually by Salisbury's final exit from office in 1902 the use of 'Prime Minister' had stuck, and was applied in Hansard lists to his successor Balfour, who did hold the First Lord post. According to Sidney Low the *Court Circular* too, possibly inadvertently, had described Salisbury as 'Prime Minister' in 1900.[25]

Second, an early reference to the post within government – not made publicly – came in 1902. At the first meeting of the Committee of Imperial Defence (CID) on 18th December of that year, 'The Prime Minister' is listed as being present, above the other politicians and military personnel who were in attendance, although below the Duke of Devonshire who took the chair. There is no mention of 'First Lord of the Treasury' and unlike the other individuals who were there the premier – Arthur Balfour – is not named, demonstrating there was no doubt about the existence of the Prime Minister and who he was, and that there were no problems of etiquette in the use of this title, at least for a private meeting of this sort. The CID was an innovation in British government since it employed what its minutes described as 'a civilian Secretary ... to keep the Minutes and Records and attend to the Secretarial work'.[26] Had a body supported in this way been established

[24] See: Sidney Low, *The Governance of England*, 1904 edition, p.154.
[25] *Ibid.*
[26] The National Archives/Public Record Office (TNA/PRO) CAB 2/1 Committee of Imperial Defence, Minutes of 1st Meeting, 18 December 1902.

earlier, then the formal title Prime Minister might have been written down in internal official files sooner, although it is only possible to speculate about the earliest date at which the term would have been used.

Third, a public document, the 1904 *Imperial Calendar* (the predecessor to the Civil Service Yearbook), referred to Balfour as 'Prime Minister and First Lord of the Treasury' (in the previous edition he was 'First Lord of the Treasury and Lord Privy Seal').

These three developments in the use of terminology can be viewed as preliminaries to the granting to the Prime Minister of a place in the official order of precedence (after the Archbishop of York) on 4th December 1905, conventionally regarded as the key moment in formal domestic recognition.[27] A mention of the Prime Minister in statute first came with the *Chequers Estate Act 1917*, which specified the endowment of Chequers as a residence for the premier, though it did not define or empower the post or office it was associated with in any way.

Just as in common usage it took longer for the *office* of Prime Minister to be acknowledged than the *title* attaching to one person, there was a similar lag in the formal establishment of the premiership as a Whitehall institution. One way of charting the development of an administrative entity is through its record-keeping habits. The earliest file in PREM, the National Archives/Public Record Office category for No.10 files, dates from 1907[28], and the papers do not become numerous until about a decade later. Before this development the disposal of papers seems to have been a matter for each individual premier, suggesting a shadowy official existence for the office of Prime Minister. In contrast, by the early twentieth century substantial official files had been amassed by institutions such as the Foreign Office and Home Office, covering their entire periods of existence – as well as containing material carried over from earlier eras.[29] Public recognition of the premiership – in the form of an explicitly labelled 'Prime Minister's Office' in the *Civil Service Yearbook* – did not take

[27] See eg: Sidney Low, *The Governance of England*, 1914 edition, p.xx.
[28] TNA/PRO PREM 5/1.
[29] *Ibid.*, FO and HO.

place until the appearance of the 1977 edition, and there never has been established a fully-official 'Department of the Prime Minister'.[30]

The process of development of the post and office of Prime Minister is reminiscent of the phenomenon identified by the German sociologist Max Weber as the 'routinization of charisma'. Weber defined a charismatic individual as someone 'treated as endowed with supernatural, superhuman, or at least exceptional powers or qualities'. He argued that if 'charismatic authority ... is not to remain a purely transitory phenomenon ... it is necessary for the character of charismatic authority to become radically changed'. This trend could manifest itself in various ways, including the establishment of a means of designating successors to the original leader; and the organisation of the administrative staff into 'offices'.[31] This analysis can be applied to the premiership, if it is adapted to allow for the possibility that the charisma associated with not one but intermittently appearing successive figures was routinised. Innovations associated with the ascendancies of politicians such as Walpole and Pitt the Younger were eventually regularised into a formally acknowledged post and institution, which could then continue to exist permanently, rather than being dependent upon the charisma of an individual. It might even be held that the charisma associated with later premiers and their followers, was subsequently incorporated as established features of the office. For instance, the collection of aides known as the 'Garden Suburb' that Lloyd George gathered around himself can be seen as being 'routinized' into the Policy Unit from the 1970s.

Vague roles

Though there has been some clarification, uncertainties about the nature of the office have survived into the twenty-first century. There remain suggestions that the post of Prime Minister even now does not exist fully in its own right, and is dependent in particular on its combination with that of

[30] See below.
[31] Max Weber, *The Theory of Social and Economic Organisation* (London: William Hodge, 1947), pp.329; 334; 337–8.

First Lord of the Treasury (and to some extent with that of Minister for the Civil Service). The sign on the front door of No.10 reads only 'First Lord of the Treasury'; and the Order in Council issued on 28th June 2007, confirming the royal swearing in of Brown at the outset of his premiership, described him only as 'First Lord of the Treasury and Minister for the Civil Service'.[32] The post of First Lord of the Treasury retains a statutory existence with 65 primary and 48 secondary laws currently referring to it (of which 14 and 12 respectively also refer to the Prime Minister).

In October 2001, when answering a written parliamentary question from Graham Allen MP about the premiership, Blair informed the Commons 'there are more than 50 specific powers conferred on the office by statute' but most concerned appointments. The roles of 'head of Her Majesty's Government, her principal adviser and as Chairman of the Cabinet are not ... defined in legislation. These roles, including the exercise of powers under the royal prerogative, have evolved over many years, drawing on convention and usage, and it is not possible precisely to define them'. Blair added: 'The Government have no plans to introduce legislation in this area'.[33]

The vagueness of the premiership is associated with a broader informality characteristic of the British constitution. In the words of Melbourne 'the work of conducting the executive government, has rested so much on practice, on usage, on understanding, that there is no publication to which reference can be made for the explanation and description of it'.[34] But even within this setting, the office of Prime Minister is distinguished by its lack of distinction. The roles of offices and departments elsewhere in Whitehall are more clearly defined. This disparity arises partly because some secretaries of state have a far greater statutory existence than the Prime Minister. In total 92 pieces of primary legislation (mainly Acts of Parliament) presently in force, refer to the Prime Minister;

[32] *Orders approved at the Privy Council held at Buckingham Palace on 28th June 2007 at 6pm.*

[33] Hansard, House of Commons (HC), Written Answers, 15 October 2001, Col. 818W.

[34] Benson and Esher (eds), *The Letters of Queen Victoria*, 3 vols, Vol. 1, *1837–1843*, Melbourne to Queen Victoria, 1 November 1841, p.358.

while the figure for secondary legislation is 422. By contrast, the respective figures for the Secretary of State for Health are 662 and 7,205; and for the Business Secretary 577 and 2,221. While other posts such as the Foreign Secretary and Chancellor of the Exchequer have even slimmer statutory bases than that of the Prime Minister, their roles have greater definition than the premier because they have clearer policy portfolios;[35] and there was not the same historic tendency to decry or deny their existence.

Though visibility may have improved slightly over time, the premiership has been a rather mist-shrouded institution from its origins to the present. It is possible to sketch the general contours of the office at different times.[36] But, while there was some awareness amongst contemporaries of the broad parameters, there have been no clear rules as to how to operate within, or change, them.

In Trollope's *The Prime Minister* the Duke of Omnium, after a short time as premier, felt that while there are 'men under him who were really at work ... with the Prime Minister ... it was all a blank'.[37] In a later passage Omnium concluded 'there was in truth nothing for him to do'.[38] Callaghan, a connoisseur of Trollope, described in suspiciously similar terms in his autobiography how, upon becoming Prime Minister in 1976:

> For the first day or two while I was making governmental changes there was a constant stream of Ministers coming and going, but once that was complete I sat back and realised I had nothing to do ... For a brief period as I sat in the Cabinet Room I savoured the suspicion that as everyone else was doing the Government's work, I could be the idlest member of the Administration if I was so minded. It was of course an illusion, although I never went to the other extreme and believed that a Prime Minister must be a workaholic.[39]

The void identified by Trollope, though Omnium viewed it bleakly, has enabled the premiership to exercise significant

[35] See below.
[36] See below.
[37] Anthony Trollope, *The Prime Minister*, Vol. I, p.161.
[38] *Ibid*, p.249.
[39] James Callaghan, *Time and Chance*, p.403.

discretion over which business to engage with and how prominent a role to play. In doing so, the role performed by the office has been conditioned and limited by the personal qualities of particular prime ministers, and the circumstances in which they operated. Herbert Asquith most famously summarised this constrained flexibility when he wrote that 'the office of the Prime Minister is what its holder chooses and is able to make of it'.[40] Others had already made similar observations. Consciously or otherwise, Asquith possibly plagiarised Algernon West who wrote that the 'work of a Prime Minister is ... very much what he chooses to make it'.[41] Asquith may have taken another cue from Low who argued in 1904 that 'the "precise" amount of authority exercised by the Prime Minister must depend upon circumstances and his own character'.[42]

Zigzag

The flexibility of the office of Prime Minister allows for, and is associated with, an historical phenomenon labelled here 'zigzag'. This term is better than the 'ebb and flow' of Professor Bogdanor, which conveys an impression of inexorable events determined by external forces.[43] 'Zigzag' captures the more erratic approaches of individual prime ministers. There is a tendency for premiers to adopt, in their manner of being prime minister, methods that distinguish them from certain stylistic features of their immediate predecessors. Harold Wilson seems to have had in mind a tendency along these lines when – in his criticism of what he termed the 'prime ministerial government thesis' – he noted that its proponents 'entirely fail to allow for almost 180-degree differences in the style of individual, indeed successive, prime ministers'.[44] Such shifts might involve a variety of different characteristics. They could include the degree of formality favoured by a particular premier. Like Blair, Melbourne caused consternation through conducting meetings from his settee. He sometimes received

[40] Earl of Oxford and Asquith, *Fifty Years in Parliament*, vol. 2, p.185.
[41] Algernon West, 'The Prime Minister'.
[42] Low, *The Governance of England*, 1904 edition, p.158.
[43] See: Chapter One.
[44] Harold Wilson, *The Governance of Britain*, p.9.

visitors expecting a more official discussion while 'lounging back nursing a sofa cushion'.[45] Peel, with whom Melbourne alternated at No.10 from 1834–46, displayed some more punctilious dispositions, including his insistence that Cabinet operate according to a written agenda.

Amongst these tendencies towards changes in the deployment of the office of Prime Minister the most significant, 'zigzag', involves the extent to which the premiership is deployed in a more or less domineering fashion. In the words of Anthony King 'The line from prime minister to prime minister is ... not straight but jagged'.[46] From the outset of the office there have been fluctuations in whether No.10 has, on the one hand, taken an interventionist approach or, on the other, left business to ministers to determine either individually or collectively. Robert Walpole was a giant operating at the highest level for more than two decades, exercising a prominent role within government (particularly from 1730) through his role as First Lord of the Treasury, doing much to create the premiership in the process. In 1742 he was followed as First Lord by Spencer Compton, the Earl of Wilmington, so weak as not to qualify as a Prime Minister at all.[47]

In his 1952 lecture *The Cabinet Council*, Arthur Aspinall identified some marked stylistic shifts – towards and away from dominance by the premiership – that occurred with changes of Prime Minister in the early decades of the nineteenth century. Pitt the Younger described the approach he favoured, and had to some extent been able to pursue, in his 1803 description of the 'First Minister'. He argued that if within government there were a 'radical difference of opinion ... the sentiments of the [First] Minister must be allowed and understood to prevail'.[48] After Pitt died in 1806 he was succeeded as First Lord of The Treasury by the Duke of Portland. Suffering ill-health and propped up by drugs, Portland could not properly manage a number of strong ministers. Further abrupt changes of direction occurred with changes of Prime Minister in the

[45] David Cecil, *Melbourne* (London: Constable & Co., 1965), pp.302–3.
[46] Anthony King, *The British Constitution*, p.319.
[47] Namier, *Crossroads of Power*, p.112.
[48] Melville to Addington, 22 March 1803, reproduced in Stanhope, *Life of the Right Honourable William Pitt*, Vol. IV, p.24.

1820s and 1830s. Lord Liverpool occupied the post from 1812 until 1827. He took a conciliatory approach, writing in 1821 that 'I have no right, nor desire, to dictate to others'.[49] His government can be contrasted with the dynamic 100 days in 1827 of Canning, whose premiership was curtailed by his death. The 'unworthy successor' to Canning, writes Aspinall, was Goderich. 'Prime Minister only in name', Goderich 'was utterly incompetent either to control his colleagues or to manage the King'.[50] He was followed in 1828 by Wellington, who had remarked the previous year: 'What is wanting everywhere is the hand of authority'[51] and approached the job with a view to providing it. Earl Grey, who came after Wellington in 1830, was a member of one of the aristocratic Whig families who 'had always regarded power as something to be shared amongst themselves rather than monopolized by an individual, and Grey had no belief in the dictatorship of the Prime Minister'.[52] Grey wrote in 1830 that:

> My Cabinet is composed of men who have all displayed high parliamentary talents. I have chosen each of them with a view to his special aptitude for the post he occupies, and I leave to each full latitude to manage his Department in accordance with his own judgement. Counsel of the Cabinet will then be a veritable counsel, and the Dictatorship is abolished.[53]

Shifts in the degree of dominance of the premiership occurring with changes of particular incumbent can be detected later in the nineteenth century, and beyond. Disraeli and Gladstone alternated in office between 1868 and 1885. The former was known for the hands-off style with which he operated the premiership: the latter the opposite. As West put it Disraeli 'had no love for detail, and accordingly in things indifferent to him used to give his colleagues their heads'. But Gladstone had 'the reputation of being an autocrat, and for good or evil

[49] Lord Liverpool to Mr. Arbuthnot, 15 June 1821, reproduced in Charles Duke Yonge, *The Life and Administration of Robert Banks, Second Earl of Liverpool*, vol. III (London: Macmillan and Co. 1868), p.147.
[50] A. Aspinall, *The Cabinet Council:1783–1835*, p.207.
[51] Duke of Wellington to Arbuthnot, 11 March 1827, cited in *ibid.*
[52] *Ibid*, p.209.
[53] *Ibid*, p.209.

his hand was heavy for many years on every field alike of administration and of policy'.[54]

In 1916 David Lloyd George sought to provide a dynamic antidote to the perceived directionless leadership of Herbert Asquith. Under Winston Churchill No.10 had a tendency to play a prominent role across government, especially when it came to the conduct of war. Under his 1945 successor, Clement Attlee, it did not. A similar distinction can be drawn between the incumbencies of Margaret Thatcher and John Major.

Causes of Zigzag

A primary cause of zigzag is that the same political circumstances that bring about the end of one premiership are likely to encourage a different form of operation by No.10 during the next tenure. Whether ousted by parliamentary realignment, cabinet coup or general election (or once, dismissed by the monarch), few premiers leave office entirely willingly and having outstayed their welcome, the style taken during their tenure is likely widely to be tainted by personal association with them, making circumstances ripe for a shift. This tendency is compounded because, often the rise to No.10 of a successor, may have been facilitated because he or she was seen as personally able to provide a desirable new approach. Assuming such assessments of them are correct, premiers will encounter circumstances conducive to the way they are disposed to act. Even if they are not naturally inclined towards operating in a way that differs from the previous incumbent, political circumstance may encourage or force them to do so.

The transitions from Melbourne to Peel in 1841; Aberdeen to Palmerston in 1855; and Lloyd George to Bonar Law in 1922 illustrate the dynamics that produce zigzag. The ground was prepared for the domineering approach of Peel by unfavourable views of the nature of Melbourne's term of office. In 1841 Charles Buller denigrated to Greville Melbourne's 'miserable apology for a Government ... a Government of departments,

[54] West, 'The Prime Minister'. For a further sketch of the distinctions between the two by West see: Algernon West, *Political England: A Chronicle of the Nineteenth Century* (T. Fisher Unwin Ltd, London, 1922), pp.108–9.

absolutely without a Chief, hating, distrusting, despising each other, having no principles and no plans, living from hand to mouth, able to do nothing, and indifferent whether they did anything or not, proposing measures without the hope or expectation of carrying them, and clinging to their places for no other reason than because they had bound themselves to the Queen'.[55]

Palmerston emerged as the successor to Aberdeen following British difficulties in the Crimean War in 1854–5. Partly influenced by his observation of this development, Bagehot described how in Britain under the:

> Cabinet Constitution at a sudden emergency this people can choose a ruler for the occasion. It is quite possible and even likely that he would not be the ruler before the occasion. The great qualities, the imperious will, the rapid energy, the eager nature fit for a great crisis are not required – are impediments – in common times ... we often want, at the sudden occurrence of a grave tempest, to change the helmsman – to replace the pilot of the calm by the pilot of the storm ... at what was the nearest to a great sudden crisis which we have had of late years – at the Crimean difficulty – we used this inherent power. We abolished the Aberdeen Cabinet ... which abounded in pacific discretion, and was wanting only in the 'daemonic element'; we chose a statesman, who had the sort of merit then wanted who, when he feels the steady power of England behind him, will advance without reluctance, and will strike without restraint. As was said at the time, 'We turned out the Quaker, and put in the pugilist'.[56]

Another Prime Minister who offered the 'daemonic element' but was eventually succeeded by a 'pilot of the calm' was Lloyd George. He offered a contrast to Asquith in 1916; but by 1922 the conditions that brought him to office – a precarious military position in the First World War – had passed. Being a less dynamic figure contributed to the attractiveness of Bonar Law as a replacement for Lloyd George. After taking over as

[55] Lytton Strachey and Roger Fulford (eds), *The Greville Memoirs: 1814–1860*, Vol. IV, *January 1838 to December 1841* (London: Macmillan & Co, 1938), diary entry for 29 September 1841, p.419.

[56] Walter Bagehot, *The English Constitution*, pp.78–9.

premier in the autumn of 1922, Bonar Law was recorded in the diary of the senior Cabinet Office staff member Thomas Jones as saying that 'L.G. was all right as a drummer in a cavalry charge in war but we did not want a drummer in a hospital'.[57] His words echoed the sentiments of Bagehot when stating that 'A Lord Liverpool is better in everyday politics than a Chatham'.[58] When Bonar Law sought the approval of the electorate that year *The Times* endorsed him and his theme of 'quiet and stability at home and abroad' and insistence 'upon an immediate return to normal procedure in methods of government', referring specifically and disparagingly to the approach Lloyd George had taken to the premiership.[59] While the basic public leadership role of the office of Prime Minister is constant, the specific way in which it is required to carry out this responsibility is subject to fluctuation.

The identification of zigzag must be accompanied by a number of caveats. It does not always apply when there is a change of holder. Neither Henry Campbell-Bannerman nor his 1908 successor Herbert Asquith, tended to lead from the front; while both Chamberlain and Churchill did. When describing the way the premiership operated during particular tenures, it is necessary to generalise but important not to caricature. Under Disraeli and Attlee No.10 sometimes took a lead over issues – including respectively the Congress of Berlin of 1878 and Indian independence; while during the Blair period there was substantial deference to the Treasury under Brown on a range of domestic policy issues. Changing circumstances can bring about shifts of style during particular tenures. The Thatcher premiership became increasingly dominant during the course of the 1980s; while under Major the premiership moved in the opposite direction. At any given time the ability and willingness of No.10 to intervene may be greater in some areas than in others: any shift is usually of overall balance. The nature of the premiership during a particular tenure cannot be fully encapsulated by placing it on a horizontal

[57] Thomas Jones, Keith Middlemas (ed.) *Whitehall Diary*, Vol. I, *1916–1925* (London: Oxford University Press, 1969), diary entry for 31 October 1922, p.220.

[58] Bagehot, *The English Constitution*, p.79.

[59] 'The Prime Minister's Manifesto', *The Times*, 27 October 1922.

measure of its prominence within government or otherwise. While zigzag relates to particular incumbencies it is not solely concerned with the individual occupying the post, but rather with the way in which all those who between them operate the premiership (among whom the Prime Minister is pre-eminent) function within the constraints and opportunities of a broader administrative and political environment. Finally, while the conduct of the office of Prime Minister is significant for the way the entire government functions, other forces are at work. The impact of a change at the centre on the whole is always subject to limitations. But despite these qualifications, substantial alterations in the degree of dynamism at No.10 have frequently occurred when there is a change of premier. This phenomenon is important for understanding both the office of Prime Minister and the way in which central government functions.

The shift from John Major to Tony Blair in May 1997 saw an exemplary occurrence of zigzag. Blair was an avowed centraliser. Such an approach to leadership was partly associated with a personal style that had already manifested itself during his time as Leader of the Opposition. Receiving his political calling relatively late in life, Blair was never completely absorbed into the Labour movement. His views on the party's organisation, orientation and policy set him in conflict with many within it. He saw his separateness as an asset. Blair's intention, encouraged by memories of damaging ideological divisions of the 1970s and 1980s, was not to balance between factions within Labour as had his predecessors, such as Harold Wilson, but to guide it in a clear direction that he had determined.[60] Blair may have been influenced too by Margaret Thatcher's dynamic tenure. Since he had no previous experience of office, he was neither conditioned by established constitutional practices nor deterred by first-hand experience of the practical difficulties of government. Blair's outlook motivated him to recruit a relatively large group of assistants upon whom he could depend. They would accompany him into power. In opposition Blair's aides encouraged him to dominate and transform his party, and they laid plans for his leading of government from the front.[61]

[60] Peter Hyman, *1 Out of 10*, pp.11 and 63.
[61] See, for instance: Anthony Seldon, *Blair*, p.134.

In March 1997 Blair served notice of his intentions once installed at Downing Street when he told the Newspaper Society 'People have to know that we will run from the centre and govern from the centre'. Peter Hennessy argued 'Blair and his inner group of advisers seemed determined to operate inside No. 10 ... as they had within the Labour Party'. It was their intention to drive 'policy and presentation from the centre around a core of delivery musts', while tolerating 'no serious resistance from ministerial colleagues or from cumbersome, traditional government mechanics'.[62] Foster referred to Blair's resolve that 'there were to be no Cabinet decisions'; instead they would be made by 'Blair and his immediate coterie of advisers', and by Gordon Brown, the Chancellor of the Exchequer, and his.[63] Blair was able to put into practice his preferred style of leadership in opposition, and at No.10 because of favourable political circumstances: electoral popularity, significant press support, and when in government a benign economic climate and large parliamentary majority.

Of all the causes of zigzag from Major to Blair none was more important than Blair's desire to differentiate himself from and avoid replicating the problems of his immediate predecessor. Major had appeared a weak premier, leading a divided Cabinet and party, and he received hostile media coverage. Alastair Campbell recorded that Blair told his first Cabinet on 8 May 1997: 'the last government had been a shambles and we had to learn from that. He said we will sink or swim together. He was serious about proper coordination through the centre, on policy and on press'.[64]

This case of zigzag brought with it various claims about the replacement of Cabinet government and the appearance of a British presidency. Chapter Two demonstrated that similar accusations have been advanced repeatedly over the centuries and that there are problems reconciling them with both each

---

[62] Hennessy, *The Prime Minister*, pp.476–7.

[63] Christopher Foster, *British Government in Crisis*, p.163.

[64] Alastair Campbell, *The Blair Years* (London: Hutchinson, 2007), diary entry for 8 May 1997, p.201. Campbell was not present but given the account by Alex Allan, the Prime Minister's Principal Private Secretary, who was there.

other and the historical evidence. Such theses often appear at times of a shift towards a more prominent No.10, be it under Wellington, Lloyd George, Wilson or Blair. Perhaps, just as in military engagements the purpose of following a zigzagging path is to confuse the enemy, it has had a similar effect upon observers of the premiership. Ironically even if presidential theories and their ilk were viable, the occurrence of zigzag which sometimes seems to prompt their assertion would not be sufficient to justify them, since they imply qualitative changes in British government, while zigzag concerns primarily the style pursued during the term of office of an individual Prime Minister. Other concepts are required to uncover and analyse developments to the substance of the institution, which *have* taken place, though not in ways that are often asserted.

Administrative Fusion and Fission

The British premiership can be viewed as a cluster of rights, functions and people centring on the individual who occupies the post of Prime Minister, who was to become in practice the most prominent provider of public leadership in the UK. This image is important for two reasons. First, it is the best means of distinguishing the person who is Prime Minister from the overall body, the premiership, of which he or she is a part. Second, it enables the discernment of two tendencies key to the development of the office of Prime Minister. Over time powers (vested legally or by convention in the person of the premier), functions and personnel may both appear within the ambit of this institution and move away from it. These processes are labelled here 'administrative fusion and fission', following the phrase used by A.H. Hanson and Malcolm Walles when describing their application to a variety of institutions across Whitehall.[65] Fusion and fission may involve rights, tasks and staff being moved around, newly created, abolished altogether, or reduced or expanded in some way. They may be measured absolutely (such as by a growth or decline in the total number of staff at No.10), or relatively (such as by a slower or faster

[65] A.H. Hanson & Malcolm Walles, *Governing Britain* (London: Fontana Paperbacks, 1980), pp.135–46.

rate of expansion or decline in the number of aides than elsewhere in government). Shifts can be complete or they may be of degree, with tasks and aides being shared more or less with other groups. Fusion and fission may consist variously of formal changes, alterations in practice and shifts in the physical location of personnel, and the distinction between the three is frequently blurred. Such movements can be executed rapidly with ease, and sometimes receive little attention because they are often carried out under the Royal Prerogative and do not require parliamentary approval. They might be soon reversed, though having possibly created a precedent for the future, or longer-lived. Fusion and fission can occur at almost or exactly the same time.

Administrative fusion and fission in the British premiership have many historical precedents. Written records in the region centring on the rivers Tigris and Euphrates date back to about 2,700 BCE. In this area the civilisation known as Sumer was initially ruled by a monarch in whom ultimate religious and political authority were deposited. Rulers were regarded as living gods. But 'the general trend throughout history was towards a gradual separation of the Palace from the Temple ... There were even times when the ruler and the priests were, it seems, in open conflict'.[66] Yet there was a subsequent attempt to reverse this process. In the following millennium the ruler Hammurabi established a larger kingdom in the same region. His period of rule from 1792 to 1750 BCE saw substantial centralisation. Amongst those drawn into his reach were the judges of the temples, who were required to describe themselves individually as 'servant of Hammurabi' rather than of a particular god.[67]

The occurrence of phenomena akin to both administrative fusion and fission have been replicated in many places and eras. The anthropologist James Frazer noted 'a successive differentiation of functions, or ... division of labour' across different ancient societies which led to the emergence of a class of public magicians. They in turn subdivided into different categories including that of 'chief' and later

[66] George Roux, *Ancient Iraq* (London: Penguin, 1992), pp.137–8.
[67] *Ibid*, pp.197–202.

'sacred king'. Subsequently there was 'a partition effected between the civil and religious aspect of the kingship, the temporal power being committed to one man and the spiritual to another'.[68]

In his study of the history of government S. E. Finer identified a tendency within what he termed the 'Palace', that is an 'autocratic and monocratic', form of regime. Where there have developed 'specialized agencies for the main tasks of government', the ruler makes decisions based on

> information which has flowed in to be processed through the specialized agencies until it finally reaches ministers, who thereupon put it, together with the policy alternatives, to the ruler. But sometimes the ruler feels that he is being pressured by these ministers and advisers and sets up his own counter-intelligence agency: a personal staff of inner counsellors.[69]

In the post-Conquest mediaeval period in England it is possible to observe similar processes in the development of the monarchy. Internal sections were set up in the royal household to perform particular functions. In time they became separate institutions, either gradually or because of deliberate intervention by the magnates. The Exchequer, the Chancery, then eventually, during the early fourteenth century, the Privy Seal, followed the same path. With immediate control over these bodies lost, the monarchy deployed new ones, which in turn themselves developed over time into separate offices of state. Repeatedly household servants were elevated from obscure positions and given responsibility for writing the monarch's private correspondence, but their posts later became public ones. T.F. Tout – credited as the first observer of this tendency of functions 'going out of court' – argued that this theory provides a vantage point from which to survey mediaeval political controversies involving royal favourites used to nullify the actions of ministerial offices

[68] Sir James Frazer, *The Golden Bough: A study in magic and religion* (Ware: Wordsworth, 1993), pp.105–6.

[69] S. E. Finer, *The History of Government From the Earliest Times*, Vol I, *Ancient monarchies and empires* (Oxford: Oxford University Press, 1997), pp.38 and 42.

and parliaments.[70] Eventually fission in the monarchy led to it becoming a husk, with the role of most prominent public leader in the UK passing from the monarch to the Prime Minister after a transitional phase from the early eighteenth to mid-nineteenth century.

The phenomena of administrative fusion and fission have occurred throughout the history of the premiership. Incidents of the former such as the Prime Minister obtaining the clear ability to remove ministers, and becoming sole adviser to the monarch about dissolutions of Parliament have been widely remarked upon.[71] Often such accumulation has been used as evidence of growing dominance over government by No.10. Such assertions are erroneous because of both faulty reasoning and use of incomplete evidence. Developments of this sort should not necessarily be assumed to equate directly with greater strength for the office,[72] and fusion has been subject to the countervailing tendency of fission.

Various functions and aides have been lost altogether or shifted away from the premiership. In the eighteenth century there was no clear distinction between party politicians and what later came to be known as 'civil servants'. Duties which would later be allotted either to junior ministers or to officials were performed by a single class of person often known as 'men of business'. They worked on behalf of individual ministers who were their patrons and with whose fates theirs tended to be clearly bound. Often the government roles of these aides ended if their employers left. Because of their personal link to the individual occupying the post, men of business serving early prime ministers were firmly within the ambit of the emergent premiership.

A slow process gaining pace in the nineteenth century saw the administrative machine separate from party politics. It developed into an entity that in practice enjoyed a degree of autonomy, notwithstanding the convention that its personnel

---

[70] Florence M. Greir Evans, *The Principal Secretary of State: A Survey of the Office from 1558 to 1680* (Manchester At the University Press, 1923), pp.10-11; 3; T.F. Tout, *Chapters in the Administrative History of Mediaeval England,* Vol. I (Manchester at the University Press, 1930), pp.20–1.

[71] For a comprehensive list of accruals see: Hennessy, *The Prime Minister,* pp.45–52.

[72] See: Chapter Four.

possessed no constitutional independence. The general principle emerged that they remained in their positions regardless of changes in particular ministers or parties of government, with whom they eschewed links in pursuit of impartiality.[73] A significant proportion of the staff associated with the office of Prime Minister came to be shared with this bureaucratic institution. Consequently functions they performed, such as advising on decisions and ensuring they were put into effect, now moved to some extent away from the premiership and towards the permanent Civil Service. This fission became most extreme from the 1920s when the convention developed that the senior official at No.10, the Principal Private Secretary, had to be a career civil servant; along with a general principle that the Private Office as a whole should comprise only, or almost entirely, permanent Whitehall staff. Another practice served to compound the tendency for divided loyalties amongst career officials. Their secure employment did not mean long-term attachment to No.10. Senior officials were loaned temporarily from departments elsewhere in government, to which they generally returned after a few years. These staff possessed a clear primary link to neither the person nor the office of the Prime Minister.

Further fission was instigated when David Lloyd George attached a secretariat to the War Cabinet he set up in 1916. It later became the Cabinet Office. He envisaged and used this staff as an instrument of control from No.10, but in time its formation meant that responsibility for managing Cabinet business, which had previously largely fallen to the office of Prime Minister[74], now resided with a body outside the immediate realm of the premiership. More fission still occurred when during the Second World War (after a similar arrangement in the First) the post of Leader of the House of Commons was separated from that of the Prime Minister. The two have never been reunited. More broadly, the role of unofficial 'imperial chancellery' associated with No.10, declined and vanished along with the British Empire itself during the twentieth century.

---

[73] See eg: Henry Parris, *Constitutional Bureaucracy*, (London: Allen and Unwin, 1969) p.41.

[74] See: *The Records of the Cabinet Office to 1922*, PRO Handbooks No.11 (London: PRO/HMSO, 1966), p.1.

What drives administrative fusion and fission in the premiership? The former phenomenon can be in part, motivated by the desire of prime ministers and their staff to expand the role of No.10 in some way; as in the account provided by Finer, the 'Palace' type of regime sought to increase its impact through the creation of new agencies. When Churchill became premier in 1940, the establishment of the Prime Minister's Statistical Section was intended to facilitate No.10's oversight of the mobilisation of national resources for the war effort. The extent to which fusion is associated with planned objectives or represents a reaction to external developments varies. Following the Labour General Election victory of 1964, the use by Wilson of a small team of economists can be seen largely as an extension of specific ideas developed in opposition. The creation of a 'Web team' during the Blair period signifies more a response to outside trends, of a technological and social nature.

As well as enabling more activity on the part of No.10, fusion which involves boosting staff support can be motivated by a desire to ease the burden of work on those within No.10. The establishment of a secretary paid from public funds in 1806, with a second added in 1812, seems to have been executed in pursuit of this objective, (although prime ministers had single secretaries, paid for by other means, before 1806). Fusion is not always a fully conscious act. When assuming new responsibilities for the premiership, such as the right to request dissolutions or dismiss ministers, it should not be assumed that those involved in doing so are necessarily fully aware of, or even concerned about, the lack of precedent for or significance of their actions. And the taking on of new staff and functions can be viewed in part as the product of ongoing tendencies common to many or all institutions, such as developing various internal specialisations over time, rather than as the outcome of the deliberate one-off deeds of individuals.

Some of the causes of administrative fusion are the same as those encouraging fission. The latter, like the former, may be motivated by the interlinked objectives of reducing the workload falling on individuals within No.10 and enabling the premiership to achieve more. The development of the

Civil Service, entailing administrative fission in the office of Prime Minister, was given early impetus by the pressure of business upon prime-ministerial aides generated during the Napoleonic wars, leading amongst other measures to what was initially an act of fusion, the establishment in 1805 of a permanent head of the Treasury not sitting in Parliament, then called the 'Assistant Secretary'. The idea of separating the role of Leader of the House of Commons from the premiership, finally permanently established during the Second World War, was prompted partly by a workload problem observed over a long period of time. In 1893 West argued that the combination of the roles was placing an undue burden upon Gladstone and expressed the hope 'that means will be devised for relieving Mr. Gladstone of some portion of it'.[75] The distancing of the leadership of the House of Commons from No.10 in both world wars, can be seen as well as intended to enable the premiership to focus on winning the conflict. John Hoskyns, the first head of Margaret Thatcher's Policy Unit, reduced the size and scope of the body, as compared with that run by Bernard Donoughue, Senior Policy Adviser to Wilson and Callaghan, to concentrate on what he saw as the core economic and industrial problems faced by the UK. The intermittent appointment of deputy prime ministers on various occasions since the mid-twentieth century, has been partially motivated by similar concerns, as well as providing a position of high political status to win the support of an influential and potentially recalcitrant cabinet colleague.

Fission may as well be encouraged by political pressure from those seeking to prise functions away from No.10. The constitutional reform programme unveiled by Gordon Brown in July 2007 promised enhanced roles for Parliament in activities closely associated with the premiership, such as engaging in armed conflict, treaty making and managing the Civil Service. It followed sustained pressure from within Parliament, including from the House of Commons Public Administration Select Committee.[76] Fission might also come

[75] West, 'The Prime Minister'.

[76] See eg: House of Commons Public Administration Select Committee (PASC), *Taming the Prerogative: Strengthening Ministerial Accountability to*

about as the direct consequence of a change in the outside world, such as the collapse of the British Empire.

To some extent fusion and fission can be seen as causing each other. The taking on by various prime ministers of economic advisers – an act of fusion – could be regarded as a means of maintaining a role in a policy field, direct responsibility for which was ceded when the office of Prime Minister was separated from the Treasury.[77] In this sense administrative fusion and fission are historical manifestations of concepts associated with 'regulation theory'. Political scientists of this school have identified a tendency for administrative decentralisation of functions to be accompanied by the introduction of regulatory bodies to monitor those activities that have been transferred away. Within this pattern both processes occur simultaneously or the latter follows the former.[78]

Just as fusion sometimes comes about as a consequence of fission, the reverse can apply. The need physically to locate staff working for the premiership outside No. 10, a form of fission, is normally prompted by an expansion in the total number of aides attached to the premiership. As discussed above, the emergence of the permanent Civil Service as an entity in its own right, entailing fission in the office of Prime Minister, was prompted to some extent by the creation of a new aide to the premier in the form of the Treasury Assistant Secretary in 1805.

The connection between the power of the premiership and administrative fusion and fission is not straightforward. The processes of fusion and fission can be interpreted as entailing the accumulation or loss of particular types of power resources, classified as constitutive resources (specific powers exercised under statute or the Royal Prerogative) and institutional resources (in the form of staff performing particular functions). These issues are considered in detail in Chapter Four.

Parliament, HC422 (London: Stationery Office, 2004).

[77] See below.

[78] June Burnham and G.W. Jones, 'More botany than physics: the application of policy network theory and other aids to systematic thought to understanding the work of prime-ministerial advisers', paper given at University of Birmingham ESRC Whitehall Programme conference 'Understanding central government: theory into practice', 16–18 September 1996, p.8.

Discovering Turning Points and Phases

From phase one to phase two

Through viewing the premiership from the perspective of administrative fusion and fission it is possible to identify a point of transition for the office of Prime Minister from a first to a second phase. It occurred during the mid-nineteenth century when direct responsibility for the Treasury moved away from the premiership. The development of the office from the eighteenth century was an uncertain process.[79] But subject to caveats about its lack of entrenchment, certain broad characteristics associated with the post can be identified in this early period. In his 1803 description of the appropriate role of the 'avowed and real Minister' Pitt the Younger argued 'that Minister ought ... to be the person at the head of the finances'.[80] Almost always the individual recognised as Prime Minister was First Lord of the Treasury, a post which until the mid-nineteenth century brought with it direct responsibility for the Treasury. If they sat in the Commons, First Lords were even more closely involved with the Treasury and its business, since they held this post jointly with that of Chancellor of the Exchequer (this post was not yet considered a first-rank position in its own right) and delivered the Budget speech. The premier was in this sense a departmental minister with a policy portfolio and relatively large staff, since in the nascent days of the premiership the Treasury was by far the largest office of government.

Prime ministers had ready physical access to the Treasury. In the 1730s the distinguished architect John Kent constructed new offices for the Treasury in the area known as the 'Cockpit' and renovated No.10 Downing Street, which became the official residence of the First Lord, and then built corridors linking the two.[81] Much later, from 1963[82], the Cabinet Office

[79] See above, this chapter.

[80] Lord Melville to Mr. Addington, 22 March 1803, reproduced in Stanhope, *Life of the Right Honourable William Pitt*, Vol. IV, p.24.

[81] See: Henry Roseveare, *The Treasury: The Evolution of a British Institution* (London: Allen Lane, 1969), pp.100–2.

[82] This date comes from: 'Cabinet Office and the Centre of Government, Submission by Lord Armstrong of Ilminster, Lord Butler of Brockwell and Lord Wilson of Dinton', May 2009.

came to occupy the old 'Kent Treasury', as it became known, which was subsumed within the 70 Whitehall complex.[83] The association between the institutions housed in the adjoining properties was by this time more complex – associated but at arm's length. It was symbolised by the locked door installed between them, used to limit but not completely to prevent access. In the formative years of the premiership the connection was simple: that existing between a minister and what was in effect his department.

Substantial patronage, political and financial, was at the disposal of the Treasury. Responsibility for finance was an important policy brief in itself and created the potential for involvement in any government actions that involved expenditure. The Treasury was a base upon which the First Lordship became established as foremost amongst ministerial offices, fulfilling the roles of coordinator of government, mediator between and manager of monarch and Parliament, and spokesman of the government in Westminster and the country at large. By the mid-nineteenth century the premiership had become secure with its head, the Prime Minister, in practice eclipsing the monarch as the most prominent provider of public leadership in the UK. The structure of the premiership was now sufficiently sound that the scaffolding which supported it while it was built – the Treasury – could safely be removed. When it was, the office of Prime Minister entered its second phase.

In 1841 Robert Peel decided not to combine the post of Chancellor of the Exchequer with that of First Lord of the Treasury when he took up the latter.[84] Peel's plan was to delegate the detailed work associated with responsibility for the Treasury to the Chancellor of the Exchequer, enabling him as Prime Minister to range across the whole of government. Such a move had been considered – but not executed – on previous occasions, including by Pitt the Younger. His motive was similar to that which drove Peel. In 1797 Sylvester Douglas recorded in his diary that Henry Dundas had suggested that

[83] See: TNA/PRO CAB 21/4768, 'Move of the Cabinet Office to the re-constructed old Treasury building Whitehall', 1958–1962.

[84] For a discussion of this event and its significance see: Paul Langford, 'Prime Ministers and Parliaments: The Long View, Walpole to Blair', pp.385–8.

Pitt the Younger 'wishes for assistance in the details of the Treasury, and has even sometimes mooted with him the practicability of having a Chancellor of the Exchequer with himself (still remaining a Commoner) first Lord'.[85]

The premiership under Peel retained ultimate control over financial policy and engaged closely in it when deemed necessary. But the long-term consequences of his innovation were that the Chancellorship of the Exchequer emerged as an office more clearly distinct from that of the First Lord, and the effective headship of the Treasury was ceded by the First Lord to the increasingly prominent Chancellor. In the decades that followed Peel's decision, politicians such as Gladstone and Disraeli, were able to establish their reputations through holding the chancellorship. Eventually by the twentieth century, the Chancellor of the Exchequer could be regarded as the second most important figure in Cabinet to the premier.[86] The historian Maurice Wright observed that up to the mid-nineteenth century 'the First Lord [was] intimately connected with Treasury business'; but 'after 1856 ... normally took no part in the formal transaction of Treasury business, unless the office was combined with that of Chancellor of the Exchequer'.[87] As usual, official recognition of this change was not swift. To the present day the First Lord of the Treasury remains technically a Treasury minister: the 2009 *Civil Service Yearbook* notes that one of the 'Lord's Commissioners of HM Treasury' is 'the First Lord of the Treasury (who is also the Prime Minister)'. Only as recently as its 1976 edition did the *Yearbook* first stipulate that, though listed as a Treasury minister, the 'Prime Minister and First Lord of the Treasury' was 'not part of the Departmental Treasury headed by the Chancellor of the Exchequer'. But despite this official tardiness the new arrangement that came about in practice during the mid-nineteenth century was soon widely recognised. In 1893 West described the position as it had developed in the post-Peel era: 'Departmentally the First Minister of the Crown and

[85] Francis Bickley (ed.), *The Diaries of Sylvester Douglas* (London: Constable, 1928), diary entry for 10 January 1797, pp.120–1.

[86] Maurice Wright, *Treasury Control of the Civil Service: 1854–1874* (Oxford: Oxford University Press, 1969), p.49.

[87] *Ibid*, p.49.

the head of the Government has nothing to do'. Premiers were 'as the French say, "without portfolio"' since 'the First Lord of the Treasury has nothing to do with the Treasury. His presidency is merely nominal, the real headship being in the hands of the Chancellor of the Exchequer'.[88]

The old nature of the premiership was remembered for a while. When Gladstone temporarily recombined the office of Prime Minister with the Treasury in August 1873, *The Times* noted that his decision to 'be his own Chancellor of the Exchequer' was 'a plan equally simple and unexpected, although not novel ... This was common enough in past generations, and we are returning in many ways to the practice of the past'.[89] But knowledge that the premier was once a 'departmental' minister was eventually buried.

The office of Prime Minister had left its embryonic first phase as a 'finance minister-plus'. Its occupants normally no longer possessed a 'department' and the staff and responsibilities that went with it. They were now supported by just two publicly-funded secretaries. The immediate policy-forming role diminished while that of overall coordination became more important. In this way the discretion already characteristic of the office increased, with No.10 ranging across government with selective interventions. The premiership could be seen as having developed a structure that entailed a more exclusive focus on its primary role of public leadership.

An important characteristic of the second phase of the premiership, when compared with the first, was the prominence of the individual Prime Minister within the office as a whole. This feature was possible in part because of the relatively small size of the No.10 staff, making it more feasible for the premier to maintain personal control over them and the work they do. The analogy offered by Kavanagh and Seldon is apt:

> Number Ten ... resembles the studio of a great Baroque artist, say Rubens. The finished product bears the master's name, but much of the painting, especially the routine work, was not

[88] West, 'The Prime Minister'..
[89] Editorials/Leaders, *The Times*, 8 August 1873.

> executed by him. But it is all executed in the style and the name of the master. The great trick of the modern premiership is that Number Ten has to act seamlessly as if everyone important in it is the Prime Minister.[90]

A source of the personal nature of the second phase premiership was the lack of a defined policy brief, enabling the office to range across different areas according to the particular interests of the Prime Minister.

By implication the establishment of a 'Department of the Prime Minister' of some kind could reduce the importance and impact of particular incumbents within the premiership. As their staff expanded they might be drawn increasingly into management tasks, including resolving disputes between aides; or conversely they might find personnel within the department supposedly serving them but developing group preferences they sought to impose upon the Prime Minister. Finally, if it took on a clearer set of regular functions – as it would in departmental form be likely to do – the premiership would be less suited to pursuing the varied personal initiatives of its head. The outcome could be a body less attuned and responsive to the particular needs of the premier.

Some of these possible developments motivated Wilson in his opposition to the idea – which he and some around him had entertained in the lead-up to his first term at No.10 – of a 'Department of the Prime Minister'. Making reference to arrangements in the US he noted:

> The president ... can hardly move for staff. (In President Lyndon Johnson's time, I was told his staff was 2500: I understand it increased still further under President Nixon.) He is pressed on all sides for signatures, approvals, ratifications – I have seen presidents badgered to sign them in the lift, an action that must be a more or less automatic reflex.[91]

Jonathan Powell, although he took part in a significant process of centralisation under Blair, wrote in 2009:

---

[90] Dennis Kavanagh and Anthony Seldon, *Prime Minister: the hidden influence of Number Ten*, p. xii.

[91] Wilson, *The Governance of Britain*, p.82.

> I do not believe the Prime Minister's Office should be allowed to grow into a monstrous new department ... it should be light and responsive to the PM's intentions. Everyone in No 10 should really know what the PM thinks first hand rather than trying to guess at it because they rarely or never see him or her, and then create havoc by calling Departments and saying "the PM thinks ..." [92]

Even advocates of a 'Department of the Prime Minister' have sometimes shown awareness of the difficulties that could arise for a Prime Minister. W.G.S Adams, head of Lloyd George's Garden Suburb, argued in evidence to the Reconstruction Committee of the Cabinet in 1918 that 'there should be a Prime Minister's Department created'.[93] But Adams was careful to state that it should not be 'an executive body interfering with the several departments of the Administration, but a body whose function is to draw together for the Prime Minister the threads of the Administration'. He stressed its work 'must be in close personal touch with the Prime Minister', and he was 'averse to the idea of a big Prime Minister's Department'. It should be 'of a particular genus necessary to the peculiar office of Prime Minister, who should not be a person in charge of an administrative department, but one who is overlooking the whole field of government, thinking about the co-ordination and development of policy, and seeking to make his team draw together as well as possible, and be as efficient as possible'.[94]

The issues raised by Wilson, Powell, Adams and others are associated with the tension (referred to above) inherent in the public leadership role of No.10. In the definition of public leadership used here, people – operating as individuals or groups – are key, supplying that which 'institutions organisations and routines' cannot spontaneously provide. Yet at the same time the premiership – of necessity as an actor within the central UK executive – is composed partly of 'institutions, organisations and routines'. Without them it could not function: a Prime Minister without a premiership would be impotent.

[92] 'House of Lords Constitution Committee Inquiry: Written evidence from Jonathan Powell, former Chief of Staff to Tony Blair', 11 June 2009.

[93] 'Proposed Statement by Prof. Adams', 7 March 1918, Parliamentary Archives, Lloyd George Papers, LG/F/74/10/4.

[94] *Ibid.*

But there exists a danger of reaching the point of negative returns, with excessive fusion serving to swamp individual premiers (and their senior aides), hampering the ability of the office to provide leadership. This issue is a concern not just at No.10 but across Whitehall and more generally a universal organisational dilemma. But it is intensified for the premiership because of the exceptional importance of the public leadership role to the office of Prime Minister.

Between the mid-nineteenth century and the Blair premiership the non-departmental nature of the premiership persisted. Existing arrangements were probably preserved partly because prime ministers sensed the problems described above that might arise from a 'Department of the Prime Minister'. Such a change would pose a threat as well to the existing order within the Civil Service, the status of departmental ministers and possibly even the status of Cabinet government; and it might lead to public criticism. Consequently there was a longstanding disposition within government to resist such a reconfiguration.

Despite the inbuilt opposition, at times it seemed possible that the non-departmental arrangement would be dispensed with, including the Lloyd George era. On 28 December 1916, shortly after he took office, in what seems to have been some kind of Freudian slip, *The Times* ran a short item noting that no New Year honours list had been issued by 'the Prime Minister's Department'.[95] On 5 January 1917 a note was circulated to private secretaries throughout the government announcing the formation of the Prime Minister's Secretariat, or 'Garden Suburb' as it became known colloquially. It described how the Prime Minister had decided 'to establish a *Department* [emphasis added] in connection with the Office of the First Lord of the Treasury'.[96] This document was as close to the formal proclamation of a 'Department of the Prime Minister' as Britain has come, although whether the reality of the Garden Suburb – a team of less than half a dozen senior aides – would have lived up to the grandiose billing of 'Department' is doubtful. On 10 January 1917 *The Times* reported:

[95] 'The New Year Honours', *The Times*, 28 December 1916.
[96] Letter sent to multiple departments, 5 January 1917, Parliamentary Archives, Lloyd George Papers, LG/F/74/2/3.

> The latest of the constitutional changes which the Prime Minister has decided to make is the establishment of an Intelligence Department at 10, Downing-street ... In time, it may develop into a definite Prime Minister's Department for the co-ordination of the activities of the administrative Departments of the State.[97]

Internal complaints were presumably voiced, leading to the decision that any idea that a 'department' was being instigated had to be denied. On 15 January *The Times* stated: 'The institution of the "garden suburb," [the first use of this nickname in The Times] as it is called ... is not, strictly speaking, the creation of a new Department, but is really an extension of the normal system of Private Secretaries'.[98] By 16 March 1917 the retreat was complete, when *The Times* referred to the Garden Suburb as 'the Prime Minister's secretariat'.[99]

Sometimes prime ministers took on portfolios – Gladstone as Chancellor of the Exchequer, Lord Salisbury and Ramsay MacDonald as Foreign Secretary, Asquith (briefly) as Secretary of State for War, Winston Churchill as Minister of Defence.[100] The premiership has long had oversight of what are now termed the Intelligence and Security Agencies. Since 1968 the Prime Minister has been Minister for the Civil Service (though the function has been delegated to others) and there was a Civil Service Department between 1968 and 1981. From the time of the Garden Suburb some prime ministers created bodies to provide a greater involvement for the premiership in departmental portfolios. The Policy Unit set up by Harold Wilson in 1974 has survived almost without interruption to the present. In 2001 it was merged with the Private Office to form the Policy Directorate, but by 2006 the two had come to be separate again. Other units have appeared, and there has been a gradual rise in the total number of staff attached to No.10, which was by 1997 in the low hundreds, although this latter figure included menial and support workers. But the teams under the direct control of the premier had yet to take on a number of the characteristics required for them to

[97] 'An Innovation in Downing-Street', *The Times*, 10 January 1917.
[98] 'Completing the machine', *The Times*, 15 January 1917.
[99] 'Political Notes', *The Times*, 16 March 1917.
[100] For Churchill see: Andrew Blick, *How to go to war: a handbook for democratic leaders*, pp.23–4.

qualify as a 'Department of the Prime Minister' which could be likened to the other great offices of state.

Amongst the necessary features were:

- An organisational structure including within it a permanent secretary and junior ministers;
- Official status as a department for management and accounting purposes with its own distinct budget;
- A body of staff at least approaching those of other great departments of state in numbers, and not overwhelmingly on short-term loan from other home departments;
- Direct and ongoing involvement in policy development and implementation; and
- A political head, like a Secretary of State, in whom are vested specific legal responsibilities for policy under statute or the Royal Prerogative; and who answers to Parliament for the exercise of these responsibilities and the activities of the departmental staff.

From 1997 the premiership came to meet these requirements to a considerably greater extent than it had before. This development involved the synthesis of the first and second phases of the office, into what was perhaps the third phase, with the large-scale staff associated with phase one used to augment the cross-departmental role that had become more prominent in phase two.

Phase Three?

Administrative fusion under Blair

The Blair premiership was characterised by substantial administrative fusion. The overall size of the staff grew by about seventy, from 121 in 1998 to 190 by 2002, where it remained. At senior level a significant increase took place within the Policy Unit, which rose from nine staff to 16 within a year of his taking office. The Strategic Communications Unit (SCU), newly formed in 1998, employed eight. One important development in his first term of 1997–2001 was the augmentation in the number of temporary civil servants appointed by his patronage, known as special advisers. The figure for Major's final year at No.10 was eight. By 2000–1 it rose to 25, peaking at 28 in 2004–5. Consequently Blair had an enlarged cadre of individuals closely linked to him. They were firmly within the ambit of the premiership rather than the impartial career bureaucracy or particular home departments.

At the same time Blair drew responsibility for administrative functions more within the realm of the office of Prime Minister. The effect of a 1997 Order in Council was formally to grant up to three of his special advisers executive authority over career officials anywhere in Whitehall. It was applied to only two: Jonathan Powell, the Chief of Staff, and Alastair Campbell, Chief Press Secretary (from 2001–3 Director of Communications and Strategy). Powell eclipsed the Principal Private Secretary as the most senior staff member at No.10; while Campbell was central to another process of establishing functions at the centre. Alongside the existing Press Office, new teams were created at No.10 for planning publicity across government through the SCU, and responding rapidly to emerging media stories through the Research and Information Office/Unit, set up in 1999.[101]

Despite the initial changes Blair grew frustrated with the progress being made, particularly over public-service reform, his domestic priority. Peter Hyman, a strategy and media aide, wrote that during his first term Blair endured 'the impotence that every Prime Minister feels when the departments over which he has some, but not much, control do their own thing'. According to Hyman, Blair expressed the view in February 1999 that 'The basic problem which I guess is not new for Prime Ministers is control. How do we drive our will down through the system, monitor progress and then achieve delivery? A stronger centre could give more direction and keep on the job until we are sure people are moving in the way we want'.[102] Andrew Turnbull, Cabinet Secretary and Head of the Home Civil Service, told the House of Commons Public Administration Select Committee (PASC) in 2004 how Blair had developed the view 'that trying to be a leader for government based on a very small private office and a tiny policy unit was not going to produce first of all the degree

[101] See: Andrew Blick, *People who live in the dark: the history of the special adviser in British politics*, pp. 251–96.

[102] Hyman, *1 Out of 10*, p.174.

of radicalism in policy thinking he was after and the delivery capability'.[103]

In search of greater support Blair turned to the Cabinet Office. There were a number of reasons for following this course of action. It built on existing practice. The premiership had responsibility for organising Cabinet. Accordingly a close relationship with the office responsible for servicing collective government was inevitable. Similarly prime ministers had long drawn upon the assistance of its official head, the Cabinet Secretary. The links between No.10 and the Cabinet Office were reinforced during the early 1980s when, following the abolition of the Civil Service Department, responsibility for Civil Service management and personnel was shifted into the Cabinet Office and the Cabinet Secretary post was combined with that of Head of the Home Civil Service. Civil Service-related functions came to be a substantial part of the work of both the Cabinet Office and its most senior official. In 2003 Lord Butler told PASC that those who held the dual post of Cabinet Secretary and Head of the Home Civil Service 'all found that the role of Head of the Civil Service became a more important one for a significantly greater part of our time'.[104] This additional purpose and altered workload represented a shift away from the collective and further into the remit of the premiership, since the Prime Minister had overall responsibility for the Civil Service (and was formally Minister for the Civil Service).

Another reason for the Cabinet Office to figure in an expansion of the premiership was the lack of a single minister at secretary-of-state level with clear overall control of the Cabinet Office, to stand in the way of it being partially or wholly commandeered by No.10. Finally there was ease of proximity. In 1963 fusion in the form of physical relocation occurred when the Cabinet Office moved to 70 Whitehall, bringing it geographically closer to the premiership. It was now connected to No.10 by the corridors John Kent had constructed in the 1730s to provide First Lords of the Treasury with ready access to their 'department' (the Treasury). Under

[103] PASC, Minutes of Evidence, 1 April 2004, Question 68.
[104] *Ibid*, 19 June 2003, Question 101.

Blair the original purpose of Kent's project was revived. The locked door, symbolically and physically dividing No.10 from the Cabinet Office, was passed through with such frequency that its meaning was lost.

Transforming the Cabinet Office into a predominantly prime-ministerial entity had long been considered. In 1984, responding to a paper by one of the present authors[105], the former Cabinet Secretary, Lord [John] Hunt, noted how at one of the annual Sunningdale Conferences of permanent secretaries, towards the end of his career, he gave a paper in which he reflected on the need for 'advice given earlier and in greater depth' at the centre of government. He was of the view that prime ministers 'want advice from someone they regard as their own'. After he put 'the pros and cons of a Prime Minister's Department ... a colleague of mine ... said "Of course, it is perfectly obvious we need a Prime Minister's Department, so long as it is still called the Cabinet Office"'. Hunt believed 'that may be the answer'.[106]

In 2001 John Prescott, the Deputy Prime Minister, gave away what was probably the view of the appropriate role for the Cabinet Office within senior government circles at the time in an appearance before PASC. When asked 'is the Cabinet Office now some big Prime Minister's department by another name?' He replied 'Is the Cabinet Office the Prime Minister's department? The Cabinet Office is the department of the Prime Minister at the end of day [sic]. Am I confused about this? ... What we have is the Prime Minister's department in the Cabinet Office ... At the end of the day there is no doubt the mountain top is the Prime Minister'.[107]

After victory in the June 2001 General Election, as well as reorganising No.10 into three 'Sides' or 'Directorates' – 'Policy', 'Communications' and 'Government Relations' – three new avowedly prime-ministerial bodies were established in the Cabinet Office: the Forward Strategy Unit, Delivery Unit and Office of Public Service Reform.[108] (In 2002 the

[105] G. W. Jones, 'The United Kingdom', in William Plowden (ed.), *Advising the Rulers* (Oxford: Basil Blackwell, 1987), pp.36–66.
[106] 'The United Kingdom: Lord Hunt of Tanworth', in *Ibid*, p.69.
[107] PASC, Minutes of evidence, 19 October 2001, Questions 64–6.
[108] HC. Written Answers, 19 October 2001, cols 1361–2.

Forward Strategy Unit was merged with the Performance and Innovation Unit, set up in the Cabinet Office in 1998, to form the Strategy Unit.) Senior European and foreign policy advisers to the Prime Minister were appointed, who were at the same time heads respectively of the European Secretariat and Overseas and Defence Secretariat in the Cabinet Office.

These innovations enabled No.10 to be involved earlier, more directly and continuously in policy from international to local level, dealing with issues from the immediate to those projected more than a decade into the future; and exercise an enhanced role in the way government was organised. The Delivery Unit played a major part in devising the objectives of selected departments as set out in their Public Service Agreements. It constantly monitored their performance on behalf of the Prime Minister, intervening to improve it if deemed necessary. The Strategy Unit took part in long-term planning in conjunction with departments across a wide range of briefs. In 2005 its first director, Geoff Mulgan, claimed: 'The majority of reports produced by the Strategy Unit ... were actually taken through Cabinet to be decisions of government ... Broadly, so far as these things ever happen in quite the way planned, they have been implemented'.[109] The Office of Public Service Reform, while it was not a great success and was quietly abolished by 2006, had a potentially huge remit, which was 'to support the Prime Minister and government departments in carrying forward the reform of public services, enhancing the competence and capacity of public services, including the civil service and local government'.[110] Under Blair the role of No.10 in external affairs, assisted by his European and foreign policy advisers and the Directorate that supported them, was considerable, most notably over the invasion of Iraq in 2003.[111]

While the Blair premiership was often portrayed as pursuing informal methods, the approaches associated with the staff and bodies established in 2001 suggest a need for a more nuanced account. A disdain for such procedure as the use of papers

---

[109] PASC, Minutes of Evidence, 8 December 2005, Question 31.
[110] 'Memorandum by the Office of Public Service Reform' (NC 03) to PASC.
[111] Blick, *How to go to war*, pp.40–52.

certainly manifested itself within the setting of meetings of Cabinet and its subcommittees. But in processes more within the auspices of the premiership than the collective – such as the dealings between the Delivery Unit and the departments, which proceeded on a basis of detailed agreements – a punctilious approach was sometimes favoured.

Another act of fusion was the most dramatic of the Blair premiership. The traditional purpose of the Cabinet Office was to provide support for collective government, serving the Prime Minister in his capacity as chair of the Cabinet. There were precedents for teams within it answering formally to premiers, such as the Efficiency Unit under Thatcher; and for No.10 to exercise significant influence over its general activities through the Cabinet Secretary who was in some senses an aide to the premier. But under Blair the formal basis upon which the Cabinet Office operated was progressively altered, drawing it definitely into his purview and creating a semi-official 'Department of the Prime Minister'.

The Cabinet Office Public Service Agreement announced in December 1998 accorded broadly with its long-established role. Its 'Aim' referred to helping 'the Prime Minister and Ministers collectively'. Within the Agreement Objective 1 was 'To provide efficient arrangements for collective decision making' while Objective 2 was 'To support the Prime Minister effectively'.[112] But the Spending Review of 2000 saw reference to 'collective decision making' removed.[113] Then with the 'Departmental Aim' issued for the year ending 31 March 2001 'Cabinet' was dropped as well. A Cabinet Office memorandum to PASC of October 2001 showed some commitment to traditional approaches. It described the 'primary role' as being 'to support collective government and the delivery of the Government's key priorities'.[114] Yet the Spending Review of July 2002 set out new, even more prime-ministerial, objectives. Number one was: 'Support the Prime Minister in leading the Government'. There was no mention of Cabinet or the collective, simply the requirement to 'Support the Government in transacting

[112] *The Government's Expenditure Plans 2000–01 to 2001–02*, Cm 4618, April 2000.
[113] *2000 Spending Review*, HM Treasury.
[114] Memorandum by the Cabinet Office (NC 1) to PASC, October 2001.

its business'.[115] The *Cabinet Office Departmental Report 2004* confirmed this position.[116] Though these changes largely escaped contemporary comment, the Labour MP and PASC member Kelvin Hopkins noted in 2005 that the 'Cabinet Office targets seem to relate almost entirely to the Prime Minister and not to supporting the Cabinet as such'.[117]

Such formal changes are significant. They can confirm and help create an aura of legitimacy around alterations in practice that have occurred, or are being or are about to be executed; and they can give impetus to future, possibly unforeseen, developments. The importance of official labels is well understood within Whitehall, where they are vigorously contested, as the testimony of Turnbull demonstrates. He regarded the title of the body of which he was the official head as an anachronism. In 2004 Kevin Brennan MP of PASC asked him 'is it really appropriate to call this organisation at the centre of government the Cabinet Office any more, should we not ... be saying, what it is on the tin these days in government?' Turnbull responded: 'You are right ... You could easily produce a new name but we have not found that necessary ... It is a historic name rather than "it does what is says on the tin" name'.[118] Two years previously Turnbull had told PASC of a possible more accurate description: 'If you go to Australia they have a thing called PMC (Prime Minister and Cabinet); they just describe it differently'. Why then not adopt a new nomenclature? As Turnbull put it:

> The renaming of [the British Cabinet Office] would carry the implication that the Prime Minister wanted this thing to work for him and in a sense he was taking it away from the support of the Government as a whole and he does not want to create that impression. He wants to get better support from it but he does not want to create the impression that this is only working for him.[119]

[115] *2002 Spending Review*, HM Treasury; Cabinet Office, *Departmental Report 2003*, Cm 5926 (Stationery Office, London, 2003).
[116] Cabinet Office, *Departmental Report 2004*, Cm 6226 (Stationery Office, London, 2004).
[117] PASC, Minutes of Evidence, 10 March 2005, Question 288.
[118] *Ibid*, 1 April 2004, Question 94.
[119] *Ibid*, 4 July 2002, Question 15.

Given that a delay of more than a century in formally acknowledging practical changes was unexceptional within Whitehall, the reluctance described by Turnbull was not surprising.

The absorption of the Cabinet Office by No.10 saw an enormous expansion in the staff attached to the premiership. In July 2002 Blair told the Liaison Committee

> my Number 10 office has roughly the same or perhaps even fewer people working for it than the Irish Taoiseach's. To put this in context, there are far fewer people than either the French Prime Minister, never mind the Elysee and the Prime Minister combined, or the German Chancellor.[120]

Blair presented these comparisons as evidence that the view that a Department of the Prime Minister was emerging was not 'constitutionally or practically correct'.[121] But his argument did not take account of those deployed beyond No.10 who supported him, for which the Cabinet Office began providing the statistics as shown in Table 2.

A figure of more than 700 cannot be explained simply by adding up the staff attached to the Strategy Unit (50–100) Delivery Unit (normally 35–40) and Office of Public Service Reform (about 25), although these bodies were all larger than previous prime-ministerial entities. Many more within the Cabinet Office had been attached to the premiership. While direct comparisons are difficult, the size of the team that was formally part of the premiership under Blair came to exceed that of any earlier equivalent by more than 500 and in excess of 300 per cent. Again some scrutiny came from PASC. In 2005 Ian Liddell-Grainger MP told Turnbull 'I am intrigued that 721 people now work in the Prime Minister's office and support him ... It seems an awful lot of people'. Turnbull responded 'But this guy is leading the government of the United Kingdom'.[122]

The number serving Blair still lagged behind those attached to certain major departments but the gap, particularly with the Treasury, was narrowing as shown in Table 3.

[120] House of Commons Liaison Committee (HCLC), Minutes of Evidence, 16 July 2002, Question 5.
[121] HCLC, Minutes of Evidence, 16 July 2002, Question 8.
[122] PASC, Minutes of Evidence, 10 March 2005, Question 312.

TABLE 2

Number of whole-time equivalent Cabinet Office staff deployed by objective

Objective	2002–3*	2003–4	2004–5	2005–6
1: Support the Prime Minister in leading the Government	705	721	758	782
2: Achieve co-ordination of policy and operations across government	372	447	478	312
3: Improve delivery by building capacity in departments and the public services	1,143	1,134	1,042	826
4: Promote standards that ensure good governance, including adherence to the Ministerial and Civil Service Codes	115	134	130	95
Total:	2,335	2,434	2,408	2,015

*Taken from restated 2003-4 figures

Source: Cabinet Office Annual Reports and Resource Accounts.

The money devoted to providing Blair with support as leader of the government grew as well. The allocation to Objective 1 in the Cabinet Office *Departmental Report 2003* was equated directly with that of the Prime Minister's Office, which cost £13,490,000.[123] The real cost must have been far higher because now the Cabinet Office as a whole was officially – if not exclusively – engaged in such duties, something tacitly conceded in later years when the recorded expense leapt up. By 2004–5 the gross budget for the pursuance of Objective 1 was £85,508,000 out of a gross operating cost for the Cabinet

[123] Cabinet Office, *Departmental Report 2003*, Cm 5926 (Stationery Office, London, 2003).

TABLE 3

Permanent staff in post for selected departments (excluding executive agencies) 1998 to 2004 (1 April each year)

	1998	1999	2000	2001	2002	2003	2004
Cabinet Office	650*	1,560	1,750	1,840	2,020	1,900	1,790
Health	3,490	3,540	3,570	3,640	3,440	3,150	2,750
Trade and Industry	4,430	4,450	4,700	4,980	4,960	4,820	4,970
Treasury	890	890	830	830	1,010	1,010	1,030

*Excluding Office of Public Service

Office as a whole of £345,870,000. The public disclosure by the government that there existed a dedicated prime-ministerial staff of more than 700, costing over £85 million a year, did not receive from commentators the attention it merited, despite ongoing media interest since 1997 in centralising or 'presidential' tendencies under Blair.

Another reconfiguration considered during the Blair period could have meant even more dramatic fusion. Powell argued in 2009 that:

> it would be sensible to give serious thought to merging the public spending part of the Treasury with the Cabinet Office in an Office of Management and the Budget under a Chief Secretary, leaving the residue of the Treasury as a traditional Finance Ministry. We looked at this several times in government but did not in the end implement it. Such a reform would make it possible to bring together the PSA targets set by the Treasury with the separate objectives set by the PM for the Delivery Unit, and ensure that the levers of management and finance are all pulling in the same direction.[124]

No doubt one of the major obstacles to the accomplishment of this plan came from the Treasury under Brown. Had it been executed, assuming that the newly created 'Office of Management and the Budget' came significantly within the remit, under its 'Chief Secretary', of No.10, it would have partially reunited the premiership with what was lost following the ceding of day-to-day control of the Treasury by Peel.

The emerging, enlarged prime-ministerial entity, began to resemble a department in another sense: that of having a political head answering to Parliament for policies and other activities in which it was involved. Despite the principle of collective responsibility, Parliament holds particular ministers to account for policy, and for the actions of staff underneath them. Though he had a reputation for avoiding attendance in the House, in July 2002 Blair instigated six-monthly evidence sessions with the House of Commons Liaison Committee, which comprises mainly the chairs of the departmental select

[124] 'House of Lords Constitution Committee Inquiry: Written evidence from Jonathan Powell, former Chief of Staff to Tony Blair', 11 June 2009.

committees. A Prime Minister had not submitted to such scrutiny since the 1930s and then only as Leader of the House of Commons. Ironically Blair used his first appearance to deny the establishment of a 'Department of the Prime Minister' – yet his involvement in such a process was evidence to the contrary. In the sessions that followed over the next five years he discussed with the Liaison Committee not only the organisation of No.10 support structures but a wide range of policies, a tacit concession that the premiership had taken on a more prominent role in their formation.

Further parliamentary accountability for the premiership was possible when PASC questioned Cabinet Office ministers, since it raised with them themes associated with the premiership, and in its regular sessions with successive Cabinet secretaries. Yet parliamentary probing of the office of Prime Minister had limits. Select committees struggled to obtain evidence from senior staff to the premier.[125] In July 2002 Barry Sheerman MP, Chairman of the Commons Education and Skills Select Committee, put it to Blair during a Liaison Committee session: 'very often when we are trying to scrutinise the Executive ... many of the decisions are ... made not in departments ... We cannot get anyone from the PIU [Performance and Innovation Unit] to come before a Select Committee, we cannot get anyone from your Policy Unit before a Select Committee'.[126] Blair's response was to insist that ministers remained the correct people to whom to speak.[127]

One important constraint on the development of the premiership in a departmental direction, was that the Prime Minister did not acquire a new basis in law for the new functions the office he headed took on. In practice the impact upon policy may have been great. But the basic constitutional position, described by Cabinet Secretary Richard Wilson in 2000 as being that 'the legal power of action rests with Secretaries of State and the financial resources are voted by Parliament to Secretaries of State'[128], remained unchanged.

[125] See for instance: Blick, *People who live in the dark*, p.284; PASC, *The Attendance of the Prime Minister's Strategy Adviser before the Public Administration Select Committee*, HC 690 (London: Stationery Office, 17 November 2005).
[126] HCLC, Minutes of Evidence, 16 July 2002, Question 16.
[127] See: Introduction.
[128] PASC, Minutes of Evidence, 9 February 2000, Question 50.

Despite this limitation a substantial break with established constitutional practice had taken place The significance of what had happened was underlined in 2009 by evidence submitted to the House of Lords Constitutional Committee, which was produced by Lord Turnbull's three predecessors as Cabinet Secretary and Head of the Home Civil Service, Lords Armstrong, Butler and Wilson.[129] Turnbull's own name was noticeably, but not surprisingly, absent, given he was the person during whose tenure the most dramatic changes had occurred. The three Lords stated:

> each of us, as Secretary of the Cabinet, has been constantly conscious of his responsibility to the Cabinet collectively and of the need to have regard to the needs and responsibilities of the other members of the Cabinet (and indeed of other Ministers) as well as those of the Prime Minister ... we consider that staff in 10 Downing Street ... should serve and be responsible to the Prime Minister alone, whereas staff in the Cabinet Office should serve and be responsible, in the case of the Secretariat to the Cabinet and its Committees, and in the case of units located in the Cabinet Office to Cabinet Office Ministers. The task of the Cabinet Office secretariat should be (as it was in the 1999 Cabinet Office Objectives) "to help the Prime Minister and Ministers collectively to reach well informed and timely decisions".

The statement further noted that, while there was 'no objection in principle to [prime-ministerial] units being located in the Cabinet Office', there was a need for it to be 'clearly established that their role is one of coordination, that their responsibilities do not overlap and that [they] do not impinge upon or conflict with the executive responsibilities of Ministers in charge of Departments'. At present, the Lords believed, these conditions were not always satisfied. Armstrong, Butler and Wilson argued further that

> the location of "two-hatted" officials combining duties in the Cabinet Office secretariat with roles as personal advisers to the Prime Minister does not sit comfortably with their roles in the

[129] 'Cabinet Office and the Centre of Government, Submission by Lord Armstrong of Ilminster, Lord Butler of Brockwell and Lord Wilson of Dinton'.

> Cabinet Office Secretariat or with the role of the Cabinet Office as the collective servant of the Cabinet. Such arrangements should in our view be discontinued and not repeated in future.

Finally it was noted:

> since departmental Ministers are accountable to Parliament for the exercise of their statutory responsibilities, the growing role of the centre, and especially the allocation of executive functions to units at the centre, tends to compromise the accountability of departmental Ministers to Parliament for the exercise of their statutory responsibilities and functions as well as to create risks of duplication, wire-crossing and confusion in the execution of policies.

Change in the office of Prime Minister

Chapters One and Two showed the idea of change has long been an important feature of debate about the premiership. The three tendencies of zigzag and administrative fusion and fission enhance such discussion in a number of ways. They indicate an important distinction needs to be made. While zigzag concerns primarily the *style* pursued during the terms of office of individual prime ministers, administrative fusion and fission refer to developments in the *substance* of the institution. The former describes expansions and contractions in the elasticity of the premiership; the latter depicts changes to the framework over which it is stretched.

The office of Prime Minister has always been sufficiently flexible to accommodate many varied features of different occupancies without there necessarily being a need for major substantive alteration. But there can be a connection between zigzag and administrative fusion and fission. A premier with a dynamic manner might achieve fusion in assertively pursuing his personal mission; a more conciliatory Prime Minister might bring about fission. But the relationship between the trends can be more complex. Peel, under whom No.10 acted exceptionally forcefully, delegated ministerial responsibility for the Treasury to make it more possible for No.10 to oversee the whole of government more thoroughly. In the process he unwittingly initiated a substantial transfer of responsibilities, staff and functions away from the premiership. Similarly Lloyd

George established a secretariat to ensure the implementation of decisions made by the small War Cabinet the premiership dominated; but the eventual outcome was the development of the Cabinet Office, which supported and institutionalised collective, not prime-ministerial, government, though it was later shifted increasingly into the orbit of No.10, particularly under Blair.

How does analysis using these concepts help differentiate and weigh the significance of change in the premiership since 1997? Some features of the Blair tenure that have been claimed as evidence of substantive development are better regarded as amounting to only stylistic fluctuations. They include the way in which Cabinet and its subcommittees were organised and their meetings conducted. The approach taken to these bodies was often associated with an attempted, and frequently successful, domination of government from No.10. Yet, in arranging them in such a way as to suit the objectives of the premiership, the Prime Minister was exercising powers long attached to his post. Similarly the emphasis placed under Blair on active media management in itself amounted only to the following of a particular style – akin to that adopted under many previous tenures – rather than a reconstruction of the premiership.

It is possible to identify a variety of substantive shifts from 1997, some of which were executed in pursuit of these stylistic dispositions. Various rights, staff and functions appeared within or moved towards the ambit of the premiership. Some of these occurrences of fusion were of greater historical significance than others. The creation of specialised bodies at No.10 proper was not new, and had been implemented on a number of occasions since the time of Lloyd George, but those formed from 1997, were distinctive in their precise functions, if not their general areas of operation, such as media handling. Although there were relatively recent precursors for prime-ministerial entities in the Cabinet Office, such as the Efficiency Unit set up by Thatcher, the Delivery Unit, Strategy Unit (and its two predecessor bodies) and Office of Public Service Reform broke new ground with the sizes of their staff and some of the particular tasks they carried out. There are earlier instances of staff performing the dual party-political and official roles later allocated to special advisers. But in the time since these latter aides were first introduced to No.10 in 1964, there was no precedent for the number employed under Blair; and the formal vesting of two special advisers – Campbell and Powell – with executive authority had never specifically been brought about in this way. Establishing Powell as in practice the most senior official at No.10, supplanting the Principal Private Secretary, broke with a seven-decade tradition of such a position being non-partisan. The appointment of two advisers (who were permanent officials) to the premier as also heads of Cabinet secretariats seemed a disjuncture with all past practice.

The recasting of the official purpose of the Cabinet Office meant, first, that the model of a non-departmental premiership that had held broadly since the mid-nineteenth century was called into question. Second, collective government, which had enjoyed specific institutional support since 1916, was now formally deprived of it. Though the Cabinet Office still in practice serviced the Cabinet and its committees, alongside other duties, it no longer did so officially on behalf of this collective body. Cabinet as an *institution*, one of its six key manifestations[130], was compromised. This fusion was remarkable not only for the distant nature of the precedent for the arrangements with which it was associated, but also for the scale of its implications for the UK constitution as a whole.

Taken together these substantive developments did not amount to the emergence of a presidency or the supplanting of Cabinet by No.10. Caricatures are not required to produce a dramatic account of the impact of the Blair period upon the premiership. In his time at No.10 there occurred a revolution, in both senses of the word. First, existing arrangements and groups in positions of authority were overturned. The way the centre of government functioned was altered significantly, and the grip of the career Civil Service on No.10 was broken. Second, the cycle turned. There was, to an extent, a return to arrangements existing before the development of an impartial Civil Service, when Cabinet was not supported by a specific

[130] See: Chapter Two.

staff, and the premiership had a direct policy role and was attached to a department in the form of the Treasury. Had the plan alluded to by Powell, to merge parts of the Treasury with the Cabinet Office been executed, the reversion would have been even more complete.

But revolutions have thermidors. By the end of his premiership certain functions which had appeared within the remit of the office of Prime Minister had moved away from it. This process was associated with a modification of style (though the general centralised approach remained the same) necessitated by a decline in the political authority of No.10, which became noticeable following the Iraq war which began in 2003, and practical concerns. In 2002, though remaining a prime-ministerial entity, the Delivery Unit moved physically to the Treasury, to facilitate the necessary close working relationship between the two. After the departure of Alastair Campbell from Downing Street in 2003 a new role was created in the Cabinet Office: that of Permanent Secretary, Government Communications, filled by a career official. Campbell's successor as the most senior party-political press officer, David Hill, was not granted the same executive empowerment as Campbell had enjoyed. Control over the development and coordination of government presentation had moved away from Blair's inner circle of partisan aides at No.10. As noted above, the Office for Public Service Reform was quietly abolished. Most significantly by 2006 the terms of reference for the Cabinet Office had shifted back towards the collective. Reflecting a decline in the political status of the premiership, and perhaps a different approach favoured by Gus O'Donnell, the Cabinet Secretary from 2005, 'Supporting the Cabinet' was once again described as a purpose of the Cabinet Office; and 'Supporting the Prime Minister' was listed without the words 'in leading the government'.[131] There was a sharp drop in the number of staff engaged in the latter activity during 2006–7, as compared with those employed in the former in 2005–6, from 782 to 531, alongside a fall in the total employed by the Cabinet Office on all of its objectives, from 2015 to 1603.

[131] Cabinet Office, *Departmental Report 2006*, Cm 6833 (London: Stationery Office, 2006).

One part of the debate about the premiership since 1997 has concerned how durable were any changes brought about to the office. Alterations of style, for which the elasticity of the institution allowed, were the product of contingencies. They were fleeting: a 'zig' followed by a 'zag'. Changes of substance could be more enduring, such as the delegation of responsibility for the Treasury by Peel in 1841 or the formation of a War Cabinet secretariat by Lloyd George in 1916. But the 'fission' occurring later on in the Blair era suggests that some of the material modifications introduced from 1997 might also be less permanent.

The transition from Blair to Brown in 2007 marked another occurrence of zigzag. Brown set out to present himself as a 'humble', more collegiate leader;[132] and political circumstances meant that the premiership could not be as prominent within government as it had for much of the Blair era. This change of style was accompanied by administrative fission. The 1997 Civil Service Order in Council which had allowed the premier to vest up to three special advisers at No.10 with authority over career officials was revoked. Brown appointed a permanent civil servant to fill Powell's Chief of Staff role, merging it with that of Principal Private Secretary. The number of special advisers at No.10 initially dropped from 25 to 18. The Delivery Unit was shifted formally into the Treasury, though reporting jointly to the Chancellor of the Exchequer and the Prime Minister. Shortly after his arrival at No.10 Brown announced a constitutional reform programme that included No.10 either surrendering outright or reducing its role in various activities. Brown retained the shift back towards collegiality in the wording of the Cabinet Office terms of reference. The number of Cabinet Office staff deployed on 'Supporting the Prime Minister' in 2007–8 stood at 399 – compared with 531 in 2006–7.

Yet while 399 was a smaller number of staff than in recent years, it was historically huge. The sessions with the Liaison Committee, including detailed discussion of policy, continued; as did the practice established under Blair of external policy

[132] Peter Hennessy, 'From Blair to Brown: The Condition of British Government', p.348.

TABLE 4

The first, second and possible third historic phases of the office of British Prime Minister

Phase: Time period	Brought about by	Characteristics	Composed of
One: Early eighteenth to mid-nineteenth centuries.	Emergence of First Lord of the Treasury as pre-eminent amongst ministers. A slow process lacking any formal recognition during this period.	'Finance ministry plus': a tentatively developing role, with direct responsibility for finance, providing a route into other policy areas and a patronage function which has been the thread running through the history of the office; oversight of gradually emerging entity of Cabinet; mediator between and manager of monarch and Parliament; with the Prime Minister as the government spokesman in Westminster and the country at large.	The Treasury, under the control of its First Lord; and various other assistants, none employed officially as part of a Prime Minister's Office.
Two: Mid-nineteenth to late-	Robert Peel's decision in 1841 to separate the post of Chancellor of	Because of separation from the Treasury and the lack of a specific policy portfolio, the overall	A small secretariat, initially with only two publicly-funded staff; and the whips. A number

twentieth centuries.	the Exchequer from that of First Lord of the Treasury.	coordination or public leadership role became more important. The prominence of the individual premier was heightened.	of informal helpers and various units established from 1916 onwards. The total number at No.10 had reached the low-hundreds by 1997. Not formally acknowledged as the Prime Minister's Office until the 1970s; though the post of Prime Minister was beginning to receive recognition from the late nineteenth century.
Three: Turn of twentieth/ twenty-first centuries onwards?	Tony Blair's expansion and reconfiguration at No.10; his establishment of units of unprecedented size and distinctive functions at the Cabinet Office and the redrawing of its formal objectives.	An augmented cross-government role, with systematic, direct and ongoing involvement in policy, implementation and organisation, though without new statutory responsibilities being taken on to reflect these changes. The Prime Minister was treated as politically accountable for government policy in sessions with House of Commons Liaison Committee.	Nearly 200 staff at No.10; and a further 580 in the Cabinet Office by 2005–6, in such bodies as the Strategy Unit (dropping to 399 in total by 2007-8). Not formally classified as a Department of the Prime Minister, but in practice displaying a number of key features of such an entity.

advisers to the Prime Minister heading secretariats within the Cabinet Office. Faced with political difficulties from the autumn of 2007, Brown responded by carrying out fusion. The number of special advisers rose, reaching similar levels – about 25 – to those of the Blair era. In January 2008 the first ever Permanent Secretary was appointed at No.10: the former Treasury official, Jeremy Heywood, whose task was described as 'helping to ensure a greater sense of cohesion between No.10 and the other Cabinet Office units engaged in supporting the Prime Minister'.[133] This role could be regarded as being intended to give greater cohesion to the premiership as a departmental entity, although located within a larger department, the Cabinet Office. The institutional churn of the Brown period could represent, not a retreat from the model established under Blair, but rather second-order structural alterations to what had developed in a number of key ways into a department. The longer it is retained in this form, the more plausible becomes the claim that the office of Prime Minister after 1997 entered its third phase as shown in Table 4.

[133] *Cabinet Office Annual Report and Accounts 2007–2008* (London: Cabinet Office, 2008) HC613, p.17.

Chapter Four

The Power Matrix

On 1 December 1868, in the wake of a Liberal General Election victory giving the party a Commons majority of more than 100, Gladstone was at Hawarden, his country home, engaged in one of his obsessions, tree-felling. A telegram arrived. It stated that Queen Victoria had written a letter for him, and inquired where it should be delivered. The implication was clear. Gladstone was about to be appointed Prime Minister, for the first time. Having opened the envelope and read the note, he passed it to his companion (Evelyn Ashley – son of Lord Shaftesbury and formerly a secretary to Palmerston as Prime Minister – who provided this account), merely saying 'Very significant'. Then after striking a few more times the tree he was attacking, Gladstone rested on his axe and uttered the words 'My mission is to pacify Ireland'.[1]

This objective was a central focus of the four Gladstone premierships of 1868–74, 1880–5, 1886 and 1892–4, with the pursuit of various initiatives including land reform and Home Rule. They involved No.10 playing a prominent role in policy, a dynamic approach sometimes exercised at the expense of Cabinet processes. Edward Hamilton, a Treasury official who had previously served as secretary to Gladstone, recorded in a diary entry for 9 March 1886 seeing Gladstone 'for some time today' about the plan the premier was developing for Irish Home Rule. Hamilton noted that the 'outside public no doubt are under the impression that the process of conception is the common work of all the Cabinet'. But the truth was that Gladstone 'still keeps the construction of the measure entirely

[1] See: Roy Jenkins, *Gladstone* (London: Pan, 2002), p.290.

in his own hands'. There were only 'occasional references' to a select group of ministers.[2]

Though No.10 might be successful in ensuring the adoption by the government of proposals it favoured for Ireland, they could not be put into effect if they required statutory expression that was denied by Parliament. Such obstruction occurred when the Commons rejected the Home Rule Bill in 1886; and when the House of Lords voted down the Government of Ireland Bill in 1893. As well as meeting with barriers to their introduction, policies could have negative political repercussions. The Home Rule proposal of 1886 prompted the resignation of Joseph Chamberlain, a prominent Liberal Cabinet member who was not one of those consulted by Gladstone over its details; and the policy was associated with a permanent split in the party. After the Commons defeat of the Home Rule Bill there followed a General Election which led to the fall of the Gladstone government. The Liberal Party did not win an overall Commons majority entirely of its own for another twenty years. Finally the efforts made by the office of Prime Minister under Gladstone to address Irish issues did not bring about the ultimate objective they were intended to achieve – the pacification of Ireland.

An assessment of the Gladstone premierships and Ireland emphasises that the power of the office of Prime Minister should be perceived from a variety of different viewpoints. From the perspective of its capacity to secure the adoption of particular courses of action by government, while minimising involvement from other parts of the executive, No.10 under Gladstone displayed substantial strength. But when analysis widens to cover the parliamentary response to such decisions, the defeats of Home Rule proposals in 1886 and 1893 suggest weakness. A similar sense of impotence emerges from observation of a longer timeframe extending beyond the immediate adoption of specific courses of action. The Government's commitment to Home Rule was followed by, and associated with, a major fissure in the Liberal Party, suggesting

[2] Dudley W. R. Bahlman, *The Diary of Sir Edward Walter Hamilton: 1885–1906* (Hull: University of Hull Press, 1993), p.30, diary entry for 9 March 1886.

that through asserting itself successfully in the short-term No.10 had undermined its own strength in the longer-term. The extent of the power exercised by the Gladstone premierships is called further into question when the outcome of the totality of the actions during these terms is measured against the ultimate goal he had set.

This consideration of the Irish policy pursued during the Gladstone terms at No.10 from varied perspectives, suggests the combination of historical and political-science methodologies can produce new interpretations of the office of Prime Minister. Such an approach is used in this chapter to clarify, modify and extend the models of resource-dependency upon which core-executive analysis rests; and generate a method for analysing power based on a consideration of objectives and outcomes.[3]

Types of resources

Chapter Two identified various difficulties with theories of a dominant premiership that have been advanced before and since 1997, including tendencies both to contradict each other, and to be incongruent with the historical data. In considering interpretations of the office and the relevant historical evidence, it identified a number of first-hand accounts of important limitations on the premiership. These descriptions – produced by practitioners including Walpole, Peel, Gladstone, Rosebery and Wilson – point convincingly to the conclusion that the premiership has always been in various ways significantly constrained. It follows that in pursuit of its objectives it has had to rely to some extent on the cooperation – either active or passive – of other parts of central government. Other groups within the executive are in turn subject to their own particular curbs, creating a network of interdependence. In this sense the idea of resource-dependency – as employed within the core-

[3] An early example of focussing on the resources or capital of Presidents of the U.S. and of the people they interact with is R.E. Neustadt, *Presidential Power: The Politics of Leadership* (New York: John Wiley, 1960), while the President of the European Commission was analysed in a framework of resources and constraints, personal factors and situational contexts by Ken Endo, *The Presidency of the European Commission Under Jacques Delors: The Politics of Shared Leadership* (Basingstoke: Macmillan, 1999).

executive school[4] – is useful as a means of explaining how different actors within Whitehall – including No.10 – operate. It stresses their lack of self-sufficiency, utilising the concept of their trading resources with one-another in order to obtain access to those that they need.

The focus of consideration here is upon the exercise of power by institutions – which comprise sets of rights and individuals performing functions – inside the executive, defined as all the national-level government departments and offices, excluding hived-off agencies. As disputes within No.10 show, inside each institution participating in Whitehall power-processes, there is a sub-game, involving individuals and groups within that body pursuing their own desired objectives. Various parts of No.10 possess some degree of autonomy, if only because of the practical need to delegate work, though the Prime Minister is clearly the most important individual figure.

If power is the ability to achieve desired outcomes, how should the objectives of an institution such as the premiership be ascertained? An institution does not have a single consciousness of its own, and the intentions lying behind its activities, exist in the minds of the individuals attached to it.[5] Most prominent in determining the objectives of No.10 are the premiers themselves. But to varying extents, influenced by such tendencies as their personal style and the size of the No.10 staff, the decisions they explicitly approve will be not their own but will be determined by the advice they receive; and they will delegate some responsibilities entirely to aides. Consequently it is necessary to consider both the desires of prime ministers and their aides – with the former the most prominent – which between them shape and determine the objectives of the premiership.

As well as differentiation within Whitehall institutions there is overlap between them. Some team members at No.10 are seconded from departments, to which they expect to return and in this sense remain attached. At the same time the premiership may draw on the support of aides not officially

[4] See: Chapter One.
[5] See: Introduction.

attached to it, such as Cabinet Office or Treasury staff. Each department and office within the executive employs permanent officials who at the same time belong to a body that can be regarded as an actor in its own right – the Civil Service. The Cabinet as well can be regarded as a player within the executive – entailing a further intersection between it and the various Whitehall departments and offices of which its members are the political heads.

While distinctions may at times be blurred, there is value in focusing upon particular institutions within the executive and the interactions between them. These bodies can be seen as exercising power through trading resources of types which include:

- **Political**, that is assets possessed by an institution as a consequence of its association – probably through the minister who heads it – with success or high public standing of some kind. They may be enhanced by such means as the winning of elections, a prosperous economy, having support within a party or amongst the wider public, or having allies within government. Thomas Hobbes captured the value of commodities of these kinds in his 1651 work *Leviathan* when he wrote that:

  what quality soever maketh a man beloved, or feared of many; or the reputation of such quality, is Power; because it is a means to have the assistance, and service of many.
  Good successes is Power; because it maketh reputation of Wisdome, or good fortune; which makes men either feare him, or rely on him.[6]

- **Personal**, that is the particular qualities possessed by individuals associated with a given institution, which for No.10 means prime ministers and their aides. In a recent comparison of the Blair tenure with that of the concurrent Australian Prime Minister, John Howard, when discussing 'power resources' the political scientist Mark Bennister referred to the importance of 'individual character, style

[6] Thomas Hobbes, *Leviathan* (London: Penguin, 1985), p.151.

and personality' to leadership.[7] Within the premiership the characteristics of premiers, such as an ability to dispose of a heavy workload, can enhance the power of the institution. During the final Gladstone premiership No.10 could not be as pervasive as during his earlier tenures because, in the words of Algernon West 'It is difficult to be an octopus at eighty-three'.[8] Effectiveness at deploying the resources at the disposal of the office they head can be a valuable asset in its own right, just as in a card game a player with a weak hand may triumph over one with a strong hand because of sheer playing skill. In describing the relationship between the Blair No.10 and Brown Treasury, Michael Barber remarked 'Spending reviews were a matter of a hard-fought card game (more canasta than poker)', though he believed 'the Treasury held the trump cards on timing and information'.[9] Other individuals not at the political head of an institution, such as No.10 aides, can bring valuable qualities such as policy expertise.

- **Constitutive**, that is responsibility under statute, under the Royal Prerogative or by convention for particular decisions or acts. The constitutive resources of some contemporary departments may often come from the specific rights provided for its Secretary of State by acts of Parliament.[10] The head of No.10, the Prime Minister, is made responsible for the Civil Service under (at the time of writing) the Royal Prerogative and is by convention manager of the Cabinet.

- **Institutional**, including the body of staff attached to a particular actor within Whitehall and the particular functions it performs. The performance of a particular task is distinct from a clear *right* to execute it, which is classified as a constitutive resource. In contemporary departments there is a large institutional resource of personnel that

[7] Mark Bennister, 'Blair and Howard: Predominant Prime Ministers Compared', *Parliamentary Affairs*, Vol. 61 No.2, 2008, p.338.
[8] Algernon West, 'The Prime Minister'.
[9] Michael Barber, *Instruction to Deliver: Tony Blair, Public Services and the Challenge of Achieving Targets*, pp.3067.
[10] See: Chapter Three.

carry out ongoing work within a particular portfolio. With the premiership during its second historical phase, from the mid-nineteenth until the turn of the twentieth/twenty-first century, there was a relatively small staff, which was unable to engage in issues to the same depth as those of the departments, but ranged more widely and freely. Over time the No.10 team expanded and policy area-specific functions were increasingly developed. Other resources that can be categorised as institutional are the information and finance possessed by institutions.

Assessment of the history of the premiership using these concepts provides insights into the development of the office of Prime Minister, some of which can in turn prompt observations about the idea of resource-dependent power-processes in general.

Resource models can be integrated with the processes identified in the previous chapter: zigzag, and administrative fusion and fission. Zigzag is driven to some extent by the combination of political and personal resources attached to the premiership and other parts of the executive. Between them they represent how the office is inclined to operate and the particular conditions in which it functions, which can constrain No.10 or permit and encourage it to act in particular ways. The zigzag phenomenon is made possible – and likely to occur – because of the nature of the constitutive and institutional resources possessed by the premiership, as is discussed below. Increases or depletions in the quantity of these latter two resources held at No.10 are brought about, respectively, by administrative fusion and fission in the office of Prime Minister.

The power of the premiership: flexible and indirect

An important characteristic of the premiership, particularly in its second, non-departmental, phase, has been its possession and use of resources qualitatively different from those held and deployed in other parts of government. As John Mackintosh wrote of the Prime Minister 'his position is a special one with powers differing in kind from those of the other senior ministers'.[11] Departments possessed resources including definite policy responsibilities (constitutive resources), based on both the Royal Prerogative and – increasingly – statutes. They held institutional resources such as teams of staff, which over time became relatively large, constantly engaged in advising on and implementing decisions and programmes within their allotted portfolios. These resources were connected with specific activities that impacted directly on the outside world.

By contrast the premiership held and deployed assets that entailed operating in a more nebulous fashion and working largely through other formally autonomous actors within the executive. These resources included responsibilities (constitutive resources), exercised by the Prime Minister – largely lacking a statutory basis – for appointing and removing ministers and allocating portfolios; disbursing other forms of patronage; organising Cabinet; requesting dissolutions; and managing the machinery of government and the Civil Service.

There have never been exact prescriptions as to how No.10 should deploy these resources, providing it with considerable scope for freedom of action when compared with the departments, since the functions of secretaries of state, particularly if set out in statute, are more precise. The opportunities for the premiership to operate in varied ways have been enhanced by another feature of its resources. While in its second phase, the office of Prime Minister did not hold institutional resources, such as a large body of staff continuously and closely engaged in specific policy areas, it possessed another institutional asset in the attribute of flexibility, enabling its potential involvement in a variety of different cross-departmental issues at short notice. This particular blend of constitutive and institutional resources brought about the elasticity of the premiership (discussed in the Chapter Three), which in turn made possible and to an extent precipitated the zigzag phenomenon.

The reserves of resources it holds and uses frequently involve the premiership inducing – but not formally instructing – other actors within Whitehall to use their ability to impact upon the

[11] John Mackintosh, *The British Cabinet*, p.428.

outside. As Geoff Mulgan, Director of Blair's Strategy Unit, told the Commons Public Administration Select Committee: 'Most of the work of government is done in departments, it has to be done in departments and can only be done in departments. The centre should not and indeed cannot take all those roles onto itself'. Bodies such as the Strategy Unit, he noted, did 'not have very much formal power, we have no budgets, we do not have tanks we can send on to anyone's lawns ... We work primarily through influence'. Mulgan concluded that any notion 'that there is some sort of Stalinist command and control centre which we are sitting in, in the midst of pulling levers and pressing buttons is a very long way from the truth'.[12]

This manner of operation can be seen as exercising power as defined by Michael Foucault, who wrote that:

> what defines a relationship of power is that it is a mode of action that does not act directly and immediately on others. Instead, it acts upon actions: an action upon an action, on possible or actual future or present actions ... It is a set of actions on possible actions; it incites, it induces, it seduces, it makes easier or more difficult; it releases or contrives, makes more probable or less; in the extreme, it constrains or forbids absolutely, but it is always a way of acting upon one or more acting subjects by virtue of their acting or being capable of action.[13]

The indirect way in which No.10 has tended to function helps illustrate an irony of power: the higher an institution is placed within an organisational hierarchy, the more distant it tends to be from the outcomes it seeks to bring about; and the more dependent it is upon the cooperation of others. This principle applies to central government in general, since decisions taken at the highest level in Whitehall can be implemented only elsewhere, either somewhere down the chain of command of the relevant departments, or by hived-off agencies, or bodies

---

[12] House of Commons Select Committee on Public Administration (PASC), Minutes of Evidence, 11 July 2002, Questions, 316-7, 320.

[13] Michael Foucault, 'The Subject and Power', in Michael Foucault, *Power: Essential works of Foucault 1954–1984*, vol III (London: Penguin, 2002), pp. 340–1.

such as local government. Within the central executive this tendency is exceptionally relevant to the premiership.

Qualitative distinctions between resources

The features that emerge when the premiership is placed in comparative perspective in this way prompt a number of observations about resource-dependency models. Many of them arise from the realisation *it is important to stress qualitative distinctions between different types of resources.*

First, *in as far as the core-executive school creates the image of a market it is most viable if seen as a barter economy*. Rather than there being a single unit of exchange, rough bargains must be struck, with one kind of resource traded for another. The outcome is based on broad judgments by the parties involved about what is in their interests and how far they can be asserted, not on precise calculations.

Second, the differentiation between kinds of resources helps respond to the observation that the core-executive model does not explain how power is wielded, but merely provides a description of the framework within which exchanges take place.[14] The suggestion by Richard Heffernan that for No.10 to exercise 'leadership with the government' varied types of resources (for him 'personal' and 'institutional') must be 'married'[15] is pertinent to this issue. It seems that *actors exercise power through possessing and deploying the correct combination of different resources*. For instance, the degree of freedom with which the premiership can utilise its right to appoint and remove ministers and allocate their portfolios is dependent in part upon the political resources it holds at a given time.

Another illustration of the importance of blending resources comes from the Blair premiership. In his first term of 1997–2001 No.10 possessed substantial resources, including immense political capital potentially providing significant leverage within Whitehall. But it lacked the institutional resources required to bring about the impact it sought upon other parts of government. Hence the accelerated fusion described

[14] Eoin O'Malley, 'Setting Choices, Controlling Outcomes', p.2
[15] Richard Heffernan, 'Prime ministerial predominance? Core executive politics in the UK', p.350.

in the previous chapter which occurred from 2001, with an enlarged No.10 performing a wider range of functions. This development meant that the office of Prime Minister now possessed institutional resources that could be used to facilitate more direct and detailed involvement in such activities as, setting and implementing performance objectives – an end to which they were directed in the years that followed. Through adding a missing component and creating the required mixture of resources No.10 was able to achieve a desired goal: it wielded power. (The extent to which the premiership achieved its higher objectives – including improved public services – is another issue, discussed below). As the Blair premiership progressed – and particularly following the Iraq War – the political resources attached to No.10 lessened, while the institutional reserves continued to expand, creating an imbalance that was the reverse of the earlier years. The ideal combination would have been the popularity of the first term combined with the staff support of the second. Here is an illustration of another key dimension to the resource-based exercise of power: *timing*.

Third, awareness of the qualitative distinctions between different assets present and employed in the executive is relevant to another supposed problem with resource-dependency models. The ability of No.10 sometimes seemingly to dominate decision-taking procedures has been used to question a theory of government based on trade-offs.[16] This apparent contradiction can be resolved in the following way. The premiership has for much of its existence monopolised certain constitutive resources, such as the right to organise Cabinet, manage the Civil Service and request dissolutions; and it can at times – because of its position as the figurehead of government – hoard political resources. The observation of these qualities leads to the conclusion that *the executive environment is to some extent analogous to a market that – like those in the real world – is imperfect rather than completely free*. Mutual dependency should not be mistaken for equality. Though all remain subject to constraint, some actors – most of all the premiership – can be at a structural advantage. When the

[16] O'Malley, 'Setting Choices, Controlling Outcomes', p.2.

office of Prime Minister forces proposals through successfully exploiting this position, the conduct of government may appear to be more a process of domination than the voluntary exchange of goods.

It is not only the possession, potential or actual, of certain resources that leads No.10 to resemble a privileged actor within an imperfect market, but the use to which some of them can be put. *The premiership can be regarded as able, more than any other executive actor, to determine and alter in its favour the framework within which transactions take place.* Resources enabling it to act in such a way include authority for drawing up, interpreting and enforcing the *Ministerial Code*, the rule book for ministers (notwithstanding the appointment of an independent investigator – with restricted scope – in 2007); for establishing Cabinet sub-committees to deal with particular subjects; and for creating and reshaping government departments. These constitutive resources can be used to deny resources to opponents of No.10 or prevent them from being used in a fashion undesirable to the premiership; and to provide the office of Prime Minister and allies with reserves of resources and the possibility to deploy them in a way that helps it achieve desired outcomes. The premiership can create amongst its opponents, a tendency analogous to the social phenomenon identified by political scientists as a 'collective action problem'[17], reducing the possibility they will unite and inflict defeat upon No.10. When it uses its constitutive resources in these ways, the office of Prime Minister can be equated with an actor within a market that – because it enjoys privileged access to relevant decision-makers – is able to bring about a regulatory environment suited to its particular objectives. Once again it may as a consequence be able to impose particular ideas rather than obtain support for them through bartering.

A final extension of the imperfect market analogy is possible. *Agreements may be struck within the executive that can be likened to cartels carving out spheres of autonomy that*

[17] For expositions and discussions of the collective action problem see: Mancur Olson, *The Logic of Collective Action* (Cambridge MA: Harvard University Press, 1971); and Keith Dowding, *Power* (Buckingham: Open University Press, 1996), pp.31–41.

lead to a reduction in competition, although probably never its elimination. Such arrangements combine a trade-off with the facilitation of degrees of dominance within areas delineated to the parties involved. In the Churchill war-time coalition government of 1940–5, No.10 was afforded significant latitude in military affairs, while the same was granted to departments (often headed by Labour ministers) dealing with domestic issues. As Harold Wilson put it 'The converse of Churchill's inevitable total absorption in the conduct of the war was his decision to leave economic and social issues almost exclusively to his principal lieutenants'.[18] In the Blair era No.10 and the Treasury had some kind of arrangement over areas of operation – although there was overlap and uncertainty – that to an extent suited both parties. Barber writes how 'the power ceded to Brown ... [gave] Blair time for other issues'[19]; while Derek Scott, economic adviser to Blair, notes: 'Tony's readiness to allow Gordon a pretty free hand over economic policy was matched by his own personalised view of foreign policy, and in particular his determination to bring European policy within No.10'.[20]

The imperfect market model can help interpret the success of the Blair premiership in securing adoption of the policy of joining the US-led invasion of Iraq in 2003. The consent of Brown to the action can be seen as associated with the cartel-like arrangement between No.10 and the Treasury, and perhaps because Brown genuinely supported the engagement. If Blair and Brown agreed over a particular course of action, only stubborn resistance from a variety of other actors – which was theoretically possible but unlikely – could have prevented it from being taken. The office of Prime Minister used the exclusive resources it possessed to discourage such an outcome through ensuring a deliberative environment favourable to its objectives. These assets included the rights to interpret the *Ministerial Code* in its stipulations over the availability of legal advice to Cabinet meetings, and to determine how collective business was handled, with

[18] Harold Wilson, *The Governance of* Britain, p.6.
[19] Barber, *Instruction to Deliver*, pp.307.
[20] Derek Scott, *Off Whitehall: A View from Downing Street by Tony Blair's Adviser* (London: I.B. Tauris, 2004), p.20.

important discussions and papers confined to an unofficial committee of allies. Underpinning these methods of operation was the considerable political capital possessed by No.10 at the time.

The allocation of resources

Consideration of the history of the premiership suggests some other characteristics of the concept of power resources. *Light is cast on how actors within the executive come to possess resources. Political resources are allotted as a consequence of circumstances beyond the executive, such as prevailing public opinion, and conditions within Whitehall, including alliances and disputes between ministers. Personal qualities upon which the premiership draws are the sum of the characteristics of the Prime Minister and No.10 aides of the day. Constitutive and institutional resources are in part historical inheritances.* In the words of Hennessy: 'History deals each new incumbent a certain hand, the bundle of customs and conventions, practices and expectations that go with the office'.[21] At any given time the premiership possesses a set of rights and staff, performing functions that it has accrued through the incidence of fusion at various points in the past (as well as having lost others through fission). This tendency lends force to arguments that, *as well as being relational, power is locational: the specific position of the premiership within a given constitutional structure is important to the wielding of power.*[22] The ability of No.10 to involve itself in the work of a variety of other departments is because of the central place it occupies within Whitehall structures, at a junction with various lines of convergence. The processes of executive fusion and fission could be seen as involving locational changes, since they encompass rights, staff or functions shifting between the ambits of different government institutions.

The discipline of history – concerned with developments over time – helps explain how the allocation of resources changes. *The attachment of extra resources to No.10 can involve their being transferred from elsewhere within the executive,* as when

[21] Peter Hennessy, *The Prime Minister: The office and its holders since 1945*, p.36.

[22] See: Heffernan, 'Prime ministerial predominance?', p.348.

Lloyd George obtained for the premiership in 1918, the right to request a dissolution at the expense of Cabinet as a whole, or *being newly-created,* as in 1805 with the establishment of the post of Assistant Secretary to the Treasury. At the same time *a reduction in the assets of the premiership can involve their shifting elsewhere,* as took place progressively with the Delivery Unit under Blair and then Brown, *or disappearing,* as with Lloyd George's Garden Suburb and Blair's Office for Public Service Reform.

Changes in the allocation of political resources can be triggered by a wide range of developments both beyond and within the executive and by interactions between them. Of all the types of resources their status is the most variable and unpredictable and the least subject to the control of any one actor, including the premiership. Sections of the media may campaign over a particular issue in a way unhelpful to No.10. The premiership may obtain the support of one or more departments in achieving a particular end or form a more general compact. A policy promoted by No.10 and adopted in Whitehall, such as the Community Charge under Thatcher, may prove unpopular amongst the general public, depleting the political capital at the disposal of the premiership. Often the quantity of political resources possessed by the premiership is relatively high at the outset of a particular tenure – the honeymoon period. There is a broad tendency for it to decline thereafter, until a particular Prime Minister can no longer be sustained in office. This general trend can be temporarily reversed by such events as a subsequent General Election victory, or the incidence of a national emergency to which No.10 is seen as having responded well.

The availability of personal resources can alter when individuals leave or join No.10, or when the characteristics of people change in some way. The most obvious shift of the former kind is the transition to a new premier, but the arrivals and departures of aides such as the economic adviser, Alan Walters for Thatcher and Alastair Campbell for Blair, made a substantial impact on the personal resources available at No.10. A shift in the latter category can come about from signs of strain in a Prime Minister, as suffered by Gladstone on various occasions because of the workload to which he subjected himself. Circumstances may bring certain characteristics in premiers to the fore. As her term of office lengthened Thatcher was regarded as increasingly assertive.

Changes in the allocation of constitutive and institutional resources take place in accordance with the interconnected processes of fusion and fission.[23]

Resources can be used to obtain more resources, as capital can be invested to accumulate. In the early stages of the premiership in the eighteenth century, Walpole's skill in handling the monarch and Parliament – a personal resource – was deployed to enhance the constitutive resources of the office of First Lord of the Treasury in fields such as patronage. The office of Prime Minister has long applied resources, including the right to represent the government as a whole publicly, and the institutional mechanisms it possesses for maintaining contact with the media in attempts – sometimes successful – to enhance the standing of No.10, thereby boosting its political resources. On occasion, responsibility for the allocation of ministerial portfolios has enabled the premiership to enhance its constitutive and institutional resources through providing the Prime Minister with additional roles – as when Gladstone made himself Chancellor of the Exchequer as well as premier in 1873 and again in 1880.

Institutional resources – such as the Statistical Section under Churchill, the Policy Unit from 1974 and the Delivery Unit from 2001 – have been used to obtain for the premiership another institutional resource – information. Often immediately after a General Election the premiership takes advantage of the political capital accrued through association with success to increase its constitutive and institutional resources. The Policy Unit was established under Wilson after the 1974 general election returned him to power; and it was expanded by Thatcher following her election victory of 1983. In the wake of the 1997 Blair accession there was included in the *Ministerial Code* a stipulation, not present in its previous incarnation as *Questions of Procedure for Ministers,* that all major departmental media appearances and public statements be cleared with No.10. At the same time an Order in Council was issued which served to grant Alastair Campbell and Jonathan Powell, No.10

[23] See: Chapter Three.

special advisers, the right to issue instructions to permanent civil servants anywhere in Whitehall.

Finally an institution can increase the relative quantity of a particular resource it possesses by depriving others of it. In 1870 Gladstone ended the right of any Cabinet minister to call a Cabinet meeting, monopolising this constitutive resource for the premiership. Through its media resources No.10 can restrict opportunities in other parts of Whitehall to build up political reserves.

Toxic resources

Resources can be toxic: they can undermine the achievement of desired objectives rather than help bring them about. Exercising a constitutive resource can place a strain upon institutional and political resources. The premiership's power over patronage can be a burden to deploy and its use can cause resentment amongst those unhappy with how they have been treated. Trollope conveyed both these problems in *The Prime Minister* when writing:

> many men were in want of many things, and contrived by many means to make their wants known to the Prime Minister. A dean would fain be a bishop, or a judge a chief justice, or a commissioner a chairman, or a secretary a commissioner. Knights would fain be baronets, baronets barons, and barons earls. In one guise or another the wants of gentlemen were made known, and there was work to be done. A ribbon cannot be given away without breaking the hearts of, perhaps, three gentlemen and of their wives and daughters.[24]

Resources can be over-deployed. Thatcher as chair of Cabinet so imposed her views upon proceedings as to create increasing resentment amongst her colleagues, eventually contributing to the ending of the Thatcher premiership. In the Blair period the use of the organisational authority of No.10 to bypass formal collective processes led to prominent public attacks upon the legitimacy of such methods. In both cases the heavy usage of constitutive and institutional resources led to a lessening in political resources. The intense deployment by the

[24] Anthony Trollope, *The Prime Minister*, Vol. I, pp.166–7.

premiership of constitutive assets may be tolerated elsewhere in Whitehall, while No.10 possesses strong political reserves – perhaps associated with electoral success. But if with waning government popularity the political resources of the office of Prime Minister are diminished, then it is likely to meet with more resentment and resistance within the executive, even leading to the ousting of the incumbent premier. In such a scenario No.10 can be seen as having been extended a line of credit by other institutions in Whitehall, but one dependent upon the premiership sustaining a high turnover of political success; with political failure the loan will be called in, possibly leading to bankruptcy.

Though it is often portrayed as a source of strength for No.10, the mere possession – rather than use of – the right to request a Dissolution can create problems. In the autumn of 2007 the Brown premiership suffered a substantial loss of political standing, partly because its head was seen publicly to consider bringing about a General Election but ultimately decided against. Further difficulties that may accompany the holding as opposed to the deployment of resources, include the occurrence of disputes between staff members – such as characterised the second Wilson tenure of 1974–6. These conflicts consume time and energy, and undermine the cohesion of the office of Prime Minister. The possession of particular assets may encourage and facilitate certain kinds of action by the premiership that are potentially detrimental. During the Second World War the role of Minister of Defence was attached to the premiership. While this decision had some merit, it made more likely the amateurish meddling in military affairs from No.10 for which Churchill is notorious.

It is possible for the possession of a large or growing quantity of a resource to damage the ability of the premiership to attain desired goals. This phenomenon is illustrated by consideration of the significance of staff numbers. While there was considerable expansion under Blair, not all around him were convinced of the value of this shift. Peter Hyman, an aide to Blair, stated: 'For the ten or so people closest to Tony, the debate was about whether we were more effective as a tightly-knit unit or whether we really gained by building up the capacity of Number 10'.[25] A larger team at No.10 may – simply because of its size, aside from the use to which it is put – prove controversial within and beyond government. It increases the likelihood of intra-institutional staff tensions and can entail a more cumbersome office, undermining the flexibility that has been important to it. In support of the latter point Jonathan Powell recalled in 2009 how:

> About 10 years ago a young official came from the German Kanzleramt [office of the Chancellor] to study how No 10 worked to establish whether there were any lessons for Germany. When he left he said to me that the one thing we should never do is try to replicate the size of the Kanzleramt with its various Abteilungs or departments in London or we would end up with an ungainly bureaucracy rather than a light and mobile centre of government.[26]

Whether in Powell's time this danger was avoided is debatable, but the point at least was well made.

If the premiership at a particular time possesses large stores of political resources, as when Blair took up office, public expectations about the impact it can achieve – possibly with encouragement from No.10 – can become unrealistic, prompting subsequent disillusion and the depletion of political resources. Similarly over-ambitious views may develop within the office of Prime Minister, contributing in time to a diminution of the same resources that, when possessed in abundance, encouraged them.

The identification of the potentially toxic nature of resources serves further to undermine many of the theses of increasing power by No.10 that have been advanced over the years, since such interpretations have often referred to the accumulation of resources by the premiership, including of a constitutive and institutional nature. Possession by No.10 of more rights or support structures, far from facilitating the achievement of objectives, as is often supposed, may lessen the chances of their being brought about.

---

[25] Peter Hyman, *1 Out of 10: From Downing Street Vision to Classroom Reality*, p.86.

[26] 'House of Lords Constitution Committee Inquiry: Written evidence from Jonathan Powell, former Chief of Staff to Tony Blair', 11 June 2009.

Beyond the core executive: objective and outcome-based power analysis

Subject to the clarifications and modifications described above the idea of resource-dependency is a useful tool for the analysis of the exercise of power by No.10 and other bodies within Whitehall, and is an improvement upon theses that claim ever-growing dominance by the premiership. It conveys an impression of mutually reliant actors trading resources that is realistic, but it is a metaphor, and as such should be treated with caution and not seen as an all-embracing explanation of political power in central government. The viability of core-executive analysis, in as far as it rests upon resource-dependency, is sustained by the historical evidence, but the core-executive school has failed to correct some shortcomings more generally associated with analysis of the power of the premiership, and has in one sense added to them. Discussions regarding the strength of the office of Prime Minister – including those in core-executive analysis – have tended to concentrate on power as wielded by one actor *over* one or more others, rather than other possible forms of its exercise; and they have focussed attention on the adoption of particular decisions, rather than on their outcomes. The latter comprise the ultimate measure of power. A particular deficiency in core-executive studies is that by definition they focus on activities and tendencies within Whitehall at the expense of a wider perspective. There are many other institutions in the outside world, including Parliament, parties, other tiers of governance and media outlets, each of which could be seen as being in possession of its own resources. As has been shown with the defeats of Gladstone's home-rule bills in the Commons and the Lords (which are not part of the national executive), external bodies can play critical parts in the exercise of power by the premiership.

Such deficiencies in analysis of the strength of the premiership can be both exposed and corrected by examination of the objectives of actors and of how far they achieve them, an apt approach, given the definition of power as the ability to achieve desired goals.

Power assessment: key questions

A number of questions need to be asked about goals and outcomes.

How ambitious was the objective?

When an assessment is made of how much power the premiership possesses, it is necessary to take into account not only how far an aim has been achieved, but how demanding the objective was. The scope of the task No.10 sets for itself varies. During tenures such as those of Melbourne (1834 and 1835–41) the primary objective seems at times to have been the modest one of getting Cabinet to agree about something, regardless of what it was. There is a tale that once, following a discussion of the Corn Laws, he told his Cabinet:

> By the bye, there is one thing we haven't agreed upon, which is, what are we to say? Is it to make our corn dearer or cheaper, or to make the price steady? I don't care which: but we had better all be in the same story?[27]

Under Pitt the Elder/Chatham, who was arguably in effect Prime Minister (though not First Lord of the Treasury) for periods during the 1750s and 1760s, aspirations were higher, involving the position of the UK as a global empire.[28] Some incumbents have displayed a tendency to set targets that seem unattainable. As well as Gladstone another 'mission impossible' Prime Minister was Blair. In 2004 Andrew Turnbull, as Cabinet Secretary and Head of the Home Civil Service, when explaining the substantial changes to the centre of government brought about in the Blair period, told the House of Commons Public Administration Select Committee: 'The real objective is simply explained, one is to produce better public services and the other is to produce a society that people are happy living in'.[29] The former purpose was a heavy burden to take on; the latter was seemingly too difficult to be achieved and – depending

[27] Spencer Walpole, *The Life of Lord John Russell* (London: Longmans, Green & Co., 1891), p.384.

[28] See eg: Stanley Ayling, *The Elder Pitt: Earl of Chatham* (London, Collins, 1976).

[29] PASC, Minutes of Evidence, 1 April 2004, Question 65.

on how it was interpreted – possibly beyond the appropriate scope of government.

How clear was the objective?
Sometimes the objectives of the premiership lack clarity. Under Thatcher No.10 promoted the monetarist doctrine, and a leading economist in this school, Alan Walters, was recruited to the staff. Yet the pursuit of this approach in office was clouded by uncertainties about how the theory would work in practice, the definition of terms, and shifting parameters. If power is the ability to achieve particular goals, it requires the actors concerned to know their desired outcome. Another way in which the clarity of objectives can be undermined is through differences of opinion or interpretation between individuals within No.10.

Was the objective reconcilable with other goals?
Different desired outcomes may contradict each other, and their simultaneous pursuance may cause one or more of them to fail. Following Wilson's ascent to office in 1964, No.10 pursued both maintenance of sterling at the rate of $2.80 within the Bretton Woods system and higher rates of economic growth – difficult goals in themselves and perhaps impossible to reconcile.

How propitious were circumstances for its attainment?
The premiership may have an objective that, even if clear, compatible with other goals and not inherently over-ambitious, comes up against particular circumstances not conducive to its attainment. Problems may be encountered in a wide variety of places, including within the executive, Parliament, the media, amongst the wider public, or internationally. Lord Shelburne had developed plans for social and political reform, that went unfulfilled because his tenure was ended after only nine months by an alliance between the leading opposition figures, Fox and North, in 1783; but some of his ideas were later taken forward under Pitt the Younger, under whom the premiership enjoyed more favourable political circumstances. Under Edward Heath in 1970–4 No.10 was initially inclined towards some kind of economic and social disengagement by government, but was

forced to reverse its stance by international oil and currency crises, soaring inflation and industrial unrest. Ambitious goals may be assisted by wider circumstances: in the Thatcher era of 1979–90 No.10 was able successfully to pursue a free-market agenda – even though it was more extensive than the one favoured by Heath – partly because it was assisted by divisions within the political left.

Assessments of the power of the premiership should take into account how well it coped with the distinctive environment within which it operated. A particular goal may be achieved under unfavourable circumstances through the effective use of specific methods, and equally the use of the wrong techniques may lead to the missing of an objective which was at the time relatively easy to obtain. As Niccolo Machiavelli, the Florentine politician, noted in *The Prince,* his political manual of 1513:

> the prince who relies entirely upon fortune will be ruined according as fortune varies ... the prince who conforms his conduct to the spirit of the times will be fortunate; and in the same way he will be unfortunate if in his actions he disregards the spirit of the times ... if one man, acting with caution and patience, is also favoured by time and circumstances, he will be successful; but if these change, then will he be ruined, unless, indeed, he changes his conduct accordingly.[30]

Where did a particular desired outcome stand in the hierarchy of objectives of the premiership?

In examining the wielding of power, it is important to determine whether a particular goal is more of an intermediary or an ultimate aim; and, if the latter, how important it is compared with other objectives within this second category. Achieving the assent of institutions such as Cabinet or Parliament to particular policy options, is the measure of the strength of the premiership, which tends to receive more attention than any other. Yet securing agreement within the executive to a decision, or of Parliament to a Bill, is usually only a means to an end. The Community Charge or Poll Tax was developed during

[30] *Machiavelli: The Prince,* translated by C.E, Detmold (Ware: Wordsworth, 1997), p.95.

the 1980s – with No.10 under Thatcher playing a leading role – as a means of changing the relationship between voters and local authorities. Obtaining acceptance for the measure within the executive and the legislature – though not easy to achieve and entailing the exercise of power – was the secondary goal. The ultimate desired outcome was not achieved because of immense public hostility.

To what extent was the decision to pursue a particular objective contested?

There is a temptation in the analysis of the power of the premiership to focus upon attempts by No.10 to achieve the adoption of courses of action to which there were active opponents, either within government or beyond. Using this adversarial approach, the success or otherwise of the premiership in obtaining the decision it sought in a particular instance, can be taken as an indicator of strength or weakness. Case studies of this sort include the initiation of the Concorde programme under Macmillan, and participation in the invasion of Iraq under Blair. In both there was resistance from within the government and – in the latter in particular – from outside, which No.10 managed to overcome.

A number of political scientists have long urged that in assessing power attention should not be solely devoted to what Steven Lukes terms 'the making of *decisions* on *issues* over which there is an observable *conflict* of (subjective) interests, seen as express policy preferences [emphases in original]'.[31] One way of widening the focus is by considering the significance of a lack of overt opposition to the following of particular paths. How might passive compliance with the premiership, when it occurs, be explained? Sometimes Cabinet members have allowed or encouraged the development of the impression that they were deceived over policies to which they offered little resistance, such as the Suez military intervention under Eden in 1956. Yet there are a range of other more credible explanations for such inaction. Those who acquiesce in a No.10 proposal may do so because they agree with it, or because they judge that defiance is not likely to be successful

[31] Steven Lukes, *Power: a radical view*, p.19.

or will generate too many difficulties. Further reasons for inaction may be that, within the institution concerned, another issue might be judged more worthy of confrontation – or compliance might be seen as part of an implicit bargain which yields benefits for other areas. Ministers at the head of departments may be unwilling to risk harming their political careers by either resigning or incurring the displeasure of No.10 through opposition. Equally the premiership may agree to certain decisions or refrain from bringing forward particular proposals for a similar range of reasons.

These patterns of interaction extend beyond the national-level executive. When determining whether to rule in or out a variety of courses of action, the premiership gives extensive attention to the possibility of hostility from a wide range of sources – including the party in Parliament and nationally, the media, public opinion, the markets, foreign allies and international institutions. An important theme here is that of anticipated reactions. C.J. Friedrich, the political scientist, who developed this concept, noted that:

> The influence of public opinion, or of parliament upon the conduct of governmental affairs is as devoid of ascertainable manifestations as the influence of a courtesan upon her royal master. Whey should this be so? Because the person or group which is being influenced anticipates the reactions of him or those who exercise the influence.[32]

In anticipating reactions it is possible for miscalculations to be made. Underestimations of the strength of opposition to an idea – such as Wilson's *In Place of Strife* proposals for trades-union reform, which were defeated by resistance within government and the labour movement as a whole – are easier to detect than overestimations. Where the premiership avoids certain activity on a basis of anticipated reactions, it may never be possible to judge whether it was correct in its decision. Arguably No.10 under Blair ceded more to the Brown Treasury than was necessary. Scott writes that 'It is a puzzle to me why the Prime Minister went along with' the desire

[32] Carl Joachim Friedrich, *Constitutional Government and Politics: nature and development* (New York: Harper, 1937), p.17.

of Brown 'to run everything on the domestic front'.[33] This tendency suggests that at times reality can be less important than perception, which can induce compliance even when unwarranted by the relative strength of two or more parties were it actively tested.

The view that power interactions should be assessed partly by what institutions do *not* do is potentially controversial. It carries with it the risk of being disparaged within the historical discipline as amounting to no more than counterfactual speculation. But non-events – such as the lack of a sterling devaluation when Wilson took up office in 1964 and the general elections that never were under Callaghan in 1978 and Brown in 2007 – can be in a sense as significant as positive occurrences.

To what extent was the objective shared?

There is a tendency – even amongst those who stress mutual dependency – to depict the power wielded by No.10 as the ability to achieve the adoption of its own particular objectives regardless of the priorities of others. While this approach has some merit, it should be complemented by others. Power can be seen as wielded by the premiership working in conjunction with other groups. Such a method may entail the modification of certain No.10 objectives, but it can at the same time increase the chances that courses of action ultimately followed will prove practically and politically viable. Sometimes the premiership may even regard incorporating the aims of others as a goal in itself, as suggested by Liverpool with his insistence in 1821 that 'I have no right, nor desire, to dictate to others'.[34] Consideration of the way the premiership cooperates with other institutions suggests it should be viewed not merely as a rampant interventionist, but as a possible mediator with, and balancer of, various different groups within and beyond the executive, through which it must work if it is to achieve desired outcomes.

[33] Scott, *Off Whitehall*, p.19.
[34] Lord Liverpool to Mr. Arbuthnot, 15 June 1821, reproduced in Charles Duke Yonge, *The Life and Administration of Robert Banks, Second Earl of Liverpool*, vol. III, p.147.

A way in which No.10 can operate inclusively is through the use of Cabinet in its various manifestations. While the strength of the premiership is often portrayed as inversely proportionate to that of Cabinet, the relationship involves an important dimension of interdependency. The 1889 statement by Morley that 'the Prime Minister is the keystone of the Cabinet arch'[35] is apt. A keystone is given essential support by the arch of which it forms a part; while without its keystone, the arch would collapse. Crucial to the link between the premiership and the Cabinet is the person of the Prime Minister, who is the senior figure within the former and the chair of the latter. Historically the two entities developed in tandem. The premiership needed collective support to bolster it against possible interference from the monarchy; the Cabinet required leadership to prevent reversion into a government of departments. This mutuality has remained a key characteristic throughout. Departments submit to No.10 as possessing authority for the organisation of Cabinet, but at the same time utilise Cabinet to gain an input into major decisions. Similarly, though the use of Cabinet can mean decisions are made contrary to the initial wishes of No.10, the possible benefits for the premiership are numerous. They arise from Cabinet in its manifestation as a *means* to various ends. It can ensure proposals are scrutinised from a variety of different departmental perspectives and from varied points of view within the governing party (or parties), helping make them more politically sensitive and practically viable. Ideas favoured by the premiership may be changed, but perhaps in such a way as to improve their chances of success. The Cabinet approach can reduce the resentment created by actors feeling excluded from decisions, making the government more united; and it can enable the resolution of disputes. Cabinet provides the possibility of recording and transmitting decisions; and assists the establishment of a consistent strategy for the government as a whole, with the most relevant people discussing key decisions together – and then implementing what has been agreed. While operating within Cabinet might lead to defeats for the premiership, it can enable No.10,

[35] John Morley, *Walpole*, p.157.

working with others, to restrain or impose courses of action upon parts of central government which are troublesome. Any of these outcomes might well be desired by the office of Prime Minister; and can enhance the ability of No.10 to attain further goals in the future.

Because of all the benefits on offer Cabinet should be seen as a potential instrument of power in the hands of the premiership. This possibility was grasped by certain more collegiate premiers, such as Attlee in 1945–51, and even by some for whom collective action was less of an objective in its own right. Under the Lloyd George stewardship of 1916–22, extensive use was made of Cabinet memoranda and meetings of both the full body and its sub-committees, and for the first time a specific staff was attached to it, responsible for taking and circulating minutes. Cabinet is a means by which No.10 can access key resources possessed across the executive – such as the knowledge, expertise and judgment of ministers and the institutional staff resources of the departments. Consequently whether or not individuals involved in operating the premiership (and across government) feel a personal affinity for the *principle* of Cabinet, they may value it in its manifestation as a *means* to various desirable ends.

In bypassing formal collective processes the premiership might on one level be regarded as enhancing its power through avoiding dilution of its objectives. But it is at the same time potentially debilitating its own strength, partly through depriving itself of the ability to deploy one of its major assets – the right to manage Cabinet. Another problem which can arise is illustrated by consideration of the aversion of No.10 in the Blair era to the extensive use of formal meetings of Cabinet and its sub-committees. Sometimes a substitute was provided in the form of processes conducted under the auspices of the premiership that *were* precisely documented[36]; but it could as well lead to a lack of clarity about decisions. Barber noted: 'when Blair and Brown talk with each other, they no doubt often get along famously, but rarely is a record kept – their relationship is intensely private – and as the details emerge, a Chinese-whispers effect sometimes occurs.

[36] See: Chapter Three.

The major cost to Blair as Prime Minister ... is the dilemmas and the sometimes downright confusion it sometimes causes in the key departments on which Blair depends, to deliver the transformation of the public services he craves'.[37] One way of avoiding this problem might have been the fuller use of Cabinet and the *procedures* associated with it.

The premiership can involve other parts of Whitehall in pursuing goals by dealing with them bilaterally or in small informal groups that do not come within the remit of Cabinet. These practices were favoured by Blair. While they can reduce the likelihood of a defeat for No.10, they are not as suited to bringing about the wider benefits associated with Cabinet, such as discussion of decisions from multiple perspectives, and the fostering of political and strategic cohesion.

If No.10 does not deal with other parts of government through bilateral methods or in informal groupings, or through the use of Cabinet, then they will be left to operate autonomously, entailing a significant reduction in the ability of the premiership to achieve objectives.

Groups outside the executive can be become partners in the exercise of power, including in the Houses of Lords and House of Commons (one of which all prime ministers have been members of), the party of government nationally (of which the contemporary premier is a leader) and what are now termed stakeholders. Although collaboration with them, as with Cabinet, may lead to modification of No. 10's plans, their involvement can provide varied perspectives on a policy issue, improve the chances that proposals will succeed, and generally facilitate goodwill towards the government. During the first Rockingham premiership of 1765–6, his secretary, Edmund Burke, carefully facilitated the participation of commercial business interests – a group of rising social importance – in policy formation. Burke's efforts were a great political success and can be contrasted with the development of Walpole's disastrous Excise scheme of 1733, which did not involve such consultation and provoked widespread protests, significantly diminishing the political standing of the premiership at the time.

[37] Barber, *Instruction to Deliver*, p.307.

To what extent was the objective achieved?
The ultimate measure of power entails assessing the extent to which a particular goal was achieved. First, it is necessary to look beyond the national-level executive and pay attention to the impact on the outside world. Second, developments over time must be taken into account. An effort which appears an immediate success may fail in the longer-term, and vice versa. The Sinking Fund for redeeming the national debt, introduced during the Pitt the Younger premiership, earned wide praise on its introduction[38] and during its first years of operation from 1786 to 1793, but in the longer-run, as a consequence of the war with France, it failed. The Citizen's Charter, the central policy objective of the Major premiership of 1990–7, was often ridiculed while he held office, but some of the basic ideas associated with it – such as users of public services being treated as consumers entitled to basic standards – took hold not only within the UK but internationally, although the worldwide reach was not part of the original plan.

Did the pursuance of an objective have side-effects?
Attempts at the exercise of power are dynamic and can have an impact beyond their specific goals. The pursuit of one objective may make it more difficult to achieve another at the same time, perhaps because both meet with opposition within government. Actions can have implications over time as well. Institutions such as the premiership seek to wield power within a framework, conditioned partly by activities of this sort carried out in the past; and these efforts in turn have an impact upon the environment within which future attempts to achieve desired goals are made. The premiership may secure the adoption of a policy which – perhaps because it proves unpopular with the public – decreases the political resources possessed by No.10, hindering it in achieving other objectives. A Prime Minister may give vent to domineering personal characteristics that help drive through particular objectives but cause increasing resentment within Whitehall or Parliament, which stimulate resistance to the premiership

[38] See eg: William Hague, *William Pitt the Younger* (London: HarperCollins, 2004), pp.226–7.

at a later date. In the longer-run, actions like Peel's use in 1841 of his authority over the allocation of portfolios to delegate the day-to-day management of the Treasury to a separate Chancellor of the Exchequer, can have immense implications for the way No.10 operates in future. Conduct in one period can contribute towards the development of structures which predispose institutions towards certain courses of action. The existence of the Policy Unit since 1974 can be seen as having increased the likelihood of attempts at involvement in the activities of the departments by No.10. A measure or a method once utilised becomes part of a repertoire of possibilities to be drawn on by No.10 under later incumbents, meaning the elasticity of the premiership has been stretched. Under Henry Pelham from 1746–54 No.10 applied the techniques of political management developed in the Walpole era. Having observed the premiership functioning in a particular way, individuals outside No.10 such as ministers and public observers may expect and encourage it to continue in a similar vein.

Conclusions

Through posing and answering these various questions, it is possible to place the premiership and its different attempts at achieving desired goals within a power matrix. Rather than suggesting crude tendencies such as an ever-stronger or ever-weaker No.10; or that some incumbencies see the possession of vastly more power than others, this model provides for each individual exertion by the office of Prime Minister to be judged on its own terms, and against the particular circumstances within which it took place. When combined with a modified resource-dependency framework, a fuller picture of how and to what effect power is exercised by No.10 can be constructed.

A theme that emerges from the application of this approach to a number of historical case studies is that when No.10 deploys resources to pursue goals in an exclusive hierarchical fashion, it does not necessarily ultimately wield more power than when more inclusive, conciliatory methods are employed. Under Chamberlain from 1937–40 No.10 drove the foreign policy of the government, drawing on resources such as the aide Horace Wilson and support from sections of the media and amongst the public. But the objective of staving off military conflict through Appeasement proved a failure, and Britain declared war on Germany in 1939. In 1956 No.10 under Eden, used its authority to determine where business was discussed in government to dominate the government's response to Egyptian nationalisation of the Suez Canal. Once again the policy pursued – engaging in military action on a fraudulent basis in the face of US opposition – was a disaster. The episode was a key stage in the demise of Britain as a global power, the opposite from the outcome sought by the Eden premiership.

By contrast the Callaghan premiership, in the face of a sterling crisis in 1976, made wide use of collective procedures, in particular full Cabinet meetings. By this means it was able to secure agreement across government, including amongst ministers of a range of different views in the Labour Party, to measures to reduce the Public Sector Borrowing Requirement, so as to secure support from the International Monetary Fund (IMF). The approach taken under Callaghan has sometimes been portrayed as dangerously misguided; and after 1976 there was a sharp decline, never reversed, in the frequency of full Cabinet meetings.[39] But the inclusive technique used, helped develop a package satisfactory to the IMF – without ministerial resignations – and proved successful in that Britain has never, so far, had to seek further assistance of this nature. Cabinet proved to be a means to an end desirable to No.10, given the difficult political and economic circumstances.[40] While Labour lost the General Election which followed in 1979, this outcome was more directly attributable to the industrial unrest of the so-called 'Winter of Discontent' of 1978–9 than to the sterling difficulties of 1976. If not handled in a collegiate manner, the IMF crisis could have ended in the collapse of the Labour government, and greater retrenchment than was enacted.

A final illustration of the advantages of an inclusive approach comes from the Blair premiership, better known for dominance from No.10. While some measures driven largely

[39] See: Chapter Two.

[40] For a discussion of these issues sympathetic to Callaghan's approach see: Hennessy, *The Prime Minister*, pp.384–9.

by the premiership met with debatable degrees of achievement, partly because they were too ambitious, a set of policies more widely developed and supported were successful. They include the National Minimum Wage; devolved government for Northern Ireland, Scotland, Wales and London; the Human Rights Act; and the Freedom of Information Act. Each in different ways achieved to a considerable extent what was hoped for by those who devised and implemented it. While No.10 played a part in these initiatives, it was far from a solo performance, with development taking place within the Labour Party and wider civil society over a long period before 1997, and starting before Blair's leadership of the party. The most successful efforts in the exercise of power under the dynamic Blair premiership came about when it was at its least domineering. At times a rival party, the Liberal Democrats, were involved in discussions at the highest levels. Even if such measures were largely regarded by the premiership as trade-offs, enabling No.10 to pursue other objectives, they can be seen in these terms alone as a success.

Chapter Five

Conclusion

The moral philosopher known in the West as Confucius, who lived in the sixth and fifth centuries BCE, is reported as once being asked whether there was 'such a thing as a saying that can lead the state to ruin'. He replied:

> A saying cannot quite do that. There is a saying amongst men: 'I do not at all enjoy being a ruler, except for the fact that no one goes against what I say.' If what he says is good and no one goes against him, good. But if what he says is not good and no one goes against him, then is this not almost a case of a saying leading the state to ruin?[1]

It can be inferred from this observation that securing the adoption of specific policies by government is a display of power only in a limited sense. There are a number of other vantage points from which power can be assessed, the most important of which is that of the ultimate outcome of official actions. The application of this analytical approach to the British premiership serves both to displace various existing theses of the office, and to help develop new interpretations. Amongst other conclusions it suggests the bypassing of Cabinet can be associated with weakness for No.10 rather than – as is often assumed – strength. This new perspective is one of a number that are made possible using the historical and political-science techniques described in the Introduction and applied throughout this book. The following conclusion sets out what has been revealed about the development, power and nature of the office of the British Prime Minister.

[1] Confucius, *The Analects* (London: Penguin, 1979), pp.120–1.

A number of theoretical distinctions are revealed. One is between the new and the perennial. Certain tendencies important to the premiership – such as the public focus upon the person who is Prime Minister as in some way the embodiment of the government, the task of managing the media, and its dependence on the confidence of the House of Commons – have existed throughout the history of the office. But the premiership is subject to change, which can be divided into two kinds: stylistic and substantive. The former amounts to fluctuation in the manner of operation within the existing framework of the office. It is most notably manifested in the often-occurring zigzag in the degree of dynamism associated with No.10 from the tenure of one Prime Minister to the next. The latter kind of change involves administrative fusion and fission – the movement of rights, functions and personnel towards and away from the premiership; or their creation or outright abolition.

Another set of differentiations involves political power. First, there is a need to distinguish between different types of power resources, which can be divided into political, personal, constitutive and institutional assets. The balance in which they are held, or the way in which they are combined when used, is important to the outcome of the interplay between the actors in any power process. Second, such resources can have different impacts according to the nature and circumstances of their deployment or possession. They can help achieve a desired objective, or they can become toxic and undermine the attainment of a particular goal. Third, power can be exercised in different ways, including unilaterally or in cooperation with others. Fourth, the wielding of power can be measured through varied means. It can be seen, amongst other ways, as the securing of consent within the government or Parliament to a particular programme; or as the attainment in the outside world of the wider, longer-term objective of the programme.

As well as revealing a series of distinctions the techniques deployed in this book provide an historical and constitutional perspective on developments, and how they have been interpreted. This outlook, taken in combination with the theoretical differentiations discussed above, makes it possible to dispel and avoid misconceptions about the office of Prime

Minister. Errors in the literature that have been produced over time include:

- mistaking the exploitation of potential already present within the premiership for material change;
- over-eagerness to identify substantive alteration when not real, and overlooking its genuine occurrence;
- identification of trends which either cannot be verified by the available evidence or, if they can, are unsatisfactorily analysed; and
- reference to the concept of power without adequate exploration of its conceptual and contextual complexity.

Conclusions about the premiership which these mistakes have been used to support include that it is becoming a presidency, supplanting Cabinet, gaining dramatically in power, or conversely becoming weaker. Such flawed interpretations must be discarded.

Although such theses often include excessive claims about the premiership being involved in the overturning of previously established institutions and practices within the UK constitution, it should not be denied there are tensions between the office of Prime Minister and the broader constitutional and political framework within which it operates. Rather than newly emerging at some point during the history of the office, they can be seen as perennial, involving a conflict between the special responsibilities attached to No.10, including for the management of Cabinet, and the broad principle of government by consent. In an article discussing the concept of prime-ministerial predominance Mark Bennister captured the ongoing nature of this tension in the liberal democratic era when noting:

> leadership does not fit into either the liberal perspective of individual rights and freedoms or the democratic perspective of collective decision-making. The issue is dealt with by attempting to constrain leadership in liberal democracies; checks and balances attempt to limit powerful individuals. Yet powerful individuals can shape and stretch existing institutions and loosen the shackles.[2]

[2] Mark Bennister, 'Blair and Howard: Predominant Prime Ministers Compared', p.336.

This phenomenon can be seen as the manifestation of a dilemma identified in accountability theory.[3] There exists a practical requirement to entrust certain institutions and individuals with particular tasks, necessarily affording them a degree of discretion in the detail of execution. Through the history of the premiership groups, including parliamentary coalitions or parties and senior ministers, have, to be more effective at achieving their objectives, been willing to submit to some extent to the office of Prime Minister. At the same time, those who vest particular responsibilities in an 'agent' such as the premiership will seek to retain some degree of control over it. Within such a framework there will always be scope for debate about whether duties are being exercised effectively and in conformance with norms; and whether mechanisms for holding 'agents' in check are adequate. The ongoing debate about the premiership, though it often focuses on the supposed exceptionality of the office, is best viewed as one particular expression of a more widespread discussion that arises in many societies as a consequence of functional specialisation.

Having identified various defects and lacunae in existing accounts, we now summarise the new interpretation of the office of Prime Minister as set out in this work. The underlying role of the British premiership is to provide public leadership. This task is its central role and is more important and relatively more resource-consuming within No.10 than anywhere else in Whitehall. After a transitional period in the eighteenth and nineteenth centuries the Prime Minister, in practice, eclipsed the monarch as the most prominent individual supplier of public leadership in the UK, subject to the emerging convention of collective Cabinet supremacy. The manner and means through which leadership is exercised by the office of Prime Minister have varied substantially; and such mutability is necessary to the effective execution of this task.

The premiership is best seen as a cluster of functions, rights and personnel centring on the person occupying the post of Prime Minister. It emerged casually and gradually from the early eighteenth century. Initially its legitimacy

[3] See eg: Richard Mulgan, *Holding Power to Account: Accountability in Modern Democracies* (Basingstoke: 2003, Palgrave Macmillan).

was challenged but during the course of the eighteenth and nineteenth centuries it became more practically entrenched. Codification of the office of Prime Minister has been slow and remains incomplete. The vague formal existence of the institution has always afforded a high degree of discretion to those, both premiers and their aides, responsible for its exercise, subject to various constraints and enticements.

Despite the opaque nature of the premiership it is possible to identify up to three main phases in its development. The shift from the first to the second came in the mid-nineteenth century with the detachment of No.10 from the Treasury, which had previously served in a sense as a 'Department of the Prime Minister'; the transition to the third arguably took place during the Blair premiership, particularly from the outset of his second term in 2001, with the establishment of an entity which resembled in many ways a departmental augmentation of the cross-government function of the office.

The premiership has monopolised certain power resources and is able at times to hoard a preponderant proportion of others. If these resources are held or deployed in the correct combination in the appropriate circumstances, No.10 can unilaterally ensure that government pursues courses of action over certain issues at particular times. Other ways in which it can help bring about such compliance, include through using its constitutive authority to change in its favour the framework within which decisions are made; and establishing cartel-like agreements with other Whitehall actors. But the ultimate objectives of the programmes proposed by the premiership may not be realised in the outside world. As well as helping to attain goals, resources and their deployment can be toxic, bringing about a negative impact. In attempting to achieve its objectives the office of Prime Minister has often been required to act in an indirect fashion, since it is dependent to an exceptional extent upon other institutions within and beyond Whitehall. They may be able to resist No.10 and their potential reactions must be taken into account when options are assessed. If the premiership works *with* institutions such as Cabinet and Parliament, such collaboration can be used as a means of achieving its objectives.

Any observer or practitioner wishing to understand the contemporary premiership must begin with the defining feature of its possible 'third phase' – the semi-official 'Department of the Prime Minister'. This entity can facilitate wider and deeper engagement by No.10 in the business of government. But it has attributes which could manifest themselves in a negative way. It could become a more cumbersome institution, meaning the premiership loses the flexibility and coherence that is the key to the performance of its public leadership role. The existence and use of a 'department' can be associated with damaging controversy within and without government about a supposedly overweening premiership. It may create the impression that the office of Prime Minister is able to achieve more than it can in practice, in turn leading to disillusion and resentment when it does not deliver what was hoped of it. From the point of view of Parliament, problems develop if No.10 is playing a more active role in policies, since accountability is primarily focused upon individual departmental ministers, not the Prime Minister.

Further potentially undesirable consequences of the existence of a semi-official 'Department of the Prime Minister' are associated with the commandeering of the Cabinet Office – or at least part of it – that the establishment of a quasi-prime ministerial department has involved. This change amounts to a diminution of Cabinet as an *institution* since Labour came to office, building on an already existing tendency for the Cabinet Office to be drawn into the ambit of No.10. This post-1997 shift should be considered in conjunction with a decline in the frequency of Cabinet as an *event* immediately after 1976; and possible trends which are harder precisely to verify or date, such as a deterioration in the quality of minutes (a Cabinet *procedure*); and declining commitment to the *principle* of Cabinet. The significance of this final change, if it has occurred, would be considerable because of the heightened importance of personal attitudes within the un-codified UK constitution. Patterns of conduct of Whitehall institutions including the premiership are determined to a significant extent by expectations: what those within them and elsewhere in the executive (and beyond it) consider to be appropriate forms of behaviour.[4] Taken together these tendencies suggest that Cabinet as a whole has been seriously undermined,

[4] See eg: Anthony King, *The British Constitution*, pp.321–2.

although not extinguished. Indeed a possibility of Cabinet resurgence appeared during Gordon Brown's tenure from 2007 when coups against him failed, and, to win support from the Cabinet, he promised to be more collegiate, but he soon reverted to his characteristic domineering style. The attempted coups and Brown's promises to change his ways, followed by his reneging on them, showed that No.10 was still only as strong within Cabinet as the Prime Minister's colleagues let it be.

Diminution of Cabinet does not correlate automatically or simply with the strengthening of No.10 inside or beyond Whitehall. The space created within the central executive by a diminished Cabinet is not necessarily wholly filled by the premiership. A weakened collective is less able to restrain not only No.10, but also other offices and departments, creating a more widespread potential for greater autonomy, as was notably enjoyed by the Treasury under Brown. Even in circumstances where the premiership is able to act to a large extent unilaterally over an issue, the ultimate outcome may not be desirable, since one of the potential values of Cabinet is to help produce decisions which – through assessing them from more varied perspectives – are more likely to end in success.

For those of the view that the potential problems linked with the existence of a semi-official 'Department of the Prime Minister' outweigh the benefits, the solution to advocate is a reshaping of the purpose of the Cabinet Office so that – except for the Prime Minister's Office, which is linked to it organisationally – it supports only the Cabinet collectively. Premiers could continue to receive support from the Cabinet Office as a whole, but solely in their capacity as chair of the Cabinet. The execution of this shift would involve redrafting the terms of reference of the Cabinet Office, and attaching to ministers collectively any bodies or posts within the Cabinet Office previously charged in part or in whole with supporting the Prime Minister, or else abolishing them. A further means of ensuring the Cabinet Office was focussed on the task of facilitating Cabinet government would be to remove from it responsibility for management of the Civil Service, perhaps through the creation of an institution akin to the Civil Service

Department that existed from 1968–81, or some kind of public service board, or returning the task to the Treasury, where it resided up to 1968. Such changes are likely to meet with bureaucratic resistance: there would probably be hostility within the Cabinet Office where permanent civil servants would fear losing some of their access to the premiership and their ability to lobby for their particular desired objectives, especially promoting and protecting the privileges of the Civil Service. It is reasonable to suppose that the attitude of three former holders of the dual role of Cabinet Secretary and Head of the Home Civil Service, Lords Armstrong, Butler and Wilson, is representative of the kind of views that would be pressed at high level. In their 2009 evidence submission to the House of Lords Constitution Committee, though favouring some enhancements to the collective role of the Cabinet Office, they judged that:

> the establishment of a free-standing [Civil Service] department was not a success. The incorporation of central responsibility for the civil service into the Cabinet Office has, we believe, worked well: it sits well with the Prime Minister's overall responsibility as Minister for the Civil Service and with the position of the Secretary of the Cabinet as Head of the Home Civil Service.[5]

If the 'Department of the Prime Minister' is not deliberately abolished through means similar to those outlined above, it may eventually end in another way. It is possible that for practical reasons overall management of this 'department' could be at some point delegated to a single minister, who then became an increasingly significant political figure in his or her own right, and under whose headship the 'department' in effect became detached from the office of Prime Minister. It would then have followed a similar trajectory to the Treasury in its separation from the premiership in the mid-nineteenth century. Future practitioners might then be tempted to create a new large-scale entity to support the office of Prime Minister.

---

[5] 'Cabinet Office and the Centre of Government, Submission by Lord Armstrong of Ilminster, Lord Butler of Brockwell and Lord Wilson of Dinton', May 2009.

Index